DAY

BY

DAY

DEVO-
TIONS

2

W9-CEK-439

Karyn Henley

Tyndale House Publishers, Inc., Wheaton, Illinois

Visit Tyndale's exciting Web site for kids at www.cool2read.com
Also see the Web site for adults at www.tyndale.com

For more information about Karyn Henley, visit www.karynhenley.com

TYNDALE is a registered trademark of Tyndale House Publishers, Inc.

Copyright © 2005 by Karyn Henley. All rights reserved. Exclusively administered by Child Sensitive Communication, LLC.

For permission to copy excerpts from this book, contact Tyndale House Publishers, Inc., P.O. Box 80, Wheaton, Illinois 60189.

Bible story excerpts—and Scripture quotations marked DBD—are taken from Day by Day Kid's Bible, copyright © 1998 by Karyn Henley. All rights reserved. Exclusively administered by Child Sensitive Communication, LLC.

Scripture quotations marked NLT are taken from the Holy Bible, New Living Translation, copyright © 1996. Used by permission of Tyndale House Publishers, Inc., Wheaton, Illinois 60189. All rights reserved.

Scripture quotations marked NIV are taken from the Holy Bible, New International Version®. NIV®. Copyright © 1973, 1978, 1984 by International Bible Society. Used by permission of Zondervan Publishing House. All rights reserved.

Scripture quotations marked ICB are taken from the International Children's Bible®, New Century Version®, copyright ©1986, 1988, 1999 by Tommy Nelson™, a division of Thomas Nelson, Inc., Nashville, Tennessee 37214. Used by permission.

Edited by Betty Free Swanberg
Designed by Jacqueline Noe

Portions of this book were first published by Tyndale House Publishers, Inc., as Sword Fighting, copyright © 2000 by Karyn Henley. All rights reserved. Exclusively administered by Child Sensitive Communication, LLC.

Library of Congress Cataloging-in-Publication Data

Henley, Karyn.
  [God's story and me]
  Day by day devotions / Karyn Henley.
    p. cm.
Originally published: God's story and me. c1998.
Includes index.
Summary: Presents daily devotional readings and prayers arranged by weekly themes covering such topics as unfailing love, forgiveness, patience, and God's promises.
  ISBN 0-8423-7486-8 (2)
  1. Christian children—Prayer-books and devotions—English. 2. Devotional calendars—Juvenile literature. [1. Prayer books and devotions. 2. Devotional calendars.] I. Title.
BV4870 .H45 2004
242'.62—dc22   2003015509

Printed in the United States of America

11 10 09 08 07 06 05
7   6   5   4   3   2   1

CONTENTS

Dear Reader,

Three letters follow each Bible verse in this book. These letters are codes for the Bible translations the verses come from. The words are a little different in each translation, but the verses mean the same thing. Reading different translations helps us understand the Bible better. Here are the letters: DBD = *Day by Day Kid's Bible*; NLT = *New Living Translation*; ICB = *International Children's Bible*; NIV = *New International Version.*

Love,

Karyn Henley

MADE FOR GOD

God loved us. That's why he chose us. He planned to make us his children through Jesus.
Ephesians 1:4-5, DBD

This week you will learn
· *why God made you;*
· *what glory means;*
· *what it means to bless someone;*
· *why we will never be able to do everything right.*

Monday

Read "In the Secret Place," page 212 in the *Day by Day Kid's Bible.* Or read this part of the story:

God, you know me.
You know when I sit down and when I get up.
You know what I'm thinking.
You know when I go out and when I lie down.
You know all my ways.
Even before I say a word, you know it all, God. . . .

You planned all my days.
You wrote them in your book,
even before I had lived one of them.
Psalm 139:1-4, 16

"MOM!" CALLED ANNA. "DeeDee won't leave me alone. I need some space."

Anna thinks her five-year-old sister, DeeDee, is cute. In fact, Anna loves DeeDee. But Anna does not want to be around DeeDee 24 hours a day, 7 days a week. The truth is, even though Anna has friends and family who love her, nobody wants to be around Anna all the time either. Nobody but God.

God loves each of us so much, he wants to be with us 24 hours a day, 7 days a week, all our lives.

God loves *you* that much. He did not make you by accident. Why did God make you? Because he knew he would enjoy someone just like you. He loves you. He made you so that he can be with you wherever you go and talk with you now and forever. God made you so he can have a relationship with you.

Dear Father God, thank you for loving me. Thank you for being with me all the time. Thank you for enjoying me. I want to enjoy you too.

Tuesday

Read "Erased Sins," page 362 in the *Day by Day Kid's Bible.* Or read this part of the story:

> *I'm the Lord. I'm your God. . . .*
> *Bring all my people. I made them.*
> *I made them to show how great I am.*
>
> *No god was made before me.*
> *There will never be one after me.*
> *I am God. Yes, I am.*
> *There is no other one who can save you.* Isaiah 43:3, 7, 10-11

THE WINNERS IN the Olympic Games stand on a stage as someone hangs medals around their necks. The flags of their countries hang behind them.

News cameras take their pictures. We say the winners are getting a lot of glory. That means everyone who is watching can see who these people are and what they have done.

God made us for his *glory*. That means he made us to show the world who he is and what he has done. How can we do that? We can enjoy what God has given us and thank him for it. We can act and speak in loving ways to show what God is like. We can tell others how good God is.

Dear God, thank you for all you give me. Help me to act and speak in loving ways so others can see what you are like.

Wednesday

Read "Abram's Travels Begin," page 9 in the *Day by Day Kid's Bible.* Or read this part of the story:

God talked to a man named Abram. God said, "Leave this land. . . . I will show you a new land to live in. . . . I'll do good things for anyone who speaks well of you. I'll send trouble to anyone who says bad things about you. Good will come to everyone on earth because of your family." *Genesis 12:1, 3*

HOW DO YOU SNEEZE? Do you know anyone who has a funny sneeze? When someone sneezes, people often say, "God bless you!" *Bless* means to bring good to someone. So when we say "God bless you," we mean "I pray that God does good things for you."

God's agreement with Abram was: "I'll bless you, and you will be a blessing." God wants the same for us. God made us so he could bring good to us and we can bring good to others. Why? Because when we do good, we show other people what God is like. When they see what God is like, they may want him to be their God too. How has God blessed you? How can you bless others?

Dear God, thank you for blessing me. Help me to bless other people by bringing good to them. Then they can see how good you are.

Thursday

Read "A Letter from Jesus," page 695 in the *Day by Day Kid's Bible*. Or read this part of the story:

Seeing you is like reading a letter from Jesus. This letter wasn't written with ink. It was written with God's living Spirit. God doesn't write on stone. He writes on human hearts. . . .

He shines brighter and brighter in us every day.
2 Corinthians 3:3, 18

THE SUN. FIRE. ELECTRICITY. All of these make light. Almost everything else in our world reflects light. Light from the sun hits glass windows and water and metal car bumpers, making them shine. Light from the bulb in your bathroom hits the mirror and the sink faucet, making them shine.

We reflect a special kind of light. We are like a mirror for God, who is the light of our lives. God loves us, so we love others. God is kind to us, so we are kind to others. God made us to reflect him the way a mirror reflects light. God wants to shine through us to the world. When we let him do that, we glorify God or bring him glory. We show the world what God is like by loving the way he loves.

Dear God, thank you for your love that shines into me. Help me reflect your love to the people in the world around me.

Friday

Read "Better Gifts," page 784 in the *Day by Day Kid's Bible.* Or read this part of the story:

Now we are part of God's family forever! Jesus died to pay for sin. So God's people are free from sins they did before. . . .

Jesus went right into heaven. He went face to face with God for us. . . .

He got rid of sin once and for all. He did it by giving himself. *Hebrews 9:14-15, 24, 26*

YOU ARE A TREASURE to God. A treasure is something you want to hold and keep. God made you so he could have a relationship with you. He made you so you could glorify him by showing who he is. He made you so he could bless you and you can be a blessing to the world. He made you to reflect him. But do you always act in a way that shows who God is? Do you always bless other people by doing good things for them?

Nobody does everything right. Why? Because we are not God. Only God does everything right. So God knew he would have to do for us what we could not do for ourselves. That's why Jesus came. He did everything right for us. And then he died to be punished for the wrong things we do. That doesn't mean we stop trying to do what's right. But it means we don't have to worry about God being angry when we do wrong. We tell him we're sorry, and we try to do better next time. Because of Jesus, God treats us as if we had never done wrong at all. That's love!

Dear God, I'm sorry for the things I do wrong. Thank you for sending Jesus to do everything right and to die for my sins. Thank you for forgiving me. Help me do the best I can to live in a way that will show how good you are.

SOME THINGS YOU CAN DO THIS WEEK

* **Make a door hanger.** Get a piece of printer paper or notebook paper and fold it in half the long way (from top to bottom). Cut the paper in half along the fold. Hold one half of the paper next to the doorknob of your room, and draw a round circle the size of your doorknob near the top of the paper. Cut out the circle so it will hang on your doorknob. On one side write GOD, draw a heart, then write ME. On the other side, write– 24/7. That means "God loves me 24 hours a day, 7 days a week."

* **Design a first-place medal.** Get a piece of aluminum foil about the size of a place mat. Set a paper plate in the middle of the foil. Wrap the foil around the plate. Turn the foil-covered plate over so you can write on the bottom of it. With a pencil that's not too sharp, write GOD in the center. Then draw a design on the foil around the word. Your pencil will dent the foil where you draw. What are some ways you can give God glory (show who he is and what he has done)?

* **Find reflections.** Walk through the rooms in your house, shining a flashlight on different objects. Which ones reflect the light well and which don't? Bumpy things break up light waves and don't reflect as well. Smooth things are better at reflecting, or sending the light waves back to you. How do we reflect God, or show what he is like?

* **Check out the moon.** The moon does not shine its own light. Instead, it reflects the sun's light. Go out at night and look at the moon. What shape is it? The light part shows which part the sun is shining on. Who were we made to reflect? How? Read Matthew 5:16.

KEEPER OF PROMISES

The Lord did exactly what he had promised. Genesis 21:1, NLT

This week you will learn

· *how keeping promises fits into God's plan;*
· *who laughed at one of God's promises;*
· *what a land of "milk and honey" is;*
· *what always wins.*

Monday

Read "Abraham's Visitors" and "Two Sons," pages 13 and 16 in the *Day by Day Kid's Bible.* Or read this part of the two stories:

Then God said, "Sarah will have a baby boy." . . .

She laughed to herself when she heard what God said. That's because she and Abraham were very old.

"Why is Sarah laughing?" asked God. "Is anything too hard for God?" . . .

God kept his promise to Sarah. She and Abraham had a son, even though they were old. The baby came just when God said it would. Abraham named the baby Isaac. *Genesis 18:10-14; 21:1-3*

A MUMMY IS the body of a person who died long ago and was dried and wrapped in bandages. Most mummies have been found in Egypt. Abraham lived at the time when people made mummies. Also at the time Abraham lived, people first started keeping chickens. Before that, chickens were wild.

God promised Abraham a son. But that looked impossible. Did those who thought it was impossible win? No. God won. He kept his promise. God's love always wins. Keeping his promises is one way God blesses us and shows he loves us. We can bless the world in the same way. We can keep our promises. That way, we can show what God is like.

Dear God, thank you for keeping your promises. Help me keep my promises.

Tuesday

Read "A World under Water," page 6 in the *Day by Day Kid's Bible.* Or read this part of the story:

"I'm making a promise to you and all the animals. It's a promise that will last forever. I'll never get rid of everything by flood water again.

"Here is the sign that shows my promise is true," said God. "I am putting a rainbow in the clouds. I will remember my promise when I see the rainbow." *Genesis 9:8-17*

THE LARGEST ANIMAL in the world is the blue whale. Blue whales can grow to over 100 feet long. The giraffe is the tallest. It can be as tall as a two-story house. The cheetah runs fastest, as fast as a car on a toll road or freeway: 62 miles an hour. When God started over with the world, he saved some of all of the living things he had made. Afterward, he made his rainbow promise.

God chose to save Noah because Noah trusted and obeyed God. Can we trust God to keep his promise, just as Noah did? When we trust and obey God, we're showing God that we love him. In the time of Noah, did evil people win over the earth, or did God win? God won. God loves his people, and his love always wins.

Dear God, thank you for loving us and taking care of us. Help us trust and obey you.

Wednesday

Read "The One We Will Serve," page 102 in the *Day by Day Kid's Bible.* Or read this part of the story:

Joshua grew old. Then he called the leaders together. "I'm old," he said. "You've seen everything God has done for you. God fought for you and pushed the nations out of this land.

"So be strong. Be careful. Obey everything the law tells you to do. . . .

"You know that God has kept all his promises." . . .

"We will serve God," said the people. "We will obey him."
Joshua 23:1-3, 6, 14; 24:24

GOD HAD PROMISED to bring his people to a land "flowing with milk and honey." In Bible times, "milk and honey" was a way of saying "blessings" or "good things." So the new land was a place where the people found more than enough good food and water. This was the land Joshua was talking about in today's reading. God had kept his promise. His people had moved into the land of milk and honey.

In a later time called the Middle Ages, people called good things "cakes and ale."

If you were talking about how much God has blessed the place where you live, instead of calling it a place of "milk and honey" or "cakes and ale," what would you call it? What are some blessings God has given you? Remember: God's plan is to bless you so you can bless others.

Dear God, thank you for keeping your promises. Thank you for blessing me and my family.

Thursday

Read "A Ladder up to Heaven," page 25 in the *Day by Day Kid's Bible*. Or read this part of the story:

That night Jacob had a dream. He saw a ladder that went all the way up to heaven. . . .

God stood at the top of the ladder. God said, "I am the Lord. . . .

"I'll be with you. I will watch over you everywhere you go. I won't leave you. I will keep all my promises to you."
Genesis 28:11-13, 15

DREAMS WERE VERY IMPORTANT to people in Bible times. In countries where people did not believe in God, someone who had an important decision to make would sometimes go to a temple or other special building to sleep. The person hoped to have a dream there that would explain what to decide. Dreams that a king had were thought to be especially important.

God often sent messages in a dream, like his message to take care of Jacob. It would have been bad for Jacob to be all alone and afraid. Did Jacob have fears that won? No. God won.

God wants you to know that you are not alone, and you don't have to be afraid. God's promise is to always be with you too. God keeps his promises. God loves his people, and his love always wins.

Dear God, thank you for keeping your promises. Thank you for always being with me.

Friday

Read "Coming like a Robber," page 777 in the *Day by Day Kid's Bible.* Or read this part of the story:

God is not slow about keeping his promise. He is not slow the way people think of being slow. He is waiting for you. . . .

He wants everybody to come into his kingdom. . . .

God keeps his promise. So we look for a new sky and space. We look for a new earth. It will be the home of people who are right with God. *2 Peter 3:9, 13*

"NO EYE HAS SEEN what God has planned. No ear has heard what God has planned. No mind has thought of God's plans. His plans are for people who love him," wrote the missionary Paul (1 Corinthians 2:9, DBD). It's a promise: God is making a place ready for us. It's a place so wonderful, we can't even imagine it. Jesus told his friends, "There are many rooms in my Father's house. . . . I'm going there to get a place ready for you. So you can be sure I'll come back for you. I'll take you with me" (John 14:3, DBD).

Does God keep his promises? Yes. Will people who are hurting and angry and dying in this world win? No. God loves his people, and his love always wins.

Dear God, thank you for making a special, wonderful place for me. Thank you for your love.

☀ SOME THINGS YOU CAN DO THIS WEEK 🌙

☀ **Have milk and honey for a snack.** You can put the honey on bread. Remember that God kept his promise to take his people to a land "flowing with milk and honey," a land of many blessings.

🌙 **Roll a piece of foil into a tight little ball.** Fill a sink or a bowl with water. Place the foil ball on top of the water. What happens? Now form another piece of foil into a boat or bowl shape. Set it on the water. What happens? Water pushes against whatever is in it. You can feel this by putting your hand in a plastic bag and gently pushing it into the water. The ball of foil was not very big, so there wasn't much water pushing against it. But the boat-shaped foil was larger. The water pushing against it was stronger, so the boat floated. Remember how God took care of Noah and the animals, and then promised to never get rid of all the people and creatures on the earth with water again.

☀ **Make a star picture.** Put lots of star stickers on a piece of paper. Then place a second piece of paper over the first one, covering the star stickers. Color over the top paper with crayons. The star shapes will show up. When you look at the star picture, remember God's promise to take care of Jacob. Remember that God keeps his promises. That's one way he blesses us and shows he loves us.

🌙 **Make trail mix.** You can mix together raisins and other dried fruit bits, plain granola, unshelled peanuts, and sunflower seeds. Sometimes people take trail mix with them when they are traveling or hiking. What do you think Jacob might have taken with him? Remember God's promise to care for Jacob. Remember God's promise to care for you, too.

GOD, ALWAYS IN CONTROL

Trust the Lord with all your heart. Don't depend on your own understanding.
Remember the Lord in everything you do.
And he will give you success. Proverbs 3:5-6, ICB

This week you will learn
· *what to think when you don't understand what's happening;*
· *who tasted a king's drink, and why;*
· *who God says he is;*
· *what it means to know that God is in control.*

Monday

Read "The Dreamer," page 32 in the *Day by Day Kid's Bible.* Or read this part of the story:

Joseph walked up to his brothers. They pulled his beautiful, long coat off. They threw him into the dry well.

Then they sat down and ate their lunch. Now along came a line of men with camels. . . .

Judah said, "It won't do us any good to kill Joseph. Let's sell him to these men." . . .

The brothers took Joseph out of the well. They sold him to the men. *Genesis 37:23-28*

LONG AGO in Joseph's time, people put their belongings in a large cloth and tied it into a bundle. To carry smaller things, they used pouches made of animal skin or cloth. They often traveled in groups of people with pack animals (like donkeys), because they were safer from robbers than if they were alone.

Maybe Joseph thought that God was not in control of his life anymore after his brothers sold him. But God was still in control, even though Joseph didn't understand.

If God is always in control, does that fit his plan to love and bless us? It does, because God loves us even when bad things happen and we don't understand.

At this point in Joseph's life, it looked as though evil had won. But his story was not over! Joseph still had hope, because he trusted that God loved him, and Joseph believed that God's love always wins.

Dear Father God, thank you for always being in control even when bad things happen and I don't understand. Help me to love and trust you no matter what happens.

Tuesday

Read "Two Strange Dreams," page 35 in the *Day by Day Kid's Bible*. Or read this part of the story:

One day two new men were sent to jail. One was the man who took the king his drinks. He was a waiter. The other was the king's baker. . . . Joseph was put in charge of them. . . .

One night the baker and waiter both had dreams. . . .

The waiter said, "My dream was about a vine." . . .

"Here is what your dream means," said Joseph. ". . . You will see the king. Please tell him about me. See if you can get me out of jail, too." . . .

But the waiter didn't tell the king about Joseph. He forgot. *Genesis 40:1, 4-5, 9, 12-14, 23*

WAITERS WHO SERVED drinks to a king were important people. Before they gave a drink to the king, they had to taste it to make sure it was not poisoned. The king's cup was probably made of gold. Although some cups were shaped like cups we use today, most cups were shaped like bowls.

Another reason the waiter was important was because he always listened when the king told about important decisions he had to make.

In jail, Joseph blessed the waiter and others by helping them. He knew that God is always in control, even when bad things happen and we don't understand. God was in control even when the waiter forgot to talk to the king about Joseph.

God blesses us by always being in control. We keep loving God and blessing others so they will come to love God too.

Dear God, thank you for always being in control, even when I don't understand. Help me to keep loving you and blessing others.

Wednesday

Read "The King's Dreams," page 36 in the *Day by Day Kid's Bible.* Or read this part of the story:

"I had a dream," said the king. ". . . I heard that you can tell what dreams mean."

"I can't," said Joseph. "But God can."

So the king told Joseph about the fat and thin cows. He told Joseph about the fat and thin wheat.

Joseph said, "Both of your dreams mean the same thing. . . . First this land will have seven years with enough food. Then there will be seven years of no food. This will happen right away. So you should find a wise man. Put him in charge of Egypt. Save food that grows in the good years." . . .

The king liked Joseph's idea. He said, "God has told this to you. You are the wisest of all. . . . You'll be in charge of all the land of Egypt." *Genesis 41:15-35, 37, 39, 41*

BY TELLING THE MEANING of the king's dream, and by showing him how to save grain for food, Joseph blessed the king and all the people of Egypt. How did this fit into God's plan? God blessed Joseph with wisdom. Joseph trusted God and blessed the king. The king was able to see God's love through Joseph.

God's plan is to love and bless us. Then we will love God and bless others so they will come to love God too.

Who won in Joseph's life: evil people, who tried to hurt him, or God? God won. God loves his people, and his love always wins.

Dear God, thank you for giving wisdom. Please make me wise and help me to bless others.

Thursday

Read "Fire!" page 49 and "Hay Bricks," page 51 in the *Day by Day Kid's Bible.* Or read this part of the story:

"I want you to go to Egypt," said God. "I'm sending you to the king. You'll bring my people out of Egypt."

"But who am I?" asked Moses. . . . "What if they ask what God's name is? Then what will I say?"

"The name is I Am Who I Am," said God. . . .

Moses told the Jews what God had said. But they didn't listen to him. Their hearts were too sad and worried.

Exodus 3:10-11, 13-14; 6:9

IF A NEW TEACHER said, "Tell me about yourself," what would you say besides your name?

When Moses asked about God's name, God answered, "I Am Who I Am." That means God will always be who he is. He lives beyond time. He lived in the past, he lives now, and he will live forever.

God, who lives beyond time, can always be in control. But he does not make us live under his control. He lets us choose for ourselves. Moses chose to follow God and let him be in control of his life. At first, the Jewish people in Egypt would not let God be in control. In fact, they got mad at Moses. But Moses kept trusting God, even when he didn't understand what was happening. It may have looked like evil was winning at this point in Moses' life. But the story wasn't over yet. Moses could keep trusting God to be in control, because he knew that in the end, God's love always wins.

Dear God, thank you for telling us about yourself. Thank you that you live forever and that your love always wins.

Friday

Read "Frogs, Bugs, and Flies," page 53 in the *Day by Day Kid's Bible*. Or read this part of the story:

Flies messed up the land. Then the king called Moses and Aaron. . . . "I'll let you worship God in the desert," said the king. "But don't go very far. Pray for me now."

"I'll pray when I leave you," said Moses. "The flies will go away tomorrow. But make sure you don't lie to us again. This time you'd better let us go." . . .

God got rid of the flies. There wasn't even one left. But the king still didn't think God was important. He didn't let God's people go. *Exodus 8:24-25, 28-32*

OUT OF THE GROUND they came—fat, buzzing cicadas (sih-KAY-duhs), also called locusts. Where Drew lived, these cicadas came only once every 17 years. But when they came, hundreds of them crawled out of holes, climbed up trees, shed their old skins, flew around, laid eggs in the trees, and then died. Drew caught them once in a while, and his cat liked to chase them. When the insects died, all their bodies made the ground around the trees black, and they began to stink.

Do cicadas come where you live? Do you have lots of fireflies or mosquitoes or ants? Can you imagine what Egypt might have been like when God filled it with frogs and flies and gnats and locusts? God was showing everyone that no one is more powerful than he is. God was showing that he is in control. Who won: the mean king or God, who is love? Did God set his people free? Exodus 12:37 says that God took his people out of Egypt. God's love always wins.

Dear God, thank you that no one is as powerful as you are. Thank you for being in control.

SOME THINGS YOU CAN DO THIS WEEK

Find the missing item. Gather ten things you might pack if you were going on a trip (like a toothbrush, a comb, socks, and so on). Then get friends or family to play a game with you. Put the ten items in a suitcase. When everyone is ready, open the suitcase and count to thirty. Everyone else should look at what's in the suitcase. Then close the suitcase and take it out of the room. Take one item out. Go back into the room and open the suitcase. See who can tell you the item that is missing. Remember how Joseph traveled in a caravan—a group of people with pack animals.

Taste some grains. Find foods in your pantry that are made from grain (crackers, bread, pasta, cereal, and so on). Put a bit of several of these foods on a plate and then try each kind, one by one, to see how the different grains taste. Although Joseph didn't understand what was happening, God was using him to save grain for a time when Joseph's own family would need food.

Find a green bush. Draw a bush on a piece of red paper and cut it out. Then glue or tape the red bush to a piece of white paper. Now get a second piece of white paper. Stare at the red bush, keeping your eyes on the middle of the bush, while you slowly count to fifteen. Then stare at the middle of the plain white paper. After a few seconds, you should see a green bush appear. This is called an afterimage. Remember the bush that Moses saw and how God was in control even though Moses didn't understand.

Make play dough. Mix one part water, one part salt, and three parts flour. Use it to form the shapes of different kinds of insects. Toothpicks can be legs and antennae. You can put designs on your insects by drawing on them gently with markers. Remember how God showed his power to the people in Egypt.

GOD COMES NEAR

How good it is to be near God! Psalm 73:28, NLT

This week you will learn
· *who God comes close to;*
· *how we hear God;*
· *who was afraid to come near to God;*
· *why we don't have to be afraid.*

Monday

Read "A Fat King," page 104 in the *Day by Day Kid's Bible.* Or read this part of the story:

God's people began to worship the fake gods from [other] nations.

Now the king of Aram brought his army in. He became king of the land. He took charge of God's people.

But God's people called to God for help. So God chose a judge for them. . . .

This judge helped the people fight the king. God helped them win. . . .

God's people began to sin again. So God let King Eglon take over the land. . . .

At last God's people called to him for help. So God sent them another judge. *Judges 3:7-10, 12, 15*

"I CAN DO IT," said Brady, holding the LEGO pieces away from Mike.

"Okay, okay," said Mike, "I was just trying to help." He shook his head at his little brother. In a few minutes, he heard Brady whining. "Do you need help?" Mike asked.

Brady nodded. "The wheels won't go on," he said. Mike sat down and began to help.

God's people sometimes act like Brady. They turn away from God and think they can take care of life themselves. That shows God that his people do not want him near. So he does not come near. For the people in today's Bible reading, that's when the enemy came. Then the people turned to God. And he came near to them again. This teaches us something very important about God: God comes near us when we come to him. How can we come near to God? We can talk to him. That's called *praying*. We can keep him in our thoughts. And we can follow his ways by obeying him.

Dear God, thank you for wanting to come near to me. Help me come near to you.

Tuesday

Read "A Voice at Night," page 124 in the *Day by Day Kid's Bible*. Or read this part of the story:

Samuel was sleeping in the worship tent. That's where God's ark box was.

Then God called to Samuel.

"I'm right here," said Samuel. . . .

"I didn't call you," said Eli. "Go back to bed."

So Samuel went back to bed.

God called again. "Samuel!"

Samuel got up again. He went to Eli. . . .

"I didn't call you, son," said Eli. "Go back to bed." . . .

God called Samuel again.

Samuel got up and went to Eli. . . .

"Go back to bed," said Eli. Then Eli told Samuel to say these words if God called again. "I'm your servant. I'm listening, God."

So Samuel went back to bed.

Then God came and stood there. He called, "Samuel! Samuel!"
"I'm your servant," said Samuel. "And I'm listening."
1 Samuel 3:3-6, 8-10

A CRICKET'S EARS are on its front legs. Most fish don't have ears, although some have inner ears that hear sound waves traveling through water. Birds' feathers hide their small ear holes. Elephants have the biggest ears. Cats, bats, and dogs can hear sounds that humans can't hear.

Most people have never heard God speak out loud. Still, God does speak to us. One way is through the Bible, where God tells us about himself and his plan. Another way is in our spirit. But God will never tell us anything in our spirit that is different from what he tells us in the Bible. For example, God would never tell us to be rude or to steal.

God loves and blesses us by speaking to us. That's one way he comes near. We show our love for God by listening to him. That's one way we can come near to God.

Dear God, thank you for speaking to me. Help me hear you.

Wednesday
Read "A Message for Mary," page 504 in the *Day by Day Kid's Bible*. Or read this part of the story:

God sent the angel Gabriel with a message . . . to a young woman. . . .

"Hello!" said Gabriel to Mary. "You are very special. God is with you! . . . You are going to have a baby boy. You are to name him Jesus. . . . He will be God's Son." *Luke 1:26-28, 31, 35*

EACH PERSON'S FINGERPRINTS are the one and only fingerprints like them in the world. Something that is the one and only thing like it is *unique* (you-NEEK).

The most unique person who ever lived is Jesus. When God promised to send Jesus, God called him *Immanuel,* which means "God with us." Before Jesus came, he lived with God in heaven. What do you think Jesus gave up to come to earth? Being "God with us" is what makes Jesus unique, the one and only person like him. It was through Jesus that God came near to all of us. He came as a baby and grew up as a human so he would know exactly what it is like to be a human being. Now when you talk with God, he knows just how you feel. He is near.

Dear God, thank you for coming to be with us through Jesus.

Thursday

Read "Ten Rules," page 66 in the *Day by Day Kid's Bible.* Or read this part of the story:

All the people saw the lightning. They heard the horn and the thunder. They saw the smoke over the mountain. They shook. They were afraid. They stayed back. "You talk to us," they told Moses. "We'll listen to you. But don't let God talk to us. We might die!"
    "Don't be afraid," said Moses. "God is testing you. He wants you to worship him. Then you won't sin." *Exodus 20:18-20*

SHERI LOVES STORMS. She loves thunder and lightning and wind. She goes to the window to watch. But some people are afraid of thunder and lightning and wind. When God came to the top of the mountain near his people, they were too afraid to listen for his voice. They told Moses to listen for them. But Moses told them that God just wanted them to respect him and know that he was the greatest. They didn't need to be afraid of coming near to God.

Why aren't we afraid to come near to God? It's because we know how much he loves us. His plan is to love and bless us. Then we love and bless others. We do kind things so they will come to love God too. God wants everyone to come near to him. He loves everyone.

Dear God, thank you for letting us know you love us. Thank you for wanting us to come near.

Friday

Read "Clean Feet," page 609 in the *Day by Day Kid's Bible.* Or read this part of the story:

Jesus got up from the table. He took a long cloth. He tied it around himself like a belt. Then he got a big bowl of water. He started washing his friends' feet. He dried their feet with the long cloth. *John 13:4-5*

WHAT KIND OF SHOE is your favorite? In Bible times, people often went barefoot, or they wore sandals made of leather or plant fiber. Some people wore soft leather boots. In cold weather, Roman soldiers sometimes wore fur-lined boots. Some people carried their shoes to make them last longer! So most people's feet got dirty from walking down dirt roads and dusty streets. Washing a guest's feet was a way to serve and bless them. It was a sign of respect.

Jesus is God's Son, the King and Master of the whole world. But he came near enough to his friends to wash their feet. That's how much he loved them. If Jesus were to walk into your house or yard, he might bring you a snack. Or play ball with you. Or help you with your homework. Even though you can't see him, he is near right now. How is he showing his love? Can you feel his hug?

Dear God, thank you for coming near to me and showing me your love. Help me to see all the ways you show your love to me.

☀ SOME THINGS YOU CAN DO THIS WEEK ☽

Make a volcano. Put a small paper cup in the center of a cake pan. Fold one edge of a sheet of aluminum foil around the sides of the cup and let the foil slope down into the cake pan to form a mountain shape. Put one tablespoon of baking soda into the cup. Slowly add one cup of vinegar. Remember how God showed his greatness with thunder and lightning when he came to the top of the mountain.

Make ears. Find a large piece of construction paper. Place a large paper plate in the center of the paper and trace around it. Cut out this circle. Then draw ears on each side of the large hole. These can be any kind of ears (big ears, silly ears, animal ears). Hold the paper up and look through the large hole so that the ears appear to be your own. Think of how Samuel heard God's voice and about how you can listen to God.

Make a design from the name IMMANUEL. First turn a piece of paper sideways and print the name IMMANUEL on it in large letters, with space between each one. Then turn each letter into a human figure. For example, draw a round head at the top of the I and make arms come out the sides. Put feet on the bottom of the I. Do this with all of the letters, using your imagination to make them look fun. Remember that *IMMANUEL* means "God with us." Jesus is Immanuel, God coming near to us.

Make sole rubbings. Hold a sheet of paper against the sole of a shoe and rub a crayon over the paper. It will reveal the pattern on the bottom of the shoe. You can "collect" footprint rubbings this way from family and friends, and even from your own shoes. Remember how Jesus came near enough to wash his friends' feet.

GOD IS TRUSTWORTHY

O Sovereign Lord, you are God! Your words are trustworthy. 2 Samuel 7:28, NIV

This week you will learn
· what trustworthy means;
· how a bunch of jars got broken;
· who tore his own coat into twelve pieces;
· why you can trust God.

Monday

Read "A Look into the New Land" and "Scared of the People," pages 79 and 80 in the *Day by Day Kid's Bible.* Or read this part of the story:

After 40 days the 12 men came back to Moses. . . .

.   "We can't fight those people. . . . They are stronger than we are." . . .

Then God's greatness came over the worship tent. God said to Moses, "How long will this go on? How long will these people treat me as nothing? I've shown them wonders. But they choose not to believe me." *Numbers 13:25-26, 31; 14:10-11*

WHY DID GOD EXPECT his people to be able to take the land? God planned to help them. But they were afraid and didn't trust God to help. That made God sad, because he is *trustworthy.* That means God is worth trusting. We can count on God. We can depend on him. This is part of God's plan. He loves and blesses us by being trustworthy. We love God back by trusting him. Then we bless others by being trustworthy ourselves. When other people learn that they can count on us, they will see God's love through us and may come to love God too. Being trustworthy is one way God shows us he loves us. It's all part of God's plan to show that his love wins.

Dear God, thank you for being trustworthy. Help me to trust you.

Tuesday

Read "Hiding on the Roof" and "Falling Walls!" pages 95 and 98 in the *Day by Day Kid's Bible.* Or read this part of the story:

"Tie a red rope in your window," the men said. "Then bring all your family into this house. That way we can save you. . . ."

"All right," said Rahab. . . .

Then the wall of the city fell down. Joshua and his men went right into the city.

Joshua called the men who had stayed at Rahab's house. "Go save Rahab," he said.

So they went to Rahab's house. They brought out Rahab and her family. *Joshua 2:17-21; 6:20, 22-23*

AT BASKETBALL GAMES, people yell for their teams so loudly that afterward we might say their shouts "shook the rafters." At football games, sometimes the cheering seems to shake the stands where we sit. But at Jericho, the shouts of God's people brought down the walls! Except for one place. Rahab's house stood. Can you imagine what it might have been like to be in Rahab's family and look out the window while all this happened? It might have been hard to trust God to save them. But God did save Rahab, because she believed in him even though she was not one of his people. This tells us that God welcomes people of all nations.

Everyone can trust God. He loves us and blesses us by being trustworthy. We love him back by trusting him. Then we bless others by being trustworthy ourselves, so others will see God's love through us and will come to love God too, just like Rahab did.

Dear God, thank you for welcoming people of all nations. Show all people how trustworthy you are.

Wednesday

Read "Sun and Moon Stand Still," page 101 in the *Day by Day Kid's Bible.* Or read this part of the story:

God sent hail down on the enemy armies.

That day Joshua prayed, "Let the sun stand still. Let the moon stand still."

The sun did stand still. The moon stopped moving across the sky. The sun and moon stopped until God's people won the fight. *Joshua 10:11-13*

HAVE YOU EVER SEEN the moon and sun in the sky at the same time? The earth turns around every 24 hours, which makes the sun look like it rises and sets. The moon goes around the earth every month. So sometimes the moon is going around our side of the earth at the same time we are turning toward the sun. Then we see both the sun and the moon.

As long as there has been an earth, the sun has come up every morning. The prophet Jeremiah wrote that God's love is new every morning. We trust that the sun will come up each day. And it does. But it's really not the sun we are trusting. We're trusting God. We know he will keep bringing a new day with more of his love. Because he is trustworthy. He is worth trusting.

Joshua trusted God, and God helped him by doing something unusual. We don't know how he did it, but God gave him a longer day. We can trust God too. He stays with us and loves us no matter what happens.

Dear God, thank you for staying with us no matter what happens. Thank you for being trustworthy.

Thursday

Read "A Night Fight," page 109 in the *Day by Day Kid's Bible.* Or read this part of the story:

[Gideon] gave each man a horn. He gave each man a jar. In each jar was a stick with fire burning on it.

"Watch me!" said Gideon. "I'll lead. You follow. Do what I do. I'll blow my horn. Then you blow yours." Gideon told his men to shout these words: "For God and for Gideon!"

They went down into the valley. They came to the enemy camp. . . .

All of a sudden, Gideon blew his horn. He broke his jar. The other men blew their horns. They broke their jars. They shouted, "A sword for God and for Gideon!" Then they just stayed where they were.

But the enemy army didn't stay. They were afraid, so they shouted and ran. *Judges 7:16-22*

HEROES ARE PEOPLE we think of as being big and strong. The big hero fights the bad guy and wins. But God often chooses heroes and leaders who are not strong or big to lead his people. Young David fought Goliath the giant. Moses, who told God he was not good at talking, spoke to the king of Egypt and led God's people out of that land. Even Samson, though he was strong, did not win over the enemy until he was blind.

Why does God choose people who are not strong to lead? Because God wants us to know that only he can win over the troubles in our lives. Only he is worth our trust. It does not matter how strong or smart we are. We need God. And he can use small things, even people who feel they are not impor-tant. He can use people like you and me, if we trust God. That's because God loves us, and his love always wins.

Dear God, thank you for using small things to get your work done. Thank you for using me.

Friday

Read "Enemies" and "One Nation Turns into Two Nations," pages 269 and 271 in the *Day by Day Kid's Bible.* Or read this part of the story:

Ahijah was wearing a new coat. But Ahijah tore his new coat into 12 pieces. He said, "Take 10 pieces, Jeroboam. God told me that he is taking the kingdom away from Solomon. God is giving 10 parts of it to you." . . .

God's words to Jeroboam long ago came true. Jeroboam became king of the 10 family groups in the north. They called their nation Israel. *1 Kings 11:30-31; 12:15*

"I DIDN'T REALLY MEAN IT." Have you ever heard anyone say that? People don't always say what they mean or mean what they say, but God does.

Things were pretty bad for Solomon. Still, Solomon could have told God he was sorry. He could have started following God with his whole heart. But he didn't. That's why God sent a message through Ahijah, who tore his own new coat and told Jeroboam that God would give ten parts of the kingdom to him. Did it happen? Yes.

God says what he means, and he means what he says. God is trustworthy. We can trust him to do what he says. God loves and blesses us by being trustworthy. We love God and bless others by saying what we mean and meaning what we say.

Dear God, thank you for saying what you mean and meaning what you say. Thank you for being trustworthy. Help me to be trustworthy too.

SOME THINGS YOU CAN DO THIS WEEK

● **Make up spy riddles.** With friends or family, say, "I spy with my little eye something that is . . . *(name a color)*." The others try to guess what you spy. If they can't guess, give other clues. Then it's another person's turn to make a riddle. Think about the spies who went into the land God promised to give them. They did not trust God to help them take the land.

● **Build model walls.** Spread a sheet across the floor. Build a model of Jericho's city wall with blocks. When the wall is built, stand back, off the sheet. March around the sheet seven times. Then gently hold on to the edge of the sheet and shake it so the walls of Jericho fall. Remember how Rahab trusted God to take care of her.

● **Play a hot-sun game.** Blow up a yellow balloon. Get family or friends together in a circle. Choose a leader to sit in the center of the circle. Give the balloon to the leader. The balloon represents the sun. The leader begins the game by tossing the balloon to someone. Then the leader closes his or her eyes while everyone else passes the balloon around the circle very quickly. Don't hold on to it for very long, because the sun is hot! After a few minutes, the leader calls, "Sun, stand still!" Whoever is holding the sun trades places with the leader. This new leader starts the next round of the game. Remember how God stopped the sun and moon in the sky. Think of how trustworthy God is.

● **Design a flag for a country.** This country can be imaginary or real. To make the flag, use markers and crayons on plain paper. You can design the flag any way you choose. If you have an encyclopedia, look up "flag" and see the flags of the different countries. Remember that God loves people from every country, just as he loved Rahab.

GOD, THE ONE AND ONLY

Turn to me and be saved, all you ends of the earth; for I am God,
and there is no other. Isaiah 45:22, NIV

This week you will learn
· *how stones burned up;*
· *what holy means;*
· *who ate grass because he thought he was the greatest;*
· *how we know that there is only one God.*

Monday

Read "Fire on Carmel Mountain," page 281 in the *Day by Day Kid's Bible.* Or read this part of the story:

Elijah prayed. "God, show that you are God in Israel. Show that I'm your servant. Show that I'm obeying you. Answer me, God. Let these people know that you are God."

Then fire came down from God onto the altar. It burned up the meat. It burned up the wood. It burned up the stones. It burned up the dirt. And it burned up the water in the pit!

The people were watching. They bowed down with their faces to the ground. "The Lord is God!" they shouted. *1 Kings 18:36-39*

THINK OF THE SMELL of meat on the grill outdoors. It smells good and makes us hungry.

Long ago, people cooked meat on altars as a gift to God. They called these gifts *sacrifices,* because they sacrificed or gave up the very best animals they had. They also called their gifts *offerings* because they offered the best they had to God.

When fire came down on Elijah's altar, God was showing that he is the One and Only God. There is no other god for us to love and follow. We don't offer meat as a gift to God anymore, but we can give him other gifts to show our love. Can you think of what you might give him? (Hint: He loves to hear you sing and talk to him. He likes it when you write a poem to him or draw him a picture. He likes it when you are kind to others and show what he is like.)

Dear God, thank you for being the One and Only God. I will give my best to you.

Tuesday

Read "Good King Asa," page 276 in the *Day by Day Kid's Bible*. Or read this part of the story:

Then Asa called to God. "There's nobody like you, God," he said. "You help people who are not strong. Help us. We trust you to help us. We fight this big army in your name. You are our God. Don't let men win against you."

So God fought the army from Cush. They ran away.
2 Chronicles 14:11-12

HAVE YOU EVER SEEN a fort? The word *fort* means "strong." A fort is a place surrounded by strong walls to keep enemies from coming in. Pioneers in America built wooden forts. Long before that, people of other nations built forts made of wood or stone.

But King Asa knew that a fort cannot always keep an enemy out. He knew that only God is strong enough to keep an enemy away. No one else can help the powerless against the mighty. God is the "One and Only."

Do you ever feel powerless? God helps the powerless. All you have to do is ask. Then wait for him to work. Isaiah wrote, "Since the world began, no ear

has heard, and no eye has seen a God like you, who works for those who
wait for him!" (Isaiah 64:4, NLT).

*Dear God, thank you for helping the powerless against the mighty. You are
truly the One and Only God.*

Wednesday

Read "What Elisha Saw," page 302 in the *Day by Day Kid's Bible.* Or read this part of the story:

Every time Aram's army moved, Elisha knew where they went. . . .
     "Go find Elisha," said the king of Aram. "I'm going to catch
him."
     So his men found out where Elisha was. Then Aram's king sent
out lots of men. They rode out with horses and chariots. They went
to get Elisha.
     It was night. . . . They got in a circle around the city.
     Elisha's helper, Gehazi, got up early the next day. He looked
out and saw the army around the city. He saw the horses and chariots. "What are we going to do?" he called to Elisha.
     "Don't be scared," said Elisha. "Our army is bigger than theirs."
     Then Elisha prayed. He said, "God, let Gehazi see."
     So God let Gehazi see. He looked out and saw another army all
over the hills. It was an army of horses and chariots of fire.
2 Kings 6:8-9, 13-17

KINGS AND COMMANDERS in Bible times often led their armies to battle
in a chariot. A chariot was a cart with two wheels. Horses pulled it, and it
could go very fast. Sometimes men would have chariot races.

God's heavenly army was ready to protect and help God's people. But
Elisha's servant could not see them until God allowed him to. Elisha's servant

probably had never seen chariots and horses of fire before! God truly is the "One and Only." He loves and blesses us by commanding heaven's armies around us. Are these armies for us or against us? They are for us. God's armies always fight for the people who love and follow God. God loves his people. And in the end, his love always wins.

Dear God, thank you for commanding heavenly armies. You are truly the One and Only God.

Thursday

Read "A Burning Coal," page 337 in the *Day by Day Kid's Bible.* Or read this part of the story:

The year Uzziah died, I [Isaiah] saw God sitting in heaven. He was above others, and he was great. His robe was so long that it filled the worship house.

Beings from heaven were flying above God. Each one had six wings. The beings covered their faces with two wings. They covered their feet with two wings. They flew with two wings. They called out to each other. "Good and right and holy is God Who Has All Power. His greatness fills the whole earth." *Isaiah 6:1-3*

DO YOU EVER go to a library? There were libraries in Bible times too. But that's about the only place books could be found. And many of the "books" were rolls of paper. There were no machines to print books, so they had to be written by hand. Even the books of the Bible were first written by hand. That meant it took a long time, even as long as a whole year, for someone to copy one book! That's why there were not many books. Besides, in Bible times only kings and leaders, rich people, and scribes (whose job it was to write things down) were trained to read and write. Women were not taught to read or write.

But Isaiah wrote down what he heard and saw. That's why we can read it today. He saw God on his throne. He heard the heavenly beings calling, "Holy!" The word *holy* means "perfect" and "awesome," and "different from other beings." What can you write about our One and Only God?

Dear God, thank you for being perfect and awesome and different from all other beings.

Friday

Read "The King Who Lived with Wild Animals," page 434 in the *Day by Day Kid's Bible*. Or read this part of the story:

I [Nebuchadnezzar] was walking on my palace roof. I said, "This is the great Babylon that I built. I built it by my strong power. It shows how great I am!"

I had hardly stopped talking when I heard a voice. It came from heaven. "Here's what will happen to you, King. You will not be king anymore. You'll be sent away from people. You'll live with wild animals. You'll eat grass like a cow. Seven years will pass. Then you'll say that God is the king. You'll know that God gives kingdoms to anyone he wants."

Right away, it happened. I was sent away from my people. I ate grass like a cow. . . .

After seven years, I, Nebuchadnezzar, looked up to heaven. My right mind came back to me. Then I praised the Most High God who lives forever. *Daniel 4:29-34*

COWS AND SHEEP AND GOATS must have been surprised to look up and see a man eating grass. And it wasn't just any man. It was the king! He had talked like he was the greatest. That was like saying he was greater than God. But the king soon learned that he was no greater than an animal in the field.

God tells us that his ways are higher than our ways, and his thoughts are higher than ours (Isaiah 55:9). God is truly the One and Only. He is the greatest. He is able to love and bless us. So we love God and bless others. Why is it important to bless others? So they will see the love of God through us and choose to love God themselves.

Dear God, you are truly the greatest. You are the One and Only God.

SOME THINGS YOU CAN DO THIS WEEK

Make paper blocks out of paper grocery bags. Open the bags. Fill each bag about halfway with old, crumpled newspaper. Close and fold the tops of the bags down to the fill line. Then tape the folded edge to the side of the bag with masking tape. Stack these blocks to make an altar or a fort. Remember King Asa's fort and Elijah's altar, and the way God showed them that he is the One and Only God.

Make a scroll. Turn a piece of paper sideways and copy a verse about God onto it, such as this week's theme verse. Or make up your own words to tell what God is like. Then tape each side of the paper to an unsharpened pencil and roll each pencil to the center of the paper. Put a rubber band around this scroll to keep it rolled. Remember Isaiah writing what he saw about God.

Make a magnetic path. Draw a path going any way you choose across a paper plate. Color grass all around this road. Set a paper clip on the plate. Hold a magnet under the plate, touching the plate so that the paper clip is drawn to the magnet. From underneath, use the magnet to lead the paper clip along the path. The paper clip needs the magnet to lead it, because the paper clip doesn't have the power to move on its own. Even if it did, it wouldn't know which way to go. God leads and directs us. His ways are greater than ours, and his thoughts are greater than ours.

Write your name. Get some washable ink or washable liquid paint, paper, and a variety of pointed, but not sharp, items to use as writing instruments. You might look for feathers, cotton swabs, sturdy toothpicks, whole carrots, pipe cleaners, sticks, etc. Dip the tip of each writing tool into the ink or paint, one at a time. Write your name with each one. Think about who wrote things in Bible times. We have our Bibles today because men wrote about what happened and about what God told them.

GOD CALLS TO US

Return, O Israel, to the Lord your God, for your sins have brought you down.
Hosea 14:1, NLT

This week you will learn
· what mercy means;
· who sent out a big army of small animals;
· who fueled his winter fire with God's words;
· what we can do when God calls us.

Monday

Read "The Bad Things Israel Did," page 323 in the *Day by Day Kid's Bible.* Or read this part of the story:

> Hear what God says. . . .
>
> "The people of Israel don't care about me.
>   They're like a cow that won't go where you lead.
> So how can I lead them to green fields?
>   How can they be my sheep? . . .
>
> "I'll be like a lion to Israel and Judah.
>   I'll take them away. There will be no one to save them.
> Then I'll wait for them to say they've done wrong.
>   They will feel so bad, they'll look for me."
> Hosea 4:1, 16; 5:14-15

MARY, MARY, QUITE CONTRARY. You may have heard that rhyme when you were younger. The word *contrary* means "opposite" or "not wanting to follow directions." Perhaps you or some of your friends have a little brother or sister who is about two years old. Then you know that when you say, "Come here," the toddler often runs the other way. That's being contrary.

God's people were contrary. They worshipped idols and trusted in their own power instead of God's power. God tried to get the people to come back to him. He was patient. He told them over and over again to come back. God let them have trouble, hoping they would learn that their idols could not help them. God tries to bring his people back to himself in every way he can. Sometimes he uses trouble. Sometimes he uses kindness.

Dear God, thank you for loving us enough to try to get us back to yourself in every way you can. Keep calling us back when we turn away from you.

Tuesday

Read "A Big, Strong Army," page 313 in the *Day by Day Kid's Bible.* Or read this part of the story:

There was never an army like this.
There will never be one like it again. . . .

Nations are afraid when they see this army.
Their faces turn white.
That's because the grasshoppers march like fighters.
They go over walls and march in line. . . .

"Even now you can come back to me," says God.
"Come back with all your heart."
God is kind and full of love.
He doesn't get angry very fast.
He doesn't want to send trouble.
Joel 2:2, 6-7, 12-13

A LOCUST IS an insect kind of like a grasshopper. If lots of locusts flew into your state, they would eat all the plants. God let locusts go into the land of

Judah, because the people did not love and obey him. He called the locusts his army. God hoped that trouble with locusts would make the people turn to him and trust in him again. God was using an army of locusts to call his people back to him.

Sometimes God lets us have hard times. He does it to get our attention or to train us so we will make better choices in how we act or talk or think. It is always best to turn to God in good times as well as in bad times. That's because no matter what happens, God loves his people. And in the end, his love always wins.

Dear God, thank you for loving me enough to call me back to you when I turn away. Help me to come to you in good times as well as bad times.

Wednesday

Read "The King's Order," page 320 in the *Day by Day Kid's Bible.* Or read this part of the story:

God spoke to Jonah again. "Go to the big city of Nineveh. Tell them what I will do because of their sin."

This time Jonah obeyed God. He went to Nineveh. . . .

Jonah called out, "Nineveh has only 40 more days. Then the city will be destroyed."

The people believed God. . . .

God saw what the people were doing. He saw how they had stopped sinning. So he felt loving and kind toward them. He didn't get rid of them. *Jonah 3:1-5, 10*

THUNDERSTORMS, WINDSTORMS, sandstorms, blizzards, tornadoes, hurricanes, hail storms. Most of us want to be safe indoors during a storm. But when Jonah was trying to run away from God, he found himself in the middle of a storm. You probably remember what happened.

God showed mercy to Jonah by not letting him drown. *Mercy* is deciding not to punish someone, even if punishment is deserved. How did God show his mercy to the people of Nineveh? God didn't destroy them. But Jonah didn't think that was fair, because the people of Nineveh had been so bad. So Jonah complained. But God helped Jonah understand his mercy. He made a vine grow up to give Jonah shade. Then the plant died, and Jonah was sorry about the plant. God taught him that if he was that sad about the plant, God cared even more about the city.

God calls us to himself so he can have mercy on us. God loves his people, and his love always wins.

Dear God, thank you for calling me to yourself and for having mercy on me.

Thursday

Read "The King in the Winter House," page 393 in the *Day by Day Kid's Bible.* Or read this part of the story:

God told Jeremiah, "Get a roll of paper. Write on it everything I told you. Write what I said about Israel, Judah, and other nations. Maybe the people will hear about it. Maybe they'll stop doing wrong and start doing right. Then I'll forgive them." *Jeremiah 36:1-3*

CAMPFIRES FEEL WARM and cozy on a chilly night. In Bible times, no one knew about electricity or gas yet. So houses did not have heaters like ours do. People heated their rooms with a fire in a fireplace or in a metal or clay box. They kept windows closed to keep cold air out. That meant smoke from the fire filled the room and made the ceiling black unless there was a chimney hole above the fire.

The king who got Jeremiah's message was sitting by one of these fire boxes. The message said, "Follow God and he will bless you. If you turn away, you'll get in trouble." But the king cut up the message and threw it into the fire box.

A few people, like Jeremiah, followed God. But most of the people worshipped idols. For hundreds of years, they had been turning to God, then turning away, then turning to God, then turning away. God had given them lots of chances to come back to him. Still, God kept calling to them. God is very patient.

Dear God, thank you for being patient.

Friday

Read "Seventy-Two Men," page 577 in the *Day by Day Kid's Bible.* Or read this part of the story:

Then Jesus said, "Come to me if you're tired. Come to me when you have too much to do. I'll give you rest. Learn by watching and listening to me. I'm thoughtful and kind. My heart is not proud. You'll find your soul can rest with me. I'll be easy on you."
Matthew 11:28-30

A MASTER CRAFTSMAN is a person who has practiced making or doing something so much that he or she is an expert, doing excellent work. A master craftsman might be in charge of teaching or directing others. A ring-master directs a circus. A Webmaster is in charge of making Web pages. A headmaster is in charge of a school. A music conductor is called *maestro*, which is Italian for "master."

Jesus' friends called him Master, and they learned from him. Jesus calls us to come and rest and learn from him. So God is still calling people to himself through Jesus. Jesus will be your Master too, if you put him in charge of your life.

Dear God, thank you for calling me to yourself through Jesus. Help me to be a good follower.

SOME THINGS YOU CAN DO THIS WEEK

Play "Contrary Children." Get together with family or friends and play this game like you would play "Simon Says," except that everyone does the opposite of what the leader says. If the leader says, "Take two baby steps toward me," everyone should take two baby steps away from the leader. If the leader says, "Pat your head," everyone should pat somewhere else. The leader does not do the movements. If the leader sees a player doing what he says to do, that player must sit down. The last player standing is the winner and becomes the leader for the next round of play. Think of how God kept calling his people to himself, even though they were contrary.

Snack on "grasshoppers." Lay a pickle slice (dill pickles work well) on a plate to make the body of the grasshopper. Cut a circle of cheese in half. Each half makes a wing to go on each side of the body. Use a green olive or a grape or a cherry tomato as the head, and stick it on with a toothpick. Remember the army of grasshopper-like locusts that God allowed to come into the land so his people would turn to him for help.

Make a fish. Cut the shape of a piece of pie out of a paper plate. The cutout place is the fish's open mouth. Tape or staple the cutout piece to the side of the plate opposite the mouth to make a tail. Color the fish. Remember how God sent Jonah to call the people of Nineveh to himself. (You may want to read the whole story of Jonah on pages 319–322 in the *Day by Day Kid's Bible*.)

Write your name in picture language. Before you do that, write your first name in large letters across the top of a piece of paper. Then, under each letter, draw something that starts with the sound of that letter. For example, draw an apple for each A in your name. Draw a flower for each F, and so on. This turns your name into a pictograph. To read a pictograph, say the sound that each picture starts with. Try writing a message in picture language. Remember the message that Jeremiah wrote for the king, calling the people to turn back to God.

GOD NEVER STOPS LOVING ME

The Lord's love never ends. Lamentations 3:22, ICB

This week you will learn
· who remembered and loved for 70 years;
· where a special place of safety and rest is;
· how much you are worth.

Monday

Read "Running Away at Night," page 422 and "Great Love," page 424 in the *Day by Day Kid's Bible*. Or read this part of the story:

> *I remember one thing.*
> > *I have hope because of what I remember.*
>
> *God has great love. So we are not lost.*
> > *God's care never ends.*
> *His care is new every morning. . . .*
>
> *God doesn't leave his people forever.*
> > *He might bring sadness.*
> *But he will show his care, too.*
> > *His love is great. It never ends.*
> Lamentations 3:21-23, 31-32

IT WAS AN AWFUL DAY, a terrible day. Nobody wanted it to happen, but it did. An enemy army came and burned down the houses. They broke down the city walls. They took God's people away to Babylon. But even then, God was loving and taking care of his people. He was using this time to teach them that the idols they had worshipped could not help them. The idols could not take care of them or rescue them.

Jeremiah wrote a poem about that sad time. He said that no matter what had happened, God still loved his people.

When things seem to be going wrong, it's easy to think that God has forgotten us. But God's love never ends. No matter what happens, God never stops loving us.

Dear God, thank you that your love for me never ends.

Tuesday

Read "Going Back Home," page 457 in the *Day by Day Kid's Bible.* Or read this part of the story:

Many people chose to go back to Jerusalem. . . .
    They praised God like King David said to do long ago. They thanked God. They sang, "God is good. His love for his people lasts forever." *Ezra 1:5; 3:10-11*

"DO YOU REMEMBER Zachary?" Mom asked.

"Who?" said Danny.

"Zachary, your friend when you were three years old. He moved away," said Mom.

"Oh, yeah. I had forgotten about Zachary," said Danny.

If we haven't seen somebody in a long time, we may forget the person, or we might not think about our friend very often. But God doesn't forget anyone. And he never stops loving. He stayed with his people after they were taken to Babylon. Even 70 years later, he still remembered them and loved them. Then he brought them back home so they could rebuild the houses that had been burned down. God's people remembered him when they were in

Babylon, and God forgave them. Did the enemy from Babylon win, or did God win? God won. God loves his people. God and his love always win.

Dear God, thank you for never forgetting me. Thank you for your love that lasts forever.

Wednesday

Read "A New Song" and "Who Is Strong?" from page 202 in the *Day by Day Kid's Bible.* Or read this part of the story:

> *God's word is right and true.*
> *You can trust him in all he does.*
> *God loves what is right and good.*
> *The earth is full of his love.*
> *His love never comes to an end. . . .*
>
> *We wait for God.*
> *He is our guard. He helps us.*
> *Keep us in your love that never ends, God.*
> Psalm 33:4-5, 20-22

UPSTAIRS in Chang-Ho's house there is a window with a wide sill. It is just the right size to make a seat for Chang-Ho. He has a pillow there, and that's where he sits to read or draw or just think. When he is sad or upset, it is a place where he goes to feel safe and restful.

You have a special place of safety and rest deep inside you wherever you go, if you trust in God. He is our safety. He is our rest. He is our help in times of trouble. He loves us always. His love will never end.

Dear God, thank you for being my place of safety and rest. Thank you that your love for me will never end.

Thursday

Read "As High As the Sky," page 206 in the *Day by Day Kid's Bible*. Or read this part of the story:

> *God's love is as high as the sky is above the earth.*
> *He has moved our sins away from us as far as the east is*
> *   from the west.*
> *God is loving and kind to people who worship him.*
> *He is like a father who is loving and kind to his children.*
> Psalm 103:11-13

HOW HIGH IS THE SKY? As far as we know, it keeps going and going, up and up into space forever. That's how much God loves us: much, much more than we could ever imagine.

Love isn't just a nice feeling about someone. Someone who loves another person wants to do things for the person who is loved. When it's Mother's Day, you want to give a gift to your mom or do something nice for her, because you love her. God's love is like that. He wants to do things for you, because he loves you. Look around. What has he given you?

And what does God want you to do? He wants you to love him back. But even if you don't, he will never ever stop loving you.

Dear God, thank you for loving me with a love as high as the sky. I love you too.

Friday

Read "Spirits," page 794 in the *Day by Day Kid's Bible.* Or read this part of the story:

Here's how God showed us his love. He sent his only Son to the world. He did it so we could live. That's love. It's not that we loved God. It's that he loved us. So he sent his Son as a gift. He sent Jesus to die for our sins. God loved us that much! *1 John 4:9-10*

TYLER TOOK the remote-control car down from the store shelf. He had wanted it for a long time. And he had saved up just enough money to buy the car. It would cost all he had saved. But to Tyler, the car was worth it.

Someone paid to buy you back from a bad-news life. What's a bad-news life? It's trying to do good but messing up and doing bad. It's growing old, getting sick, and dying without knowing God and his love. That's bad news. So Jesus paid to get you out of bad news and into good news. The good-news life is God forgiving you for messing up and then staying close to you so he can always take care of you.

How much did Jesus pay? He paid with his whole life. He died for your sins so you could be free from them and live with God forever. Wow! God loves you that much! You are worth a lot!

Dear God, thank you for sending Jesus to die for my sins. Thank you for loving me that much.

SOME THINGS YOU CAN DO THIS WEEK

Take an imaginary walk. Imagine walking over different kinds of paths. First, walk across a room as if you were going barefoot across hot sand, then as if walking through puddles of water, then on ice, then on pillows, then through prickly grass, then on gravel, and last through squishy mud. If you do this with friends or family, you may play Follow the Leader for each of these. Remember how the enemy army took God's people to Babylon. But God and his love never left them.

Make a picture frame. Glue your picture in the center of a small paper plate. Around the edge of the plate, write "God will never stop loving me." Try to get the words to go all the way around the plate, even if you have to write it more than once, because a circle has no end, and God's love has no end. (You can make this as a gift if you want. Instead of using your picture, use a picture of the person you're giving the gift to.)

Interview your mom or dad or your grandparents. Ask them to tell you about their earliest memories. Ask them to tell about when they were children. God has never left them. God never left his people in Babylon. He was with them and remembered them for 70 years. Then he brought them back to their own land.

Make direction cards. On one index card, write the word EAST. On another, write WEST. Put the EAST card on a wall or window that is on the east side of your room. Put the WEST card on a west wall or window. When you look at them, remember that God has moved your sins away from you as far as the east is from the west.

GOD DOES NOT CHANGE

I the Lord do not change. Malachi 3:6, NIV

This week you will learn

· *what we see outdoors every day that will wear out like clothes;*
· *who wanted to go to a place with burned gates;*
· *what the four living beings in heaven say;*
· *how special it is that God will always be the same.*

Monday

Read "A Land That Brings Joy," page 485 in the *Day by Day Kid's Bible*. Or read this part of the story:

"I'm the Lord. I don't change. So I've kept you around. You've turned away from me over and over again. You haven't kept my laws. But come back to me. Then I'll come back to you," says God. *Malachi 3:6-7*

"IF YOU DON'T LIKE THE WEATHER, wait a day and it will change." That's a saying that's true in most places. Some days are sunny, some are cloudy, some are rainy, some are hot, some are cold. Everything changes. Even huge mountain rocks wear down in the rain and wind.

But God is greater than everything. He does not change. Think about who God is. He is strong, wise, kind, loving, giving, beautiful, and interested in you. Will that ever change? No. He is your God forever, always loving you with his never-ending love.

Dear God, thank you that you never change. Thank you for loving me forever.

Tuesday

Read "Angels," page 778 in the *Day by Day Kid's Bible*. Or read this part of the story:

> *Lord, in the beginning you made the earth.*
> > *Your hands made the sky and all of space.*
> *They won't last forever.*
> > *But you will.*
> *They will wear out like clothes.*
> > *You'll roll them up as if they were a robe.*
> > *They will be changed like you change clothes.*
> *But you stay the same.*
> > *Your life never ends.*
>
> Hebrews 1:10-12

HOW ARE A POPSICLE, a soccer ball, and a pair of socks alike? None of them last forever. Which will probably last the shortest time? Which will probably last longest?

The earth has lasted a long, long time. So has the sky. But God, who made them, was around long before they were made. And he will be around long after they are gone. He will be the same God forever that he has always been.

You and I will change though. The biggest change for you and me will be when we go to live with God and get new spirit bodies. We'll still look like ourselves, but we'll be well and strong, and we'll live forever with God. It will be more wonderful than we can imagine. And God will not have changed a bit. He will be the same loving, giving, wise, caring God he has always been. And one very special change for us: We'll be able to SEE God!

Dear God, thank you for planning for us to change so that we can see you someday. And thank you that you never change. Thank you for loving me forever.

Wednesday

Read "Burned Gates," page 490 in the *Day by Day Kid's Bible.* Or read this part of the story:

The king had never seen a sad look on my face before. So he asked, "Why are you sad?" . . .

I told the king, "It's because of Jerusalem. It's the city where my people lived. It's a pile of sticks and stones. . . .

"If you're happy with me, let me go to Jerusalem. Let me build the city back up."

The king . . . was glad to send me.

I went to Jerusalem. I stayed there for three days. Then I went out into the city at night. . . .

The leaders didn't know what I had done. . . .

I told them how God had been with me. . . .

They said, "Let's start building!" So they began.

Sanballat and Tobiah heard about this. They began making fun of us. . . .

"God will help us finish this," I said. "We are his servants. We will start building Jerusalem again."
Nehemiah 2:1-4, 6, 11-12, 16, 18-20

ROBBERS, FLOODED RIVERS, muddy roads. These are some of the dangers Nehemiah and his friends may have faced as they traveled back to Jerusalem. But Nehemiah trusted God to take care of him, because he knew all the things God had done in the past, and he knew that God never changes.

It can be the same for you today. You can think of all the ways God has taken care of you in the past. Even if you have had hard times, you know that God has helped you get through the hard times. And because God never changes, you can know that God will keep taking care of you. He will keep blessing you in wonderful ways. He will keep helping you. You can depend on his love, because God doesn't change. What a great God we have!

Dear God, thank you that you never change. Thank you for showing me that you will always take care of me and love me.

Thursday

Read "Yesterday, Today, and Tomorrow," page 791 in the *Day by Day Kid's Bible.* Or read this part of the story:

God has given us a promise. "I'll never leave you." So we say what the psalm says.

> *"God helps me.*
> *I won't be afraid.*
> *What can people do to me?"* . . .

Jesus is the same today as he was yesterday. He will always be the same. *Hebrews 13:5-6, 8*

THUNDERHEADS ARE CLOUDS that billow up tall like mountains in the sky. They have dark bellies and bring summer storms with lots of rain. Cumulus clouds are the puffy, white summer clouds. Cirrus clouds are wispy, icy winter clouds. Stratus clouds make such thick, gray skies that the clouds seem to never end.

A cloud hid Jesus as he went back to heaven. His friends were watching. Jesus had just said, "I'll always be with you." How could Jesus always be with them after he left?

When Jesus was a man on earth, he could be in only one place at a time. But now his Spirit can be with all of us at the same time. We can't see him, but we know him in our own hearts. We can read about Jesus in the Bible. And we can know that he is the same loving Jesus who is with us now. That's because, just like God the Father, Jesus the Son does not change. He will love us forever.

Dear God, thank you for sending Jesus, your Son, to us. Thank you, Jesus, that you are with us right now!

Friday

Read "An Open Door," page 803 in the *Day by Day Kid's Bible.* Or read this part of the story:

Suddenly, my spirit was meeting with God's Spirit. I saw somebody sitting on the King's throne in heaven. . . .

Four living beings were in the middle, around the King. . . .

These living beings always call, "Holy, holy, holy. God is clean, sinless, and holy. He has all power. He is holy. He lived before. He lives now. He will always live." *Revelation 4:2, 6, 8*

EVERGREENS ARE TREES that are always green. Everblooming plants always have flower blossoms. Everlasting flowers have been cut and dried so they won't lose their color. But an evergreen tree won't live forever. Everblooming plants blossom only during the warm seasons. Even everlasting dried flowers grow old and crumble away.

But God lived before time began: *He was.* He lives now: *He is.* He will always live: *He is to come.* And he has made a way for us to live forever with him by believing in his Son, Jesus. So when we pray, we can tell God what the living beings in heaven always tell him: Holy, holy, holy are you, Lord God Almighty. You were. You are. You are to come!

Dear God, you are holy, holy, holy. You were. You are. You are to come. Thank you that you have made a way for me to live with you forever.

SOME THINGS YOU CAN DO THIS WEEK

* **Make mug mats.** Get four 3-inch by 5-inch index cards and some colored felt. Trace around the cards on the felt, then cut out the four felt rectangles. Glue one felt rectangle onto each index card. You can glue rickrack or other trim around the edges of the felt to make a border. Nehemiah served drinks to the king, and it was God who gave the king a kind heart toward Nehemiah. The king let Nehemiah go back to build up the walls of Jerusalem. Remember: God always took care of Nehemiah. God does not change.

* **Sprout a bean.** Get a package of dried beans. Line the sides of a clear plastic jar or cup with paper towels. Slip several beans between the paper towels and the sides of the jar so you can clearly see the beans. Put enough water into the jar to get the paper towels wet, but not so much that water is standing in the jar. Now place the jar in a sunny spot. Keep the paper towels damp from day to day. Watch how the beans change. You can plant these in a garden later if you want. Remember that every-thing changes except God. He never changes. He will never stop loving you.

* **Be a cloud watcher.** From your window or from outdoors, watch how the sky changes as the clouds float across it. Try to figure out what some of the clouds look like. Imagine what it might have been like to watch Jesus go up into the sky until clouds hid him. Then think about him being with you, and talk with him without speaking out loud. Remember that Jesus is with you always, and that he is the same yesterday, today, and forever. He will always love you.

* **Dry some flowers.** If you have flowers blooming in a garden, ask for permission to pick two or three. Gently place them between two pieces of paper. Then carefully place the paper on a hard surface like a counter or a big book, and place a heavy book on top. Leave the flowers for a few days before taking them back out. You can also just lay the flowers out to dry and watch what happens. Remember that everything changes. But God never changes. His love for you lasts forever.

GOD'S SECRET PLAN

God's secret plan . . . is Christ himself.
In him lie hidden all the treasures of wisdom and knowledge. Colossians 2:2-3, NLT

This week you will learn
· *about God's secret plan;*
· *how someone was healed when someone else spit;*
· *who is sometimes called the name of a farm animal;*
· *who helps us to be loving and full of joy.*

Monday

Read "Crowds," page 529 in the *Day by Day Kid's Bible.* Or read this part of the story:

"A person who is sad is like a bent plant," wrote Isaiah. "My servant won't hurt bent plants. A person who is glad is like a glowing candle. My servant won't blow out glowing candles.

"My servant will stand up for what's right," wrote Isaiah. "He will win. The nations will hope in his name." *Matthew 12:17, 20-21*

TELEVISION, RADIO, THE INTERNET, cell phones, newspapers, magazines. We get our news in many different ways. Which ways does your family like to get news?

In Bible times, they didn't have any of these ways of getting news. Most of the time, news got around when people told each other what had happened. Sometimes people would write down something they wanted others to know.

In today's reading, Matthew quotes from Isaiah, who lived hundreds of years before Jesus was born. Isaiah wrote what God told him. So people who heard or read what Isaiah had to say knew God was going to send a servant. What they didn't know was God's secret plan. God's plan was to come to earth as a man himself, by sending his own Son. Jesus was God-Man. Nobody expected that. God sent Jesus to show us just how much he loves us. So Jesus gives courage to sad people. He shares the joy of glad people. He loves everyone.

Dear God, thank you that your secret plan was to send Jesus. And you did it!

Tuesday

Read "Seeing for the First Time" and "How Could This Happen?" page 574 in the *Day by Day Kid's Bible*. Or read this part of the story:

As Jesus walked along, he came to a man who couldn't see. He'd been that way since he was born. . . .

[Jesus said,] "It happened so God can show his power. I have to do God's work while it's day. Night will be coming. Then nobody can work. While I'm here, I'm the Light of the World."

Then Jesus spit on the dirt and made some mud. He put it on the man's eyes.

"Go," said Jesus. "Wash the mud off in the pool."

The man went to the pool. He washed the mud off. When he came back, he could see! *John 9:1, 3-7*

It's the black part of your eye, the pupil, that does the seeing. Your pupils grow larger when it's dark so they can let in more light. When the sun is shining, they get smaller to keep out the light that's too bright.

Jesus said, "I am the Light of the World." Just as light shows us the way to go when it's dark, Jesus shows us the way to live. Darkness hides things. Satan is evil, and he likes to hide; he is afraid to be seen. But light shows everything. Jesus shows us all that is good. He is never afraid to be seen. God's secret plan is no longer a secret, because Jesus shows us God's power and love. God is much stronger than Satan. His love always wins.

Dear God, thank you that Jesus is the Light of the World. Thank you for sending Jesus to show us your goodness.

Wednesday

Read "Water from a Well," page 518 in the *Day by Day Kid's Bible.* Or read this part of the story:

Jesus was on his way to Galilee. He went through the land of Samaria. He was tired. So he stopped at a well and sat down. . . .

It wasn't long before a woman came to the well. . . .

"Someday true worship will come from the spirit," said Jesus. "In fact, the time is already here. God is spirit. So worship must come from the spirit. It must be true. That's the way the Father wants it."

Then the woman said, "Someday the Promised One is coming. He will be able to tell us all about it."

"I am the Promised One," said Jesus. *John 4:3, 6-7, 23, 25-26*

"THE ICE CREAM TRUCK'S COMING!" called Victoria. Corey dug into his top drawer and grabbed the quarters he kept there. Then he ran outside to the curb where Victoria was waiting. The ice cream truck was nowhere to be seen. But Corey didn't have to ask his sister how she knew it was coming. He could hear its sing-song tune coming from around the corner.

How did the woman in our reading know that the Promised One was coming? Hundreds of years before, God's prophets had written that God would send a Promised One, the Messiah, or the Christ. The names *Messiah* and *Christ* both mean "Chosen One" or "Promised One." God had chosen and promised Jesus from the very beginning. Jesus is the Promised One God sent to show how much he loves us.

Dear God, thank you for keeping your promise to send Jesus.

Thursday

Read "The Shepherd's Voice," page 576 in the *Day by Day Kid's Bible*. Or read this part of the story:

"The sheep follow the shepherd," said Jesus. "They know his voice. They'll never follow a stranger. . . .

"I am the Good Shepherd," said Jesus. "I know my people. They are my sheep. My sheep know me, just like the Father knows me. I know the Father. I will even die to save my sheep."
John 10:4-5, 14-15

TEREN HAD TWO SISTERS and a brother. His mother and father would call the children to come by whistling a tune of four notes. Sometimes when Teren would hear the whistle, it was time for dinner. Sometimes it was time to get ready to go somewhere. Teren and his sisters and brother knew they were to come when they heard that whistle.

Jesus said we are his sheep. How do we know his voice? God lets us know by his love. If we have a thought like, "I'm stupid," that's not love. So we know it's not from Jesus and we don't listen to that voice. But when we have thoughts about how much God loves us, that's Jesus' voice. When we think about kind and loving things to do, Jesus is telling us to do the loving thing. Jesus, who came to earth as God's secret plan, shows us God's way of perfect love.

Dear God, thank you for showing us the way of love through Jesus.

Friday

Read "The Lamb of God," page 514 in the *Day by Day Kid's Bible.* Or read this part of the story:

John saw Jesus coming. "Look!" said John. "It's the Lamb of God. He takes away the sin of the world! This is the man I was talking about." . . .

Andrew and his friend heard what John said. So they followed Jesus.

Jesus turned around and saw them. "What do you want?" he asked.

"Teacher, we want to know where you're staying," they said.

"Come and see," said Jesus. *John 1:29-30, 37-39*

SOMETIMES WE DESCRIBE people by using animal names. In one book the writer describes a girl as being "rabbity." Maybe she has big front teeth, or maybe she's a bit nervous and jumpy. If we said that someone is a lion, we might mean that person is a brave leader. If we said, "That little boy is such a monkey," we might mean he's funny or he climbs everything.

John called Jesus a Lamb.

In Bible times, people burned a gift of lamb meat on an altar as a way of telling God they were sorry for their sins. Then God sent Jesus to die for the sins of all people. That's why Jesus is called the Lamb of God. Before Jesus died, people had to offer lambs over and over again, whenever they sinned. But Jesus died once, for all people and for all the bad things we do: sins we did in the past, sins we do today, sins we'll do in the future. Jesus is the Lamb of God.

Dear God, thank you for sending Jesus to be the Lamb of God who takes away my sins.

SOME THINGS YOU CAN DO THIS WEEK

Check out your pupils. Look in a mirror at the size of your pupils (the black part of your eyes). Now close your eyes and cover them with your hands. Count slowly to 20, then take your hands off and open your eyes, still watching the mirror. What happened to your pupils? They were larger just after you opened your eyes, because they had been trying to see more in the dark. But they quickly got smaller because of the light in the room. Remember how Jesus healed the blind man and said, "I am the Light of the World."

Make up a secret code. Write the letters of the alphabet down one side of a piece of paper. Next to each letter draw a shape that you want to stand for that letter. For example, next to the A, draw a triangle pointing up. By the B, draw a circle. By the C, draw a moon. By the D, draw a triangle pointing to the right. With that code, the word BAD would look like a circle, a triangle pointing up, and a triangle pointing right. Go though all the letters this way. Then with your code, write your name or write a note to someone. Remember that the message about Jesus' coming was written by prophets hundreds of years before he came.

Make a sheep face with a small paper plate. Draw dark eyes and a dark nose. Glue cotton balls all around it except on the eyes and nose. Then glue the plate to the center of a piece of colored paper. On the colored paper, write, "Jesus is the Good Shepherd. I am his sheep."

Make up animal riddles. Without saying the kind of animal you are thinking about, describe that animal to friends or family. Ask them to guess what animal you are describing. Then someone else describes an animal, and you guess. To change the game, act out an animal without saying anything. You can add the animal's sound if you want. Remember why Jesus is called the Lamb of God.

JESUS DOES WHAT GOD DOES

Whatever the Father does, the Son also does.
For the Father loves the Son and tells him everything
he is doing. John 5:19-20, NLT

This week you will learn
· who sounded like he knew what he was talking about;
· who got lost, but not really;
· how John could tell who Jesus was;
· who cares about you.

Monday

Read "Father and Son," page 526 in the *Day by Day Kid's Bible.* Or read this part of the story:

"My Father is always at work," said Jesus. "He is even working today. So I'm working too."

The leaders didn't like to hear this. So they tried to find a way to kill Jesus. They thought he didn't care about the worship day. What's more, he was calling God his own Father. He was making himself the same as God.

Jesus talked about himself. He said, "The Son can't do anything by himself. He only does what he sees his Father do. Whatever the Father does, the Son does too."

"The Father loves the Son," said Jesus. "He shows the Son everything he does." *John 5:17-20*

DID YOU TIE YOUR SHOES on Sunday? Did you untie them?

God told his people to rest on the worship day and not do any work. But the Jewish leaders made all kinds of rules about what was work and what was not work. These were not God's rules. They were the leaders' rules. One of the rules said you were not to tie or untie a knot on the worship day. And you were not to carry certain things, like mats. So when Jesus healed a lame man on the worship day, the leaders said that was bad, because healing was work. And when the man carried his mat like Jesus told him to do, the leaders were even more angry.

But what made them most angry was Jesus calling God his own Father. He was making himself the same as God. But he *is* the same. He does whatever God does. Jesus came to show us what God is like.

Dear God, thank you for sending Jesus to show us what you are like.

Tuesday

Read "What Did You Come to See?" page 538 in the *Day by Day Kid's Bible.* Or read this part of the story:

Now John, the one who baptized people, had some followers. . . . He told them to ask Jesus a question. "Are you the one we've been waiting for? Or should I look for someone else?". . .

Jesus said, "Go back to John. Tell him everything you've seen. Tell him everything you've heard. People who couldn't see before can see now. People who couldn't walk before can walk now. . . . Poor people are hearing the Good News." *Matthew 11:2-5*

IN *The Prince and the Pauper,* a book by Mark Twain, two boys who look very much alike trade places. The boy who is a prince wears the poor boy's clothes and takes his place. The poor boy puts on the prince's clothes and lives in the palace. In the end, they both want to trade back. But the people don't know which boy is which. How do they find out who the true prince is? They ask him where the Great Seal is. The Great Seal was used to stamp the sign of the kingdom on orders and messages to show that they were really from the king. Only the true prince would know where the Great Seal was.

Jesus said John would know that Jesus was the Promised One by seeing and hearing about what Jesus did and what he taught. Jesus did things that only God could do. Jesus shows us what God is like. He shows us God's great love, the love that always wins.

Dear God, thank you for showing us your great love by sending Jesus.

Wednesday

Read "Many Sick People," page 523 in the *Day by Day Kid's Bible*. Or read this part of the story:

The worship day came. Jesus went to the town's worship house. He started teaching there.

People were surprised. Jesus didn't sound like any other teacher of the Law. He sounded like he knew what he was talking about. *Luke 4:31-32*

JELISA'S TEACHER was sick for a week. So Mrs. Capps came to teach. When she taught the science lesson about birds, Jelisa asked her a question about bird feathers. The answer wasn't in the book. Mrs. Capps tried to answer the question, but Jelisa wondered if Mrs. Capps really knew what she was talking about. Jelisa missed her regular teacher, who loved birds and seemed to know all about them.

When people listened to Jesus, they could tell that he knew what he was talking about. He didn't have to prove things. He just told people the truth, and they knew in their hearts that it was the truth. In fact, when a man with an evil spirit saw Jesus in the worship house, he yelled, "I know who you are! You are God's Holy One!" Even evil spirits know that Jesus is God's Son.

Before this time, God was the only one called the Holy One. But Jesus is God's Son. He came doing what God does and loving like God loves. So Jesus is the Holy One too.

Dear God, thank you for sending Jesus, the Holy One, to show us your love.

Thursday

Read "In the Big City," page 510 in the *Day by Day Kid's Bible*. Or read this part of the story:

Joseph and Mary began to look for Jesus. . . .

At last they found Jesus. He was in the worship house, sitting with the teachers. He was listening to them. He was also asking them questions. Everyone was surprised by how much he understood. They were surprised at his answers. . . .

Mary said, "Son, why have you done this to us? We've been worried. We've been looking for you."

"Why did you have to look for me?" Jesus asked. "Didn't you know I would be in my Father's house?" *Luke 2:44-49*

GIRLS DID NOT GO TO SCHOOL in Bible times. Schools were for boys only, so Jesus went to school with the other boys. Most schools met in worship houses. The teacher was always a man called a *rabbi* (RAB-buy). The people spoke Aramaic and Greek, but the teachers taught the boys to read Hebrew, because the Scriptures they studied were written in Hebrew. Jesus must have done well in school. But he knew more than his teachers did about God. That's because he is God's Son!

"Didn't you know I would be in my Father's house?" said Jesus. He meant that God was his real Father. Talking about God and living like God's Son was his real job. Jesus was letting Mary and Joseph know that he was going to grow up to be like his real Father in heaven. He would do what his Father did.

Dear God, thank you that your Son, Jesus, is just like you. Help me get to know Jesus better.

Friday

Read "Up in a Tree" and "By the Side of the Road," page 593 in the *Day by Day Kid's Bible*. Or read this part of the story:

Zacchaeus was making things right. "Look, Lord," he said to Jesus. "I'll give half of everything I own to poor people. . . ."

    "Someone has been saved today at this house!" said Jesus. "This is why I came. I came to look for people who lost their way. I came to save them!". . .

    "I want to see!" said Bartimaeus. "All right," said Jesus. "You are well because you believe in me!"

    Right away, Bartimaeus could see. *Luke 18:41-43; 19:8-10*

THE TALLEST ANIMAL in the world is the giraffe, about 18 feet tall. The tallest tree is a California redwood that is 367 feet, 6 inches tall. The shortest trees are bonsai trees, which grow to be only a few inches tall. The tallest person in recent times was a man from Illinois who was 8 feet, 11 inches tall. The shortest person was a man in India who was not quite 2 feet tall.

We don't know how short Zacchaeus was. But we do know he was a tax collector, and people didn't think much of him. Bartimaeus couldn't see. In Bible times, someone who was blind couldn't do many things, so people didn't think this person was very important. Do you think people expected Jesus to care about Zacchaeus or Bartimaeus?

Everyone found out that Jesus cares about all people, just like God does.

Jesus does what God does. Do you ever feel as though you are not impor- tant? Jesus thinks you are important. He wants to spend time with you. He loves you.

Dear God, thank you that Jesus cares about me just like you do.

SOME THINGS YOU CAN DO THIS WEEK

Play mirror partners. Get a friend or family member to help you. Face each other and decide which of you is A and which is B. A should start moving his or her arms slowly. B must try to copy A exactly, trying to keep up with A's movements as if B were a mirror to A. After a few minutes, trade. B starts the movement, and A is the mirror. If you want to trade again, expand the movements to head and legs as well as arms. Remember that Jesus is like a mirror picture of God. He does what God does.

Make a poster of some names for God. On poster board or a large piece of paper, write these words all over, making some words sideways, some straight across, some large, some small, some in different colors: Artist, Maker, Right One, Care Giver, Promise Keeper, Protector, Wise One, Ruler, Everlasting One, Powerful, Trustworthy, Our Hope, King, Giver, Living God, Love, Holy One, Fair Judge, Commander of Heaven's Armies, Merciful, Patient, Glorious, Majestic, Great, Our Shelter, Deliverer, Forgiver, Shepherd, Most High, Provider, Our Peace, Healer, One Who Sees Me, Master, I Am. These are some names we can call God. They are also names we can call Jesus.

Make a Bible-times pocket-sash. In Bible times, people didn't have pockets in their clothes. So they made long pockets by folding their belt or "sash" so that the opening was at the top. Get a strip of fabric about four feet long and six inches wide. Color designs on it with fabric markers. Then fold the width of the belt in half to make the belt three inches wide. Tie your belt around your waist with the fold at the bottom, the open side at the top. This makes a pocket. You can tuck coins or notes or tissues inside your pocket-sash. Jesus was a carpenter. Maybe he carried nails or a whittling knife in his pocket-sash.

Make a hand tree. Lay one arm on a piece of paper so that your whole hand and part of your arm is on the paper. Spread out your fingers. Trace around your arm, hand, and fingers. Now look at the tracing. The arm is the trunk of a tree; the hand and fingers are branches. Draw Zacchaeus up in the tree, and draw Bartimaeus on a road beside the tree.

JESUS HAS AUTHORITY

Even the wind and the waves obey [Jesus]!
Mark 4:41, NIV

This week you will learn
· what authority is;
· what Jesus has authority over;
· why pigs jumped into a lake;
· why people said, "Who is this man?"

Monday

Read "The Captain's Servant," page 537 in the *Day by Day Kid's Bible*. Or read this part of the story:

There was once a Roman army captain. . . . He sent some Jewish leaders to meet with Jesus. . . . He wanted Jesus to make his servant well. . . . The message said, ". . . Just say the word. Then I know my servant will be well again. You see, I know about being in charge. . . . I'm the boss of many other men. I tell one to come, and he comes. I tell another one to go, and he goes. . . ."

Then Jesus sent word to the captain. "You believed I would make your servant well. I will do just what you believed." At that moment, the captain's servant got well. *Luke 7:1-2, 6-10*

WHEN YOU'RE SICK, how do you like to be treated? Some people like to get a lot of attention. Other people like to be left alone. The Roman captain must have loved his servant a lot to send men to ask Jesus to heal him. The captain knew that both he and Jesus were men of authority. They were in charge, the ones who must be obeyed. The captain had authority over the men in his army. And he believed that Jesus had authority over sickness. Was the captain right? Yes. Jesus has authority over sickness. He can tell it to leave, and it will leave.

Dear God, thank you that Jesus has authority over sickness. (Pray for Jesus to heal people you know who are sick.)

Tuesday

Read "The Storm," page 550 in the *Day by Day Kid's Bible.* Or read this part of the story:

A roaring storm blew in. . . .

Jesus' special friends woke him. . . . Jesus got up. He spoke firmly to the wind. He spoke firmly to the waves. He said, "Be quiet. Be still."

Then the wind died down. Everything became still. . . .

Jesus' friends . . . said to each other, "Who is this Jesus? The wind obeys him! The water obeys him!" *Mark 4:37-41*

RIVERS, SEAS, MOUNTAINS, trees, animals, flowers, grass, clouds. All these are part of the natural, created world called *nature.* Most of nature is not under people's control. Volcanoes, snowfall, earthquakes, and lightning are not easy to control. Even weeds are not easy to control. But nature is under someone's control. That control is called *authority.*

Jesus is the one who is boss. He can tell nature what to do and what not to do. After all, he is the Maker of nature. The Bible says, "By him all things were created" (Colossians 1:16, NIV). Jesus has authority over nature.

Dear God, thank you that Jesus has authority over nature. Thank you for protecting and taking care of me.

Wednesday

Read "The Man Who Lived by Graves," page 551 in the *Day by Day Kid's Bible*. Or read this part of the story:

Jesus and his friends landed their boat. Jesus got out. A man came up to meet him.

    This man was controlled by a bad spirit. . . .

    Jesus said, "You bad spirit, come out of this man!" . . .

    Then Jesus asked the spirit, "What's your name?"

    "Many," answered the spirit. "There are many of us." . . .

    Pigs were eating on a hill nearby. "Let us go into the pigs," said the bad spirits.

    So Jesus let them. . . . Then all the pigs ran down the hill. They jumped into the lake and drowned. . . .

    The people went out to see it for themselves. It wasn't long before they reached Jesus. There was the man, sitting with Jesus. He had been controlled by bad spirits. But now he was dressed. His mind seemed to be working just fine. *Mark 5:1-3, 8-15*

SAY THE OPPOSITE of these words: *love, give, build, open, up, out, happy, night, clean.* We know that God loves. He gives. He makes and builds. But there is someone who wants the opposite of what God wants. The devil, or Satan, hates. He kills and steals and destroys (John 10:10). God is good. The devil is evil. God's kingdom is called the Kingdom of Light. The devil's kingdom is called the kingdom of darkness (Colossians 1:12-13). Thinking about the one who wants to kill and steal and destroy can be a bit scary. But we don't have to be afraid of evil. Why? Because Jesus has authority over evil. Remember: God will never stop loving you. And God's love always wins.

Dear God, thank you that Jesus has authority over evil. Keep me away from evil. And no matter what happens, help me remember that you are always in control and that your love always wins.

Thursday

Read "The Sick Little Girl," page 551 in the *Day by Day Kid's Bible*. Or read this part of the story:

Some men came to Jairus. "Your little girl has died," they said. . . .

Jesus didn't listen to them. He told Jairus, "Don't be afraid. Just believe."

People were crying loudly at Jairus's house.

Jesus went in. . . .

Jesus held the girl's hand. He said, "Little girl, get up."

Right away, the girl got up and walked! *Mark 5:35-36, 39-42*

HOW DO YOU KNOW if something is alive? It moves, breathes, eats, and grows. It can make other live things like itself. Think about how seeds look. Some look like rocks. Others look like dried twigs. If you didn't know about seeds, you might think they were dead.

The day that Jairus's little girl died, most people already knew that Jesus could heal sick people. That day, they learned that Jesus could also make a dead person come back to life. Why is that so amazing? Because after people die, their bodies don't come back to life again. They can't unless God raises them. Where did Jesus get this authority over death? From God. Jesus is God's Son. He has "complete authority in heaven and on earth" (Matthew 28:18, NLT). Jesus has authority over sickness, nature, evil, and death.

Dear God, thank you that Jesus has authority over death.

Friday

Read "Perfume," page 539 in the *Day by Day Kid's Bible.* Or read this part of the story:

Now there was a sinful woman in town. She heard that Jesus was having dinner at Simon's house. So she went there. . . .

    She stood close to Jesus, at his feet. Then she began to cry. Her tears dripped on Jesus' feet. They made his feet wet. So she wiped his feet with her long hair. . . .

    Simon saw this. He said to himself, "Jesus can't really be a prophet. If he was, he would know this is a sinful woman." . . .

    "This woman has lots of love," said Jesus. . . .

    Then Jesus said to the woman, "Your sins are forgiven."

    Now other people at Simon's house began to talk among themselves. "Who is this man?" they asked. "He even forgives people's sins." *Luke 7:37-39, 47-49*

NIKKI SPILLED some grape juice on her white shirt. She tried to wash it off with water, but it wouldn't come off. It left a blue spot. She showed it to her mother. Her mother used a special spot remover on it and carefully washed it. When she was done, the juice spot was gone, and Nikki's shirt was as good as new.

The sinful woman who went to see Jesus had done many wrong things. Every sin was like a dirty spot inside her that she couldn't get rid of. But Jesus forgave her. The woman had come to Jesus with lots of sins, and she left with none. We can bring our sins to Jesus too. Jesus has the authority to forgive sins.

Dear God, thank you for giving your Son, Jesus, the authority to forgive sins. Please forgive my sins.

☀ Some Things You Can Do This Week 🌙

● **Make a nature montage.** Gather some magazines that have pictures of animals, flowers, mountains, deserts, rivers, and other living things. Cut out some of those pictures and glue them onto a piece of paper. Use this montage to remind you that Jesus has authority over nature.

🌙 **Make waves.** Get a large, clear plastic jar with a lid that screws on. Pour water into the jar until it's about one-third full, and add cooking oil until the jar is about half full. Next, add three drops of blue food coloring. Put the lid on the jar tightly and shake it to mix in the food coloring. Then hold the jar sideways and gently rock it back and forth. Watch the waves that form. With scissors, cut a square of bubble wrap about one inch by one inch. Pretend it's a boat. Open the jar and drop the "boat" in. Then put the lid on again. Rock the jar and see what happens to the boat. Remember that Jesus stilled the wind and waves.

● **Look inside a bean seed.** Get some dried beans. Soak a few of them in water for at least 30 minutes. Open the bean by gently pulling it in half. Ask for help if you need it. Sometimes putting your fingernail in the crack helps it open. Look at the tiny bump that is visible inside. This will grow into a plant. The rest of the seed is used as food for the plant to eat while it grows. A seed is alive even though it looks dead. Remember that Jesus has authority over death.

🌙 **Find your pulse.** Your heartbeat is called your pulse. You can find your pulse in one of these places: 1) Press your hand against your chest a little to the left of the breastbone. 2) Press gently against one side of your neck toward the front. 3) Press the fingers of one hand on the inner wrist of the other hand. Which place do you feel your pulse the best? In Thursday's reading, the people could tell that the little girl had died because she stopped breathing and her heart stopped beating. She had no pulse. Remember that Jesus has authority over death.

JESUS, TEACHER AND STORYTELLER

[Jesus] taught them many things by parables.
Mark 4:2, NIV

This week you will learn
· what a parable is;
· how to feed your spirit;
· who is the wisest rabbi;
· who is like a vine.

Monday

Read "Lost and Found," page 583 in the *Day by Day Kid's Bible.* Or read this part of the story:

Jesus told some stories.

"Suppose you're a shepherd. You have 100 sheep. But one of them gets lost. Wouldn't you leave the other 99 sheep out in the open? Wouldn't you look for the lost sheep until you found it? Then you'd be so happy. . . .

"It's the same way in heaven," said Jesus. "The angels are very happy about one sinner who is sorry." *Luke 15:3-7*

THERE WAS NO TELEVISION in Bible times. No movies. No DVDs or videos. No CDs or tapes or radio. And only a few books were written on scrolls. So people would get together and tell stories.

Jesus liked stories. He told stories that had hidden meanings, like riddles. These kinds of stories are called *parables.* People who really wanted to know about God would listen to the parable. Then they would figure out what the story meant.

Jesus told what today's reading means: We sometimes call people "lost" if they are not in God's kingdom. God is like the shepherd. He has lots of people around the world who are in his kingdom. But he also loves all the people who aren't in his kingdom yet. He wants everyone to come to him. So he looks for "lost" people. The angels are glad when lost people are found and come into God's kingdom.

Dear God, thank you that Jesus taught us by telling parables. Help us to understand them.

Tuesday

Read "Bread from Heaven," page 558 in the *Day by Day Kid's Bible.* Or read this part of the story:

"Here's God's work for you," said Jesus. "Believe in me, because God sent me. . . .

"I am the Bread of Life," said Jesus. "Come to me. Then your heart will never be hungry. Believe in me. Then your spirit will never be thirsty." *John 6:29, 35*

WHY DO OUR BODIES need food? Food has vitamins to make us grow healthy and strong. It gives us energy. Food keeps our bodies alive.

Our spirit is the part of us deep inside that loves and knows things. Just as our bodies need food to stay alive, our spirits also need food to stay alive. But it's not the kind of food our body uses. Our spirit needs Jesus' love and forgiveness, Jesus' peace, and Jesus' wisdom. So when Jesus said, "I am the Bread of Life," he gave us a riddle to figure out. What he meant was that he can keep our spirits alive and healthy.

Praying feeds our spirits. Reading the Bible feeds our spirits. Worship feeds our spirits. Anything we do to welcome Jesus into our lives feeds our spirits. Jesus is the Bread of Life. He keeps our spirits alive and healthy.

Dear God, thank you that Jesus is the Bread of Life. Feed my spirit with the love of Jesus.

Wednesday

Read "Birds' Food and Flowers' Clothes," page 534 in the *Day by Day Kid's Bible*. Or read this part of the story:

"Why worry about clothes?" said Jesus. "Look at the flowers in the field. They don't work. They don't make their own clothes. King Solomon had beautiful clothes. But his clothes weren't as wonderful as one of these flowers. That's the way God dresses the grass in the fields. The grass is here today and gone tomorrow. So God will give you clothes too, won't he?" *Matthew 6:28-30*

RABBI IS THE JEWISH WORD for "teacher." Some people called Jesus "Rabbi" because he taught many things. And when Jesus taught, he would often help people learn from things they saw around them. Jesus said that when people see birds, they should remember that God takes care of them. Besides birds, Jesus used salt, light, and flowers to help people understand about God. Were Jesus' teachings true only in Bible times? No. Jesus' teachings are also true today in your life. Jesus is still teaching us through the Bible and through his Holy Spirit in our hearts. Jesus was, and is, and always will be the wisest rabbi, the wisest teacher.

Dear God, thank you that Jesus is such a good teacher. Thank you for teaching me how much you love me.

Thursday

Read "Ten Lamps," page 604 in the *Day by Day Kid's Bible*. Or read this part of the story:

"In the middle of the night, a voice called out. 'Here comes the groom! Come and meet him!'

"All the young people woke up. They lit their lamps. But the foolish ones had run out of oil. . . .

"The foolish people went to the store. While they were gone, the groom came. The young people who were there went with him. They went to the wedding party. The door closed behind them. . . .

"So watch. You don't know when I'll come," said Jesus. *Matthew 25:6-10*

MOST LAMPS WERE round clay bowls in Bible times. The bowl had a spout on it that held a wick, which is a string like a candle has. One end of the wick went down into the oil in the bowl. The other end of the wick burned when it was lit. The foolish people in today's reading went to the store to buy oil for their lamps. It was probably olive oil. But it might have been nut oil or fish oil.

In many stories, a lamp that is shining means life. A lamp that is not lit means death. God's ways of love lead to life. So if we are following God's ways, we will be ready when Jesus comes back. Jesus is like the groom in the story. Someday he will come to take us with him. We'll live with him forever.

Why did Jesus use stories like this? His stories make it easier for us to remember what he wants to teach us.

Dear God, thank you for showing us your ways of love that lead to life. Thank you for this story that Jesus told to remind us to be ready when he comes back to get us.

Friday

Read "The Vine," page 612 in the *Day by Day Kid's Bible*. Or read this part of the story:

"I'm like a vine," said Jesus. "You are like the branches. . . .

"You'll grow a lot of fruit if you stay in me. . . .

"Be like a branch that grows a lot of fruit. Show everyone that you are my followers." *John 15:5, 8*

THE TALLEST SUNFLOWER ever grown was 25 feet tall! That's as tall as a house! And the flower on it was 32 inches across. That's almost as wide as a yardstick! Sometimes you can see a building or a tree trunk covered with ivy vines. Watermelons and squash grow on vines. So do some flowers.

But the flowers would stop blooming and the fruit would stop growing if they decided to jump off the vine and try to grow by themselves. That's what this teaching from Jesus means. If we stay with Jesus and let the meaning of his words stay in us, then it's as if we are staying connected to the vine. Good things will grow from our lives, just like good fruit grows from a branch connected to a vine. Some of the good things that can grow in us are love, joy, peace, patience, and kindness.

Dear God, thank you for making me like a branch growing from Jesus the Vine. Keep me connected with Jesus so I can grow good things in my life.

SOME THINGS YOU CAN DO THIS WEEK

- **Design a book cover.** Think of your favorite book or story. Then pretend you are designing the cover for that book. Draw the cover (including the title) on a piece of paper. Remember the kinds of stories that Jesus told, called parables.

- **Play Pin the Flame on the Candle.** Draw a simple unlit candle on a big piece of paper or on poster board. Stick the paper or poster board on a wall, with the top of the candle about as high as your shoulders. On another piece of paper, color and cut out a small flame of fire. Get friends or family members together. Line up some distance away from the poster. Blindfold the first person and give him or her the paper flame with a circle of tape, sticky side out, on the back of it. Turn the person around three times and head him or her in the direction of the poster. Have the person stick the flame where they think the top of the candle is. Remember the story Jesus told about the young people and their lamps.

- **Make a "stained glass" candle.** Draw a large candle on a piece of printer paper. To create a stained glass look, draw lines to divide the blank space around the candle into large sections. Then use different colors of crayons to fill in the candle and the spaces around it. Lay your paper on top of a sheet of waxed paper a bit larger than the paper with the candle. Put baby oil or cooking oil on a cotton ball and rub the oil over the picture. Now light can shine through it. You can hang it in a window. Let it remind you of the story of the young people and their lamps.

- **Watch celery drink.** Get one stalk of celery with its leaves. Fill a large plastic or paper cup about halfway with water. Stir in a few drops of food coloring. Then put the celery into the colored water. Leave the cup on a counter, windowsill, or table. You can check it once in a while to see how the celery drinks up the water. Remember how Jesus said that he is like a vine and we are like branches.

JESUS, OUR BRIDGE

There is only one God and one Mediator who can reconcile God and people.
He is the man Christ Jesus. 1 Timothy 2:5, NLT

This week you will learn
· *what a mediator is and what reconcile means;*
· *how a person can be a bridge;*
· *what God's new special promise is.*

Monday

Read "Listen and Learn," page 750 in the *Day by Day Kid's Bible.* Or read this part of the story:

[God] wants everybody to be saved. He wants everybody to know the truth. There is one God. There is one person who talks to God for people. That's Jesus. He gave his life to buy us back from sin. *1 Timothy 2:4-6*

BEFORE BRIDGES, travelers had to stop when they came to a wide river or a canyon. They had to find a place in the river that was shallow enough and narrow enough to get across. They had to go around canyons. But now we have bridges everywhere. They go over not only rivers and canyons, but also highways and railroad tracks.

A person can be like a bridge. For example, if a friend treated you badly and you didn't want him to come to your house, your friend could send someone to you. This person could let you know that your friend is sorry and wants to be friends again. We call a person like that a *mediator.* A mediator goes between people to help them understand each other.

Jesus is our Mediator. He is like a bridge between us and God. He died for us to make things right between us and God. That's what *reconcile* means.

When we ask Jesus to forgive our sins, he reconciles us to God. He brings us to God.

Dear God, thank you for sending Jesus to be the Mediator, the bridge between you and me. When I believe Jesus died for my sins, I'm reconciled to you.

Tuesday

Read "Hot Air," page 441 in the *Day by Day Kid's Bible.* Or read this part of the story:

> *Then Bildad spoke.*
>
> *". . . Look to God.*
> > *Beg him for help.*
> *Be good and right.*
> > *Then he will help you."*
>
> *"I know that's true," said Job.*
> > *"But how can a person be sinless before God? . . .*
>
> *"God is not a man.*
> > *So I can't answer him like I'd answer a man. . . .*
> *I wish someone would make peace between God and me.*
> *I wish someone could take God's anger away from me.*
> > *Then I'd talk to him without being afraid.*
> > *But right now, I can't."* Job 8:1, 5-7; 9:1-2, 32-35

YOU KNOW SOMETHING that Job didn't know when he said the words you just read. Job lived a long time before Jesus came. So Job didn't know that someday God would do exactly what Job wanted. Job said, "God is not a man." But you know that God came to earth as the man Jesus. Job said, "I wish someone would make peace between God and me." That's just what Jesus did. He did for us what we could not do for ourselves. He obeyed God perfectly. And he died to be punished for our sins. So now we are sinless. That's the answer to the question Job asked: "How can a person be sinless before God?" Job didn't know. But you know. If we believe in Jesus and let him forgive us, we are sinless before God. That's how Jesus is our Mediator, the bridge that takes us to God. Now you can do what Job was afraid to do. You can talk to God.

Dear God, thank you for sending your Son, Jesus. Thank you that Jesus made peace between you and me. Thank you that he came so I can be sinless and talk to you without being afraid.

Wednesday

Read "The Son of God," page 617 in the *Day by Day Kid's Bible.* Or read this part of the story:

The leaders at the worship house had a meeting. They brought Jesus in. They said, "If you are the Promised One, then tell us."

"I could tell you," said Jesus. "But you won't believe me. From now on I'll be sitting by God's right hand."

"Then you are God's Son?" they asked.

"You're right," said Jesus. *Luke 22:66-70*

IF YOU WERE GOING TO TELL a visitor to sit in the best seat in your living room, which seat would it be? If you put a visitor at the best place at your dinner table, which place would that be?

In the days of kings and queens, the best place was beside the king's right hand. If the king asked you to sit there, it would be a great honor. It would mean that you were a very special person to the king. It would mean you were his right-hand man, and he was honoring you because he could not do without you. So when Jesus told the leaders that he would be sitting by God's right hand, he meant that God would honor him.

Jesus is with God always. That's good news for us. It means that Jesus has brought us close to God. Jesus is like a bridge. He takes us to God.

Dear God, thank you for giving Jesus the place at your right hand. Thank you for bringing us close to you.

Thursday

Read "Like a Shadow," page 784 in the *Day by Day Kid's Bible*. Or read this part of the story:

Here's the point. We have a high priest. It's Jesus. He sat down beside the King in heaven. He serves in the true house of God. It's a house that is set up by God, not by people. . . .

But Jesus' job is greater than the priests' job. God has made a new special promise. . . .

> *"I'll be their God.*
> > *They'll be my people.*
> *I will forgive their sins.*
> > *I won't remember their sins anymore."*
> Hebrews 8:1-2, 6, 10, 12

"SARA," WHISPERED JOSH, "ask Dad if we can go get ice cream after dinner."

"You ask him," said Sara.

"He might tell me no, because I haven't finished my homework yet," said Josh. Josh wants Sara to be a mediator, to go between him and Dad.

Remember when Moses went up the mountain to talk to God? The people told Moses they didn't want to come close to God. They wanted Moses to go to God for them. Someone who talks to God for other people is called a *priest*. A priest is a mediator. Before Jesus came, a priest offered meat on the altar and talked to God for the people. They needed a priest, because their sins kept them away from God.

Jesus is like a priest for us. He offered himself to God and died as punishment for our sins. So God has forgiven and forgotten our sins. Our priest, Jesus, has led us right to God. He has reconciled us to God. He is the mediator, the bridge that takes us to God.

Dear God, thank you for sending Jesus to be our priest. Thank you that he brought us close to you.

Friday

Read "Super Great Power," page 738 in the *Day by Day Kid's Bible.* Or read this part of the story:

God loved us. That's why he chose us. He planned to make us his children through Jesus. He wants to. He is happy to. So we praise him for his powerful, kind love.

God's kind love for us is free because of Jesus. Jesus forgives us for the bad things we do. God's love flows over us. His love brings us all his wise thinking and understanding. *Ephesians 1:4-8*

MAKE A FIST with one hand. Your heart is the size of your fist. Now open your hand and place it over your heart to feel your heartbeat. Is this the heart people mean when they say, "I love you with all my heart"? They are really talking about your mind and spirit, the part of you that loves and knows.

God loves us with all his heart. That's why he sent Jesus. When Jesus died for our sins, God adopted us into his family. God's family is a big family. People from all the different nations will be in this family, because Jesus is our Mediator. He makes people right with God. Jesus helps God understand us, and he helps us understand God.

Dear God, thank you for loving me so much that you brought me back to yourself through Jesus. Thank you for making it possible for me to be part of your family.

Some Things You Can Do This Week

Build a bridge. Make two stacks of blocks or books about six to eight inches apart. Try making a bridge over the stacks by using a handkerchief. Stretch it across the gap between the stacks and try rolling a toy car across it. Next try paper as the bridge. Then cardboard. Then wood. Which made the best bridge? Remember that a mediator is like a bridge, bringing peace between two people or helping them understand each other. Jesus is the Mediator between us and God.

Paint with cotton. You will need cotton swabs (like Q-tips), watercolor paints, paper cups with water, paper, and paper towels. Using the cotton swabs as paintbrushes, paint a picture of a river or a canyon with a bridge across it. Remember that Jesus is the bridge between us and God.

Make a dip-color heart. Work where it won't matter if you drip the colored water. Wear an old shirt. Spread newspaper over the space where you will work. Now place a paper towel on the newspaper and carefully draw a heart on it with a permanent marker. Get four plastic or paper bowls and fill each bowl halfway with water. Add a bit of liquid paint to the water, one color of paint for each bowl, and stir the paint into the water. Fold your paper towel in half. Then fold it in half again. Dip each corner of the folded towel into a different color of paint for a few seconds, letting the towel soak up some of the watery color. When each corner has been dipped, gently unfold the towel and lay it on the newspaper to dry. Remember that God loves you with all his heart.

Draw a throne on an index card. Glue the card to the center of a piece of blue paper. Now draw a large cloud that fills up a piece of plain white paper. Cut it out. Then cut the cloud in half. Lay the two halves over the index card, fitting the halves back together again. Tape the outside edge of each half cloud to the blue paper. Then you can open the cloud from the center to show the throne behind it. Remember that Jesus sits at God's right hand in heaven.

JESUS CAME TO UNDO THE WORKS OF THE ENEMY

The Son of God came for this purpose: to destroy the devil's work.
1 John 3:8, ICB

This week you will learn
· what Jesus came to do and what he came to undo;
· what the thunder said;
· what happens when you choose.

Monday

Read "God's Children," page 793 in the *Day by Day Kid's Bible.* Or read this part of the story:

There is no sin in Jesus. People who belong to him will stop sinning. People who keep sinning have not seen Jesus. They don't know Jesus. . . .

People who sin belong to Satan. That's because Satan sinned from the start. The reason Jesus came was to get rid of Satan's work. *1 John 3:5-6, 8*

ANOTHER NAME FOR SATAN is the devil. Jesus said that the devil was a killer from the beginning and has always hated the truth. He is a liar (John 8:44). He wants to kill and steal and destroy (John 10:10). Jesus came to get rid of Satan's work. So what did Jesus come to get rid of? Lying, killing, stealing, and destroying. That means Jesus came to bring honesty, giving, creating, and all things that bring life. Jesus came as God's secret plan to undo the works of the devil. God's Son, Jesus, is stronger than the devil because Jesus has God's love. And God's love always wins.

Dear God, thank you for sending Jesus to undo the works of the devil.

Tuesday

Read "The Woman Who Couldn't Stand Up Tall," page 546 in the *Day by Day Kid's Bible.* Or read this part of the story:

One worship day, Jesus was teaching in a town's worship house. A woman there was all bent over. She couldn't stand up tall. A bad spirit had kept her bent for 18 years.

Jesus saw her. He called her to come over to him. He said, "You're now set free from your sickness." Then he put his hands on her. Right away, she stood up tall. She praised God.

The man in charge was mad. . . .

Then Jesus said, ". . . Satan kept this woman bent over for 18 years. Shouldn't she be set free on this worship day?" *Luke 13:10-16*

"I'M JUST STUPID. I'm ugly. I'm dumb." Sometimes thoughts like these come to our minds. If we listen to them, our head bows. Our shoulders droop. We may not be as bent over as the woman Jesus healed, but we still feel bad. These kinds of thoughts don't come from Jesus. They come from our enemy, Satan, who is called the accuser. An accuser always points out what's wrong. But Jesus doesn't accuse. He points the way to what is right.

When Jesus lived on earth and met someone who had done wrong, he said, "You are forgiven. Go now and stop living in sin." Today we can hear Jesus tell us in our thoughts: *I love you. You are beautiful to me. You are wise, because you trust in me and you let me teach you.*

Jesus came to undo the works of the devil. So when you have thoughts that accuse you, think about what Jesus says about you. He will never stop loving you. Jesus is God's Son. And his love always wins.

Dear God, thank you for Jesus' love. Help me not to listen to thoughts that accuse me of the wrong things I've done. Help me to accept Jesus' forgiveness and listen to his words of love instead.

Wednesday

Read "Seeds and Dirt," page 546 in the *Day by Day Kid's Bible*. Or read this part of the story:

"Some people hear the message about God's kingdom. But they don't understand it," said Jesus. "Then Satan comes. He takes away what was planted in that person's heart. This is the seed that fell on the path." *Matthew 13:19*

SUNFLOWER SEEDS were the favorite treat for the birds and squirrels in Maria's yard. Every morning her mother would scatter the seeds on the back porch. Then Maria and her mother would watch. Sometimes even a chipmunk came to eat. Then Maria decided to plant a few of the seeds. They sprouted and grew tall. A bright yellow bloom opened at the top of the stalk, and it made more seeds for the birds.

Like a flower, God's message of love can grow and become beautiful in people's hearts. Why doesn't everyone understand the message? Because Satan lies to people. He says things like this: "God is mean and angry. He doesn't love you. You can be wise by yourself. You don't need God." But Jesus came to undo the works of the devil. When Jesus died for us, he showed us how much God loves us. God wants the best for us. He is the only one who can give joy and peace and love that lasts forever.

Dear God, thank you for loving me. Thank you for your Son, Jesus, who makes your message of love grow in my heart.

Thursday

Read "A Seed," page 598 in the *Day by Day Kid's Bible.* Or read this part of the story:

A voice came from heaven. "I have shown how great I am. And I will show how great I am again."

People who were standing there heard the voice. Some of them said it was just thunder. Other people said it was an angel talking.

"This voice was for you, not for me," said Jesus. "It's time for the world to be judged now. It's time to chase away Satan, the world's sinful prince. I'll be lifted up from the earth. Then I'll draw all people to me." *John 12:31-33*

THUNDER COMES after lightning. Lightning contains electricity, and it pushes the air out when it flashes, making the sound of thunder. Thunder never hurts anything. It just rumbles or booms. Christopher's mom always told him it was one way God said, "Look at my great power!"

When the people around Jesus heard thunder, it really was God talking. In a voice that sounded like thunder, God told Jesus that he would show his greatness. God had shown his great love by creating the world. He was going to show it again by forgiving the sins of all people forever. When would that happen? When Jesus died, taking the punishment for people's sins.

Now when Satan tries to accuse us by saying, "Look at the sin of that person," God can say, "What sin? That person has no sin. His sin has been forgiven and forgotten." That's how the world's sinful prince has been chased away. Jesus came to undo the works of the devil. God's love always wins.

Dear God, thank you for your love that always wins.

Friday

Read "Like a Fog," page 765 in the *Day by Day Kid's Bible*. Or read this part of the story:

Let God lead you. Turn away from Satan. Then he will run away from you. Come close to God. Then he will come close to you.
James 4:7-8

A CHAIR DOESN'T WORK for you until you choose to sit in it. Then it holds you up. It takes over and does the work for you. Food doesn't work for you unless you choose to take it, put it in your mouth, and eat it. If you eat it, then it takes over your body and gives you energy. It works in you. If you take medicine, it takes control of infection and "bugs" and makes you healthy again. But if you took poison, poison would take you!

Someone once said, "What you take, takes you." That's the way it works with sin, the bad things we do. If a person chooses to take actions that are bad, then sin takes over and works in that person. Sin breaks us down, making us angry and sad. It does what Satan does: It lies, kills, steals, and destroys our souls. But if we choose to follow Jesus and take him into our life, then Jesus takes over and works in us. He brings love and life forever. Jesus came to undo the works of the devil. Who do you choose to follow?

Dear God, I choose Jesus. Thank you for giving me love and life that will never end.

Some Things You Can Do This Week

● **Make a mobile.** Get four index cards. Write COME on one, CLOSE on one, and TO GOD on another. Draw a cross on the last card. Roll up a piece of strong tape like duct tape, sticky side out, and tape the back of the card with the cross to a clothes hanger just below the hook. Cut two 8-inch pieces of string and one 6-inch piece. Punch a hole in the top center of the other three cards. Tie one end of each 8-inch string to the index cards that say COME and TO GOD. Tie one end of the 6-inch string to the CLOSE card. Tie the other end of each string to the bottom of the clothes hanger from left to right: COME CLOSE TO GOD. Remember that if we turn from Satan, he'll run. If we come close to God, he'll come close to us.

☾ **Make a pasta necklace.** You'll need three long, tube-shaped pieces of dry pasta. With a sharp marker, write one of these words on each piece of pasta: GOD'S LOVE WINS. Cut a piece of thread about two feet long. Slip the pasta tubes onto the thread so the words are in order. Tie the thread so it slips comfortably over your head. If you prefer, make a bracelet instead of a necklace. Remember that God is more powerful than Satan. God loves, and his love always wins.

● **Learn to tie knots in different ways.** Look for "knots" in a book or an encyclopedia. Ask an adult to help you if you want. Knots have different names. The cow hitch, slipknot, and overhand knot are fairly easy. Sometimes knots get so tight they are hard to undo. Remember that Jesus came to undo the works of the devil.

☾ **Make a bird feeder.** Cut an orange in half. Eat the insides. Then set the halves upright like cups. Poke two holes close to the rim on opposite sides of each cup. Thread string or strong thread through the holes and tie it to make a handle for your orange-basket. Fill the basket with birdseed or shelled peanuts. Hang it by the handle on a tree. Remember the story Jesus told about the seed that fell on the path, and the birds that came and ate it.

LIGHT AND DARK

Whoever hears my word and believes him who sent me
has eternal life and will not be condemned;
he has crossed over from death to life. John 5:24, NIV

This week you will learn
· what we need to be saved from;
· what eternal life is and when it starts;
· why a Bible-time slave might have had a pierced ear;
· why John got in trouble and what Jesus showed him.

Monday

Read "Kingdom of Light," page 733 in the *Day by Day Kid's Bible.* Or read this part of the story:

God saved us from the kingdom of darkness. He brought us into the kingdom of light. It's his Son's kingdom. . . .

Jesus is in charge of everything. He made everything in heaven and on earth. He made things we can see and things we can't see. He made kings, powers, rulers, and anyone in charge. Everything was made by him and for him. *Colossians 1:13, 15-16*

FLASHLIGHT TAG is like hide-and-seek, but you play it at night outdoors or in a room that's dark. The person who is doing the seeking shines a flashlight around. And when the light shines on somebody who is hiding, that person has been found, or tagged.

Darkness is simply the absence of light. Anytime a flash of light, such as a flashlight, shines into the darkness, that darkness is moved aside. But is there such a thing as a "flashDARK"? We cannot flash darkness to move light aside. Darkness is here only if light leaves.

In our world, there are only two kingdoms: the kingdom of darkness and the kingdom of light. We can't see these kingdoms, but we know they are there. God rules the kingdom of light, which is full of life. Satan, who tries to kill, steal, and destroy, rules the kingdom of darkness. These two kingdoms, light and darkness, are the only choices we have. People are in one or the other. There is no in-between. Of course, Satan is not as strong or as wise as God. To be on the winning side, we want to be in God's kingdom, because we know that God's love always wins.

Dear God, thank you for your kingdom of light. Thank you for your love.

Tuesday

Read "A Night Visit," page 516 in the *Day by Day Kid's Bible.* Or read this part of the story:

"God didn't send his Son to blame the world," said Jesus. "He sent his Son to save the world. People who believe in him will not be blamed. But people who don't believe are blamed already. That's because they don't believe in God's only Son.

"Here's what people have to choose," said Jesus. "They have to choose between light and dark." *John 3:17-21*

LOGAN'S SOCCER TEAM practiced on the field while they were waiting for the other team to get there. They practiced and practiced and waited and waited. The other team never came. So Logan's team won, because the other team didn't show up. We call that "winning the game by default."

That's the way it is with the two kingdoms of darkness and light. If people don't choose the kingdom of light, then by "default" the kingdom of darkness wins in their lives. You see, none of us is good enough to live forever with the almighty, perfect God. Everyone chooses to do wrong sometimes. So we're all part of the kingdom of darkness because of the wrong we do. That's why God sent Jesus to save us. When people hear about Jesus, they can choose to let Jesus save them from the kingdom of darkness and bring them into his kingdom of light.

Dear God, thank you for sending Jesus to bring us into your kingdom of light.

Wednesday

Read "The Room Upstairs," page 608 in the *Day by Day Kid's Bible.* Or read this part of the story:

Jesus picked up the cup of wine. "This shows God's new special promise," he said. "It's a promise made with my blood. I will give my blood for you." . . .

Jesus knew it was time to leave the world. It was time for him to go to his Father. He loved his friends very much. They were his own people here in the world. He was about to show how much he loved them. *Luke 22:20; John 13:1*

DO YOU HAVE PIERCED EARS? Does anyone you know have pierced ears? In Bible times, some people were slaves. But a master could keep a Jewish slave for only six years. Then the slave had to be set free. If a slave wanted to stay with his master for the rest of his life, he had to have his ear pierced. This was a sign of his special promise to his master.

Long before Jesus came to earth, God made a special promise to Abraham. God said he would bless Abraham's people, the Jews. There would be as many people in his family as there were stars, and they were to promise that they would trust and obey God. God kept his promise, but the people did not keep their part of the promise. They did not trust and obey God. So God gave a new promise. He would forgive everyone by sending Jesus to take the punishment for all sins. Now, to keep our side of the promise, we are to believe and follow Jesus and his ways. Then we are in God's kingdom of light, so we have *eternal life.* That means God is always with us, and we are always with God. Eternal life lasts forever, but it starts right now for people who believe in Jesus.

Dear God, thank you for making a new promise to forgive us when we follow Jesus.

Thursday

Read "A Chariot Ride," page 643 in the *Day by Day Kid's Bible.* Or read this part of the story:

Philip ran up to the chariot. He heard the man reading the book Isaiah wrote. "Do you understand what you're reading?" Philip asked. . . .

The man was reading this part of Isaiah:

> *He was taken like a sheep to be killed.*
> *A sheep is quiet while the farmer cuts off its wool.*
> > *He was quiet too.*
> *They treated him like nothing.*
> > *What they did to him was not fair. . . .*

Philip told about the part that the man was reading. He told the man about Jesus' Good News. *Acts 8:30, 32-33, 35*

HOLLY'S FAVORITE BASEBALL TEAM scored a run. Holly cheered. But the way they made the point was by the batter bunting the ball. He tapped it without swinging the bat. He knew he would be out. But he did it so the runner on third base could run home and score. The batter made what is called a "sacrifice hit." He gave up something important to him (hitting the ball and running to first base) so his team could score a point.

Sacrifice is giving up something very important so someone else can get good out of it. Philip told the man in the chariot about the most important sacrifice in the world. Jesus gave up his life so we can be free from sin and have eternal life starting now. We can come out of the kingdom of darkness and move right into the kingdom of light! It's all because of God's great love. His love always wins.

Dear God, thank you for Jesus. Thank you that he sacrificed his life so I can be free from sin and have eternal life starting now.

Friday

Read "A New Heaven and a New Earth," page 822 in the *Day by Day Kid's Bible.* Or read this part of the story:

A loud voice came from where the King was. "Now God will live with people. That's where his house will be. They will be his people. He will be their God. God will wipe all their tears away. They won't die anymore. They won't cry anymore. They won't hurt anymore. The old way of doing things is gone."

The King said, "I'm making everything new!"
Revelation 21:3-5

JOHN, ONE OF JESUS' FRIENDS, got in trouble for teaching people about Jesus. But instead of being sent to jail, John was sent away to an island that he was not allowed to leave. One day while John was worshipping, he heard a loud voice behind him. When he turned around, he saw Jesus. Jesus showed John some things that are going to happen. Jesus told John about heaven and the end of time. John learned that no matter what happens, God's love and blessings will last forever. God and his love are greater than any other power anywhere.

Troubles may come your way as long as you live, and it might look for a while as though evil is winning. But remember what God has taught you through the Bible: He loves you. And in the end, his love will win, no matter what happens.

Dear God, thank you for inviting me to live with you in heaven. Thank you for loving me. Help me always to remember that no matter what happens, your love will win.

SOME THINGS YOU CAN DO THIS WEEK

Design a flag for the kingdom of light. You can make your flag with crayons and markers on paper, or with fabric markers on a piece of light-colored cloth.

Draw and color heaven as you picture it from the way John tells about it. You can read some of his words about heaven from Revelation 4 or from "An Open Door," page 803 in the *Day by Day Kid's Bible.* Press down hard as you color with crayons. When you have finished, paint lightly over your picture with watercolor paint. The waxy crayon-picture will show up through the watercolors.

Create seals. Flatten some play dough on a paper plate. Press different small objects (like the top of a screw, different kinds of bottle caps, old jewelry, buttons, etc.) into the dough to see the design they make. In Bible times, kings sealed important papers with their own seal that was on a ring they wore. The papers often had promises from the king. Remember that Jesus sealed God's promise of eternal life with his own death on the cross.

Draw star constellations. Look up "constellations" in an encyclopedia or a science book. These are groups of stars that make pictures in the sky. With star stickers, try to copy some of the constellations on a piece of paper. Or you can use a dark piece of paper and draw the stars with a white crayon or chalk. God promised to make Abraham's family so large that there would be as many people as stars. Remember God's new promise made by Jesus.

THE TRADE

[Christ] never sinned, but he died for sinners that he might bring
us safely home to God. 1 Peter 3:18, NLT

This week you will learn
· what *redeem* means;
· how someone bought a wife;
· what Jesus traded with us;
· how to get God's free gift.

Monday

Read "A Night in the Barn" and "A Deal at the City Gate," pages 113 and 115 in the *Day by Day Kid's Bible*. Or read this part of the story:

"Hello, friend," called Boaz. . . . "Naomi came back from Moab. She is selling the land that once belonged to our family." . . .

"Then I'll buy it," said the man.

"Ruth, the woman from Moab, comes with the land," said Boaz. "When you buy the land, you have to marry her."

"Then I can't buy the land," said the man. . . .

Back then, people made a deal this way. One person would take his shoe off. He would give it to the other person. So that's what the man did.

Then Boaz told all the people listening, "You see this. Today I'm buying the land from Naomi. And Ruth will be my wife."
Ruth 4:1-10

HAVE YOU EVER been to a pawn shop? Think of something you love so much that you want to keep it forever. Now imagine that your family needs money, so you sell your treasure to the owner of the pawn shop. But you love your treasure so much that you work hard and earn enough money to buy it back. We would say that you *redeemed* it.

Boaz redeemed Ruth. He loved her so much that he bought the land to save her from having to marry a man who didn't love her.

Jesus *redeemed* us. We were made to belong to God. We are his treasure. But because we do wrong, we live in the kingdom of darkness. God loved us so much that he paid to buy us back. How did he pay? By sending his own Son, Jesus, to take our punishment for our sins. Jesus did that when he died on the cross. That's why we say that Jesus is our Redeemer. He traded with us, taking our death and giving us his life.

Dear God, thank you for sending Jesus to redeem me.

Tuesday

Read "The King of the Jews" and "Skull Hill," pages 620 and 621 in the *Day by Day Kid's Bible*. Or read this part of the story:

"Nobody can blame me for killing [Jesus]," said Pilate. "I'll have nothing to do with it. You are the ones choosing this."

"That's fine," said all the people. "We'll take the blame."

So Pilate gave them what they wanted. He let Barabbas go free, and he gave Jesus to them so they could have him killed. *Matthew 27:24-26*

THE WORD *forgive* is made of two other words. What are they? The first is "for" and the second is "give." What would those words say if they traded places? *Give for.* What did God *give for* us in order to *forgive* us? He gave us his only Son, Jesus.

God forgives even the worst sin, because Jesus took the blame for our sins and was punished in our place. Barabbas had killed people, and he probably would have been killed on a cross. But Pilate made a trade. All of a sudden, Barabbas found himself free, even though he did not deserve to live. And Jesus died on the cross, even though he did not deserve to die. That's the same trade Jesus makes with everyone. He died for each of us so we can be free from sin. He took our badness and gave us his goodness. He took our death and gave us his life.

Dear God, thank you that Jesus traded places with me so I can have his goodness and life.

Wednesday

Read "Close to the Cross" and "Open Graves," pages 622 and 623 in the *Day by Day Kid's Bible.* Or read this part of the story:

Inside the worship house there hung a big, long cloth. It hung in front of the Most Holy Place. It kept people out of that room. But at the moment Jesus died, it tore in half. The tear started at the top. It ripped all the way down to the bottom. *Matthew 27:51*

JEFFREY WENT TO a homeschool group. Before they ate lunch, all of the students who believed in Jesus bowed their heads and thanked God for the food. They always ended by saying, "In Jesus' name. Amen." Jeffrey's friend Bradon did not believe in Jesus. One day, Bradon asked, "Why do you say, 'In Jesus' name. Amen'?"

Do you know why? Think of today's reading. In the worship house was a room called the Most Holy Place. No one was allowed to go in except the high priest. He could go in only once a year to meet with God. Nobody else could meet that closely with God. A heavy cloth hung in front of that room to keep people out. But when Jesus died, the cloth tore in half from top to bottom. That means people no longer need a priest to talk to God for them.

All people can go straight to God in prayer, because Jesus brings us to God. That's why we say, "In Jesus' name." And *Amen* means, "Yes. Let it happen."

Dear God, thank you for making a way for me to come straight to you. In Jesus' name. Amen.

Thursday

Read "Running to the Grave," page 626 in the *Day by Day Kid's Bible.* Or read this part of the story:

Mary turned around. She saw a man. . . .

 Mary thought he was the gardener. She asked, "Did you take Jesus' body away? If you did, please tell me where you put it. I'll come and get it."

 "Mary," said Jesus.

 Mary looked at Jesus. "Teacher!" she cried. . . .

 Mary hurried to find Jesus' friends. "I've seen Jesus!" she said. *John 20:14-18*

WHEN MELANIE WAS FOUR years old, a Sunday school teacher told the class that they could ask Jesus to come into their heart. When Melanie got home, she told her mother she wanted to do that. So they prayed, asking Jesus to come into Melanie's heart. After the prayer, Melanie was surprised. She didn't feel anything inside. She said, "It doesn't itch." Her mom asked what she was talking about. Melanie said, "Jesus has a beard. I thought when he came into my heart, his beard would make me itch inside."

What does it mean to have Jesus living in us? That's a mystery, even to adults. Part of the answer is this: God brought Jesus back to life. Then Jesus went back to heaven and sent the Holy Spirit to earth. When we believe in Jesus, he trades our old sinful spirit for a new sinless spirit. Then the Holy Spirit joins our spirit and lives within us.

Dear God, thank you for loving me and living in me.

Friday

Read "No More Night," page 823 in the *Day by Day Kid's Bible.* Or read this part of the story:

The Spirit says, "Come on!" . . . Whoever hears it should say, "Come on!" If you're thirsty, come. If you want to, you can have living water. It's free. . . .

Jesus says these things are true. He says, "Yes. I'm coming soon." Yes! Amen! Come, Lord Jesus. *Revelation 22:17, 20*

ONCE THERE WAS a very good actor who was in lots of movies. He was so good, he was chosen to get a special award that many actors wish they could get. But lots of people were surprised when the night came for him to get his award, because he would not take it. He didn't want it. So he never got the award.

Jesus invites us to come to him. His Spirit asks us to come. God has a free gift for us: an eternal life of love and joy and peace. But we have to choose to take it. How do we take it? "If you use your mouth to say, 'Jesus is Lord,' and if you believe in your heart that God raised Jesus from death, then you will be saved" (Romans 10:9, ICB). All each one of us has to do is ask Jesus to be our Lord and Savior.

Dear God, thank you for your free gift of eternal life.
(Perhaps you have not asked Jesus to be your Lord and Savior yet. You can do that now if you want. A parent or any other adult who loves Jesus will be glad to help you know what to say.)

☀ SOME THINGS YOU CAN DO THIS WEEK ☽

- ☀ **Make shoe prints.** Get a piece of foil larger than your foot. Place it on a soft carpet or a pillow. Carefully step on it. The imprint of your shoe will show up on the foil. You can get friends or family to do this too, and then compare the designs. In the story of Boaz and Ruth, you will remember that the man took off his sandal as a sign that he was agreeing to let Boaz redeem Ruth. How did Jesus redeem us?

- ☽ **Make a forgiveness painting.** With a white crayon, write the word "Forgiven" on a white piece of paper. Press down hard on the crayon to make the letters thick and waxy. Paint over the paper with red water-color paint. Isaiah 1:18 says that even though our sins are red, they will become white like snow or wool. What do you think that means?

- ☀ **Float some pepper.** Fill a pie pan or cake pan halfway with water. Sprinkle pepper across the top of the water. Pretend the bits of pepper are all your sins. The pepper in the water makes the water impure, just like our life becomes impure when we sin. Now take a bottle of dishwashing liquid and drip just one drop onto the water right in the middle of the pan. What happens? Just as the liquid soap chases the pepper away, Jesus' death gets rid of our sin.

- ☽ **Make a profile.** Lay your head sideways on a large piece of paper. Get a friend or family member to help you. They can trace around your head to make a profile of your face. Write JESUS inside the profile. Jesus loves you so much, he wants to live in you.

FAITH

Faith is being sure of what we hope for and certain of what we do not see.
Hebrews 11:1, NIV

This week you will learn
· what faith is;
· what language God speaks;
· the difference between belief and faith;
· the shape and size of a shield.

Monday

Read "Faith," page 786 in the *Day by Day Kid's Bible*. Or read this part of the story:

We have faith. So we understand that God made the world and all of space. He told it to happen, and it happened. He made things we see out of things we don't see. . . .

    People who come to God have to believe two things. First, they must believe that God really lives. Then they must believe that God brings good to people who look for him. *Hebrews 11:3, 6*

CAN YOU SEE GRAVITY? If you drop a ball from an upstairs window, will it go up or down? How do you know? You can't see gravity, but you can see what it does. It's the force that pulls the ball down.

We can't see God, but we can see what he does. More than that, we know that God's love is the best kind there is. Because of his love, he always does what's best for us. We are sure of that. *Faith* is being sure and steady. It is trusting what you know deep inside. We can have faith in Jesus because he is faithful. When we accept Jesus to be our Lord and Savior, we take his godly love to be our love, his godly goodness to be our goodness, his godly faithfulness to be our faithfulness. Then we can be sure of God and steady in trusting and following him.

Dear God, thank you for your kind love and your faithfulness. Thank you for helping me to be sure of you and to be steady in trusting and following you.

Tuesday

Read "God's Way," page 201 in the *Day by Day Kid's Bible.* Or read this part of the story:

> *The sky shows how great God is.*
> *Every day it tells about God.*
> *Every night it shows what he is like.*
> *No matter what language people speak,*
>   *they can understand what the sky tells.*
> *All over the world, people can see it. . . .*
>
> *God's way is the best.*
> *It keeps us strong.*
> *We can trust God's rules. . . .*
> *God's commands shine clearly,*
>   *giving our spirits light.*
> Psalm 19:1-4, 7-8

Gloire à Dieu. Gloria a Dios. Tsan Mai Shun. Bwana Asifiwe. Mezhdan la Raab. All of these mean "Praise the Lord" in other languages: French, Spanish, Chinese, Swahili (African), and Arabic. God understands every language, and he can speak every one. Most people can understand only one or two. But there is one language God speaks that talks to everyone, and that's nature.

In the Bible, Paul wrote, "God clearly showed who he is. He showed his greatness. People can see his greatness by looking at what he made. So there

is no reason for people not to believe" (Romans 1:19-20, DBD). When we study the stars or gaze at a big mountain or a waterfall or see a butterfly drinking from a flower, we know deep down that there is a God. We also know that he is beautiful and wise and very, very loving. His Spirit speaks to our spirits at those times and says, "Yes. It's true. I am love." And what do we know about that? Love always wins. It is good to have faith in our God of love.

Dear God, thank you for clearly showing me who you are. Keep showing me every day so I can love you more and more.

Wednesday

Read "Two Men Who Could Not See," page 553 in the *Day by Day Kid's Bible*. Or read this part of the story:

Two men who could not see began to follow Jesus. They called out, "Jesus, be kind to us! Make us well!" . . .

"Do you believe I can do this?" Jesus asked.

"Yes, Lord," they said.

Then Jesus touched their eyes. He said, "You believe. So you will see."

And they could see again. *Matthew 9:27-30*

"WHEN I WAS LITTLE, I believed that new shoes would make me run faster," said Miguel. "But now I believe I'll never run as fast as my friend Greg." The kind of believing that Miguel is talking about can change. What he believed changed as he grew older. And what he believes now about not being as fast as Greg might be right, or it might be wrong. It's just what he thinks. That's what makes belief different than faith.

Belief can be about anything, even God. But *faith* is only about God and your spirit. A belief can be right or wrong. And you can believe many things.

But the Bible says there is only one faith, and it is right, because it is all about who God is. What you believe can change. But faith does not change, because God does not change. Faith is being sure and steady about what you know deep inside yourself about God and his love.

Dear God, thank you for letting me know about you and your love. Thank you for the gift of faith.

Thursday

Read "Believing the Promise," page 705 in the *Day by Day Kid's Bible*. Or read this part of the story:

Abraham knew he was too old to have children. In fact, he was almost 100 years old. . . . But he believed God's promise anyway.

Abraham's faith was strong. He believed God had the power to do what he promised. That's why God said Abraham was right with him. . . .

We can believe in God also. When we do, God says we are right with him. *Romans 4:19-25*

WHEN GRANDMA ELLEN turned 100 years old, her family had a big birthday party for her. She walked slowly. She had a hard time hearing everyone. She couldn't see very well. But she was happy to be 100. She wrote a poem about it and read it to everyone. Now if anyone had told her she would have a baby, she would have laughed. Everybody at her party would have laughed.

That's just what happened when Sarah heard that she would have a baby. Sarah laughed. God said, "Why did Sarah laugh? Is anything too hard for the Lord?" Abraham didn't laugh. He believed God's promise. He had faith in God. And God was faithful. God kept his promise.

Is it easy to have faith all the time? No. We all have times when we are tempted not to believe God. That's why we need Jesus. Jesus does for us what we cannot do for ourselves. The Bible says that when we are faithless, he stays faithful (2 Timothy 2:13). That shows just how much God loves us.

Dear God, I'm sorry for times when it's hard for me to believe you. Thank you for showing how much you love me by sending Jesus to be faithful even when I am faithless.

Friday

Read "Putting on God's Armor," page 744 in the *Day by Day Kid's Bible.* Or read this part of the story:

Be strong in God. Be strong in his great power. It's like putting on God's heavy, metal armor. Then you can stand up against Satan's plans. . . .

Days filled with sin may come. But you'll be able to keep your place in God's kingdom. After you do everything you can, you'll still be standing. So stand firm. . . .

Hold faith like a shield in front of you. *Ephesians 6:10-16*

SHIELDS WERE ROUND or rectangle-shaped in Bible times. They were usually covered with leather, although some had metal on them. When a soldier held a round shield in front of himself, it covered about half of his body. The rectangle shield covered almost all of the body. Sometimes it was so big that a soldier had to have a helper carry the shield for him. Goliath had a helper to carry his shield. Since Goliath was nine feet tall, his shield must have been very big.

Faith is our shield. How? Remember that God said if you turn away from Satan, Satan will run from you. But if you come close to God, God will come close to you (James 4:7-8). Faith is your closeness to God. No one can protect you better than God. God told Abraham not to be afraid. "I am your shield" (Genesis 15:1, NIV). If your faith is in God, he is your shield. He loves you, and his love always wins.

Dear God, I choose to have faith in you. Thank you for being my shield.

Some Things You Can Do This Week

- **Draw cartoon eyes.** On a piece of paper, trace around two dimes placed side by side with a little space between. These will be cartoon eyes. Draw a line across the middle of each eye. Make a black dot in the half of each eye below the line. Draw around the two dimes again at another place on the paper. This time make a black dot in each eye in the top half of the circle. Make two more circles, and put the black dot in the center of each. Try making other eyes with different expressions. Eyes not only allow us to see, but they also help us to express feelings. Remember how the blind men believed Jesus could heal them, and he did.

- **Trick your eyes.** Use a cardboard tube from a roll of paper towels. Look through the tube with one eye. Keep the other eye open too. Now hold your right hand up, resting it against the side of the tube, with your palm toward your face. Slowly move your hand toward you and away from you until you see a hole in your hand. If you believe what you see, you believe you have a hole in your hand. But this is just a trick. Remember the difference between belief and faith.

- **Make a "domino" game.** Get 19 index cards. Write one word from this week's verse in the center of each card, and put "Hebrews 11:1" on one card. Line the cards up in order from end to end. Now design a border to the right of the first word ("Now"), and make a matching border on the left of the second word ("faith"). Draw a different border at the right of the card that says "faith" and a matching border to the left of the card that says "is." Keep designing these cards so that the right border of a word matches the left border of the next word. When the cards are finished, mix them up. Find a person to put the cards in order by matching their borders. Since a person doesn't have to read to do this, a young brother or sister could do it. Then you can read the verse.

- **Make faith rolls.** (Be sure an adult is with you to help as needed.) In a big bowl, mix three cups of flour, one package of quick-rising yeast, one-half teaspoon of salt, and one-third cup of sugar. In a saucepan, mix one-half cup of butter or margarine cut into slices, one-half cup of milk, and one-half cup of water. Heat this until bubbles start to form around the edges and the butter is melting. Pour it into the flour mixture and stir. In a small bowl, beat one egg with a fork. Add it to the batter and mix it in well. Add a little flour, up to one cup more, just enough so the dough is not sticky. Cover the bowl with a clean towel and let it rest for ten minutes. Grease a baking sheet. Shape a handful of dough into the letter *F*. Shape more dough into the letter *A*. Shape an *I*, a *T*, and an *H*. What have you spelled? Place these on the baking sheet. Make other rolls into more letters or into balls. Cover them with the towel and let them rise for 30 minutes. Heat the oven to 400 degrees. Bake the rolls for 15 minutes. As the dough rises and while it bakes, you can see FAITH grow. Real faith grows by coming closer to God and by trusting and obeying him.

WHAT IS WORSHIP?

God is spirit, and his worshipers must worship in spirit and in truth. John 4:24, NIV

This week you will learn
· what worship is;
· what people should have smelled but didn't;
· the name that no one ever said out loud;
· how we can be a living gift.

Monday

Read "Solomon Bows and Prays," page 226 in the *Day by Day Kid's Bible*. Or read this part of the story:

The priests came out of the Most Holy Place. Then some of the priests played horns. Others sang. Some played cymbals, harps, and lyres. They all cheered for God. They sang, "God is good. His love lasts forever." *2 Chronicles 5:11-13*

☽ ☀ ☽ ☀ ☽ ☀ ☽ ☀ ☽ ☀

IN SUNDAY SCHOOL, a teacher asked a class of five-year-olds, "What is worship?" One little girl stood up and said, "Worship is . . ." Then she blew a kiss up toward God. That is a good way of thinking about worship. It's like blowing a kiss to God. It's a hug from us to God. It's our way of telling God we love him. *Worship* is letting God know that we respect him and we wonder about him because he is so great. Worship is showing God that we think he is the greatest. That's what King Solomon and the priests did in today's reading. They all sang. And Solomon held his hands up toward God as he prayed, "There is no God like you" (1 Kings 8:23, NLT).

Dear God, there is no God like you. I love you.

Tuesday

Read "The Big, Burning Oven," page 431 in the *Day by Day Kid's Bible*. Or read this part of the story:

The fire had not hurt the three friends at all. Their hair wasn't burned even a little bit. Their robes weren't burned. They didn't even smell like smoke.

"Praise the God of Shadrach, Meshach, and Abednego!" said the king. "He sent his angel. He saved his servants! They trusted him. They didn't obey me. They wouldn't worship another god. They even knew they might die for it. They worship no one but their God. So I'll make a new rule. Nobody will say anything bad about their God." *Daniel 3:27-29*

WHAT KINDS OF FOOD do you like to smell? What do you enjoy smelling outdoors in the spring? What can you smell inside in the winter when it's cold and people build fires in their fireplaces?

In today's Bible reading, when the three friends came out of the fire, what was strange about the way they smelled? They did not smell like smoke. King Nebuchadnezzar learned that God is the greatest. The three friends knew that. They would not worship anyone but God. God's thoughts are higher than ours, and his ways are higher than our ways. And he loves us more than we know. Worship is our way of telling God we love him. Only God is great enough to be worshipped.

Dear God, you are the greatest. I worship you.

Wednesday

Read "Idols," page 363 in the *Day by Day Kid's Bible*. Or read this part of the story:

> *"I, the Lord, say this.*
> *I am the first. I am the last.*
>   *There's no other God but me."*
>
> *People who make idols are nothing. . . .*
> *They don't stop to say,*
>   *". . . Should I bow down to a wooden block?"*
> *The people can't save themselves.*
>   *They don't know to say, "Isn't this wooden idol a lie?"*
>
> *"Remember this, my people," said God. "I made you, and I won't*
> *forget you."* Isaiah 44:6, 9, 19, 21

TRINA WENT TO CHINA with her mother to visit a friend. The streets were crowded with small cars beeping, little trucks honking, and people on bicycles riding everywhere. In the park, some people were out walking their pet birds and hamsters by carrying them in cages. Trina walked with her mother and their friend to a garden-like yard. Priests in yellow robes were walking around. Inside a wide building on the other side of the yard sat a high, wide, golden idol of a round-faced man. People were bowing to this idol and praying. Trina knew, just like you know, that this idol could not hear prayers. It could not help people.

But sometimes we think other things can help us more than God can. So an idol can be anything that is more important to you than God. It is something you think can help you more than God can. What do people in our country think might help them more than God? Money? The right friends? The best school? Sports? The way we live shows who or what we worship.

Dear God, I don't want to make anything more important than you. Nothing can help me more than you can. I choose to worship you.

Thursday

Read "Stick with Each Other," page 712 in the *Day by Day Kid's Bible*. Or read this part of the story:

Think about God's kind love. Then give yourself to him. Be a living gift. Be special and clean. Make God happy. This is the way your spirit worships him.

Don't be like people of the world. Be changed by letting God make your mind new again. Then you'll know what God wants. You'll know what's good. You'll know what makes God happy. You'll know what's right. *Romans 12:1-2*

LONG AGO, THERE WAS a queen named Victoria in Britain. Because Britain owned many other nations, Queen Victoria ruled over many countries around the world. If you had been British back then, and if you had traveled to South Africa, guess who would have been your queen? Victoria. What if you went to India? Victoria was queen. What if you went to Hong Kong? Victoria was queen. Whether you were eating breakfast, going to school, or sleeping at night, in these countries Victoria was queen. That's the way it is when you live in a kingdom.

We do live in a kingdom: God's kingdom. So as God's children, every bit of our lives is worship, because no matter where we are or what we are doing, God is on the throne of our hearts. We are a living gift to him. We do all things to honor God and show how great he is. That's worship.

Dear God, I am glad to live in your kingdom. I worship you as my King.

Friday

Read "The Deep Earth in His Hand" and "Wake Up the Morning," page 189 in the *Day by Day Kid's Bible.* Or read this part of the story:

Come!
Let's sing with joy to God!
Let's shout out loud to the one who saves us.
Let's come to him, giving thanks. Let's worship him with music and
song. . . .

Come!
Let's bow down in worship. Let's bow before God our Maker.
Psalm 95:1-2, 6

THE FIRST HALF of the Bible was written in a language called Hebrew. If you were reading Hebrew, you would read a line from right to left instead of the way we read our language, left to right. In Hebrew, there are no vowels, no letters for the *a, e, i, o,* or *u* sounds that our language has. And there is one word that the Hebrew people would never say. In English it looks like this: YHWH. Can you sound it out? It is the name they called God. Out of respect for God, they would not say his name. Instead, they called him LORD.

We have many names for God: Father in heaven, Almighty, Creator, Most High. Can you think of other names we use to describe God? Like David, when we worship, we can tell about what God has done, and we can tell him the special names we like to call him.

Dear God, you are my Lord, the Almighty, my Creator, my Father in heaven. You are the Most High. You have done great things, and I worship you.

☀ SOME THINGS YOU CAN DO THIS WEEK ☾

☀ **Draw an object** or picture that tells something special about your life or who you are. For example, if soccer is an important part of your life, you could draw a soccer ball. Or if you take piano lessons, draw a piano or keyboard. You can draw something that shows a hobby or friends or school or a collection of some kind. You can draw more than one thing if you want. Then put your drawing(s) into a box and gift wrap it. This is a reminder that you give your life to God. You are a living gift. That's worship.

☾ **Make a model of an altar.** Gather at least fifteen small rocks or pebbles. Glue five of them next to each other to form a circle on a paper plate. Glue five more on top of the first five. Glue the last five on top of those. This makes a small model of an altar. People built altars in Bible times as places of worship. People offered meat, grain, fruit, and wine on altars. The oldest kinds of altars were made of mud bricks. Sometimes they were just mounds of dirt. But most of the altars in the time before King Solomon were built of stone.

☀ **Use stencils** of alphabet letters to write the Bible verses of Psalm 100 on paper with colored pencils. This psalm talks about five things we might do in worship. What are they?

☾ **Try writing your name** by leaving out the vowels (a, e, i, o, and u). Try writing a note that way. See if someone else can read it. Remember that this is the way Hebrew is written, except they have different letters than we do. They also read from right to left. Can you write the same note from right to left on your paper?

WAYS TO WORSHIP

Praise the Lord for the glory of his name. Worship the Lord because he is holy. Psalm 29:2, ICB

This week you will learn
· different ways to worship;
· what a khalil, a nebel, and a toph are;
· seven words for praise.

Monday

Read "My Shepherd" and "Be Still," page 185 in the *Day by Day Kid's Bible.* Or read this part of the story:

Be still and know that I am God.
Nations will call me great.
The earth will call me great.
Psalm 46:10

THERE ARE MORE THAN 200 billion billion stars. (You're not seeing double. The two "billions" is correct!) That's what the people who study the stars say. That means that if each person in the world were to count different stars, each person would have to count over 50 billion stars without counting the same star twice! The sun is our nearest star. It is 100 times as big as our earth, but it's only a medium-sized star.

Close your eyes for a minute and think about the stars. Think about God's greatness and wisdom as the Maker of the stars. The Bible tells us that God knows the number of stars and calls each of them by name. Thinking about God and his greatness is called *meditating.* The Psalms, the old songs of God's people, say, "We meditate on your unfailing love" (Psalm 48:9, NLT). Being still and thinking about God is one way to worship.

Dear God, you are great and wonderful. I will be still and think about you.

Tuesday

Read "God Talks from a Storm" and "Do You Know?" pages 446 and 447 in the *Day by Day Kid's Bible*. Or read this part of the story:

> God said, "Who is this?
>   Who is talking without knowing what he is saying? . . .
>
> "Where were you when I made the earth?
>   Do you understand it? Then tell me.
> Who marked how big it would be?
> What was the earth built on? . . .
>
> "Did you ever tell the morning what to do?
>   Did you show the sunrise where to start?"
> Job 38:2-6, 12-13

BEFORE YOU READ this next part, go and pour a bit of salt into your hand. Then look at one grain of salt. Each grain has many, many atoms inside it. Everything is made of tiny, tiny atoms. Even you! These tiny atoms have space in them. If you took all the space out of the atoms in your body, you would be no bigger than that grain of salt! That's amazing. God made the sun, moon, stars, huge mountains, and tall trees out of atoms that are so tiny, we can't even see them! Wow! Worship is thinking about God, seeing all he's done, and saying WOW! We can say WOW in a whisper, in a shout, in a song, in a prayer, or in many other ways. Anytime we think or say WOW about God, that's worship.

Dear God, WOW! You are amazing and wonderful!

Wednesday

Read "Praise Him!" and "Dancing," pages 213 and 214 in the *Day by Day Kid's Bible.* Or read this part of the story:

> *Praise God from heaven high above.*
> *Praise him, all you angels.*
> *Praise him, armies of heaven.*
> *Praise him, sun and moon.*
> *Praise him, you stars that shine.*
> *Praise him, you high heavens.*
> *Let everything God made praise him.* Psalm 148:1-5

IMAGINE ADAM AT the beginning of the world. There were no musical instruments. What would Adam have heard that sounded like music? Birds, animal calls, wind, shaking leaves, brooks, and rivers. Maybe Adam sang his own music. One of the first instruments in the world was the flute. At the top of one of David's songs (Psalm 5), there's a line that says it's for flutes. David wanted flutes to play along with this song he wrote. Some other instruments the Bible talks about are the *khalil* (kah-LEEL), pipes or flute; *shophar* (SHO-far), ram's horn; *kinnor* (KIN-nor), lyre; *nebel* (NEB-el), harp; *toph* (toff), tambourine.

Do you play an instrument? Even your voice is an instrument. How can you use music to worship? If your music comes from your respect, wonder, love, and thanks for God, it's worship.

Dear God, I love you, and I will worship you with music.

Thursday

Read "A Sad Prayer and a Happy Answer," page 121 in the *Day by Day Kid's Bible.* Or read this part of the story:

Hannah got up. She was very sad. So she went to the worship tent to pray. She cried to God. She asked God for a baby boy. She promised she would let her son serve God. . . .

God remembered Hannah's prayer. She had a baby boy. . . .

Hannah prayed. "My heart is full of joy. I'm strong in God." *1 Samuel 1:9-11, 19-20; 2:1*

SYLVIE DECIDED TO be a spy. A prayer spy. She watched for times when people prayed, besides the times when they were at church. Here's what she found out. Her family prayed before eating, because they were thankful. Her grandmother prayed when she got the sad news that a friend was moving away. Sylvie heard her dad's voice coming from his room one night, and when she peeked in, he was on his knees praying, asking God for wisdom at work. Her mother said, "You're amazing, God!" when she saw a beautiful sunset. Praying is a way to tell God we respect him, love him, thank him, and feel amazed by him. That's worship. Sylvie found out that people can worship no matter where they are and no matter how they feel. Hannah worshipped by praying when she was sad, and by praying again when she was happy.

Dear God, thank you for letting me talk to you no matter how I feel. I will worship you in prayer.

Friday

Read "Wonderful Love," page 213 in the *Day by Day Kid's Bible.* Or read this part of the story:

I will bow before you, my God the King.
I will praise you every day.
I will worship your name forever. . . .

My mouth will cheer for God.
Let everyone praise his name forever. Psalm 145:1-2, 21

IN OUR LANGUAGE, we have one word for "praise." But in Hebrew, the language King David spoke, there are seven words that our Bibles call "praise." One word is *hallal.* That means to rave or talk with excitement. Does *hallal* sound like some word you know? Another word for praise was *yadah.* That means to lift up hands. *Barak* means to kneel and say that God has all power. *Tehillah* means to sing out freely, without planning to. *Zamar* means to play stringed instruments. *To'dah* means to thank and praise God for what he is going to do. *Shabach* means to shout. All of these are words in the book of Psalms, the songs of the Bible. These are all ways to worship, to tell God how great and wonderful he is.

Dear God, I praise you. You are great and wonderful.

SOME THINGS YOU CAN DO THIS WEEK

* Draw a big window that almost fills a page of printer paper or notebook paper. Divide the window into seven sections as if it were a stained-glass window in a church building. In each section, write one of the Hebrew words for praise with a dark crayon. Then color each section a different color with lighter crayons so the words show. Now put the paper on top of a piece of wax paper. Dip a cotton ball or cotton swab into baby oil or vegetable oil, and rub it over the drawing. Hang the drawing in a window to let the light shine through it.

* **Go outdoors on a cloudless night** and study the stars. Think about how huge, how vast, space is and about how much greater God is. Wonder about God. Meditate on him and what he has made.

* **Make an instrument.** Get a comb. Cut a square of tissue paper as long as the comb and about twice as wide. Fold the tissue paper around the comb with the teeth of the comb at the fold. Place your lips against the fold of the tissue paper with your mouth slightly open. Blow gently and hum. You should hear a buzzing melody.

* **Play a tape or CD** of praise and worship music while you draw, paint, or work with play dough. As you do, think about God. Worship is expressing our wonder and love for God, to God. When we do this with our art, we are worshipping.

LORD

The God who made the world and everything
in it is the Lord of heaven and earth. Acts 17:24, NIV

This week you will learn
· what Lord means;
· who worshipped God before they knew him;
· what a plumb line is;
· the difference between fact and opinion.

Monday

Read "Paul Visits Many Towns," page 665 in the *Day by Day Kid's Bible.* Or read this part of the story:

Paul stood up. He said, "I see that you think about the spirit world. I walked around your city. I looked carefully at what you worship. I even found an altar with a different sign. It says, 'To a God We Don't Know.' I'll tell you about this God you don't know.

"God made the world and everything in it," said Paul. "He is the Lord of heaven and earth." *Acts 17:22-24*

IN THE DAYS OF CASTLES and kings, there were people who were called lords, like Lord Percy and Lord Nevill. The word *Lord* in front of their names meant that they were in charge of something and there were people who served them. Even today in England, some people are still called "Lord." The word really means ruler or authority, the one in charge. But in the Bible, the word *Lord* is used most often to mean YHWH, the name of God in the Hebrew language. In that case, *Lord* means the "Ruler of everything," the "One who has authority over everything," the "One in charge of everything": God. As Paul told the people in Athens, "He is the Lord of heaven and earth."

Dear God, You are Lord, the Ruler of all. You are my Lord.

Tuesday

Read "Lions!" page 456 in the *Day by Day Kid's Bible*. Or read this part of the story:

King Darius sent a letter to all his people. . . .

> *"I'm making a new law.*
> > *All people must look up to Daniel's God.*
> > *He is the living God.*
> > *He lives forever.*
> > *His kingdom will never end.*
> > *He does wonders in the sky and on the earth.*
> > *He saved Daniel from the lions' power."*
>
> Daniel 6:25-27

MATT AND JOSEPH were trying to see how high they could jump. Matt said, "I wish earth's gravity had less pull, like the gravity on the moon. If we were jumping on the moon, we could go much higher before gravity pulled us down."

Joseph laughed and said, "I don't believe in gravity. There's no such thing."

"Why don't you believe in gravity?" asked Matt.

"Because I've never seen it," said Joseph.

Have you ever seen gravity? Have you ever seen air? How do you know gravity is real? How do you know air is real?

Some people say there is no God. They can't see him. Kings and presidents and other leaders may think there is no one in charge of them. But God is Lord. Like King Darius said, God is "the living God. He lives forever. His kingdom will never end."

Dear God, thank you that your kingdom will never end. You are Lord!

Wednesday

Read "Living in the Light," page 792 in the *Day by Day Kid's Bible*. Or read this part of the story:

Jesus is the One Who Does What's Right. . . .

How do we know that we really know him? We obey what he tells us. . . .

Here's how we know we are in Jesus' kingdom. We act like Jesus acted. *1 John 2:1-6*

THE TOWER OF PISA is a famous tower in Italy. It's famous because it's not straight. It leans about 17 feet to one side. In fact, it leans over just a little more each year. A few years ago it was in danger of falling over, so the tower was straightened by about 20 inches. Now it should be okay for up to 200 years.

In Bible times, when people were building a wall, they would dangle a plumb line in the air beside the wall to make sure they were building it straight. A plumb line is an easy tool to make. It is simply a string or cord with a weight at the bottom of it. Builders today still use plumb lines to make sure that what they build is straight. What happens if walls are not built straight?

Jesus is like our plumb line. He is the one we measure our lives by. When we want to do something, we know that if Jesus would do it, then it's okay for us to do it. If Jesus would not do it, then we shouldn't do it. That's because God has put Jesus in charge. Jesus is Lord.

Dear God, thank you for putting Jesus in charge. He will be my plumb line. He is Lord.

Thursday

Read "A Hole in the Roof," page 524 in the *Day by Day Kid's Bible.* Or read this part of the story:

[Jesus] told the sick man, "Your sins are forgiven."

Some teachers of God's laws were watching. They thought, "How can he say that? Only God can forgive sins."

Jesus knew just what they were thinking. He said, ". . . Is it easier to say, 'Your sins are forgiven'? Or to say, 'Get up, take your mat with you, and walk'? I have the right to forgive sins here on earth. You'll see."

Then Jesus looked again at the man who couldn't move. He said, "Get up. Take your mat with you. You can go home now."

The man stood up. He picked up his mat. Then he walked out with everyone watching him. *Mark 2:5-12*

IN THE TIME JESUS LIVED on earth, people thought that if they did something bad, then bad things would happen to them. But if they did good, they thought good things would happen. So if a person was sick, everyone believed it was because he had sinned. Then Jesus came and healed people. So everyone began to wonder. If you weren't sick anymore, was your sin gone too? When Jesus saw the man who couldn't move, he said, "Your sins are forgiven." This was new. Nobody had ever come forgiving people's sins. Then Jesus proved that he had the right to forgive sins. He proved it by doing something everyone could see: He healed the man. The people could see that Jesus was Lord over both sickness and sin.

Dear God, thank you that Jesus is Lord over sickness and sin.

Friday

Read "Shining like Stars," page 746 in the *Day by Day Kid's Bible*. Or read this part of the story:

> *All people will bow down when they hear Jesus' name.*
>   *Everyone in heaven will bow.*
>   *Everyone on earth and under the earth will bow.*
> *Every voice will say that Jesus Christ is Lord.*
> Philippians 2:10-11

"MATH IS HARD," said Andy. "No it isn't. It's easy," said Jaylee. Who is right and who is wrong? Both of them are right, because they are telling their opinions. An *opinion* is something that may be true for one person, but not true for another person. But if Jaylee said, "2 + 2 = 4," and Andy said, "No, 2 + 2 = 6," then somebody is wrong, because they are talking about a fact. A *fact*, like 2 + 2 = 4, is true all the time, even if another person does not agree with it. Jesus is Lord. That's a fact. Someone might not agree with it, but it's still true. Jesus is Lord. And someday, everyone will bow down and say so.

Dear God, thank you for making Jesus great and giving him the highest place. Jesus is Lord!

SOME THINGS YOU CAN DO THIS WEEK

Write LORD across the top of a piece of paper, leaving space between each letter. Then set a timer for three minutes. Write as many words as you can of things, people, or places that start with these letters. Write words that start with *L* under the *L*, words that start with *O* under the *O*, and so on. For example, under *L* you might write Lemon, Light. Under *O*, you might write Orange. After the timer rings, look at your list. These are all people, places, or things that Jesus is Lord over.

Make a Lord of the Nations picture. From a newspaper or magazine, cut out several pictures and headlines of things that are happening in other nations. Tape or glue these onto a piece of paper. Across the top or bottom of the paper write, "O LORD . . . you rule over all the kingdoms of the nations" (2 Chronicles 20:6, NIV).

Make a door hanging. Cut a piece of paper in half lengthwise. Set one half aside. Turn a paper or plastic cup upside down and set it toward the top on the other half of the paper. Trace around it. Then cut out the traced circle. On the bottom part of the paper, write JESUS IS LORD. Color or paint designs on this paper, then hang it on a doorknob.

Be a seal detective. Look on cans and boxes in your pantry and refrigerator to see if you can find anything that is marked with a seal of approval, like "FDA Inspected" or "Good Housekeeping Seal of Approval." Then look at some of the different logos (the symbols or drawings) that represent each brand. For example, Nabisco products have a triangle; Keebler shows a tree. The makers of these products hope their brands are so good that when you see these symbols, you will buy their products. Imagine that you can give your official approval. On a piece of paper, draw a seal you would put on products that met your standard for good quality. God has a seal of approval that he wants to place in our lives: Jesus. When we ask Jesus to be our Lord and Savior, God makes us pure and gives us his approval.

JESUS: THE WAY, THE TRUTH, THE LIFE

Jesus answered, "I am the way and the truth and the life.
No one comes to the Father except through me." John 14:6, NIV

This week you will learn
· how to live longer than the oldest man who lived on earth;
· how someone can be a leader and a servant at the same time;
· why Jesus is called "the Way, the Truth, and the Life."

Monday

Read "Out of the Grave," page 589 in the *Day by Day Kid's Bible.* Or read this part of the story:

"I hold the power of coming alive again," said Jesus. "I am new life. People who believe in me will live even after they die. People who live and believe in me will never really die. Do you believe what I'm saying?"

"Yes, Lord," said Martha. "I believe that you are the one God promised to send. You are God's Son." *John 11:25-27*

A LIFE SPAN is how long something is alive. The bristle-cone pine trees in the western part of the United States are said to live longer than anything else on earth. One of these trees is believed to be 4,600 years old. That means it was over 2,000 years old when Jesus was born! Tortoises live the longest of all animals. Scientists think tortoises can live up to 200 years. And the Bible tells the name of the man who lived the longest: Methuselah. He lived 969 years! But Jesus said that we can have eternal life. How long is eternity? It never ends. We can live with God forever, because Jesus has the right and the power to give us eternal life.

Dear God, thank you for Jesus' power to give us eternal life. Thank you for making a way for us to live with you forever.

Tuesday

Read "Bread for Everyone," page 556 in the *Day by Day Kid's Bible.* Or read this part of the story:

Jesus took the five rolls and the two fish. He looked up to heaven. He thanked God. Then he began to hand out the rolls. He gave them to his helpers. There were a lot more than just five rolls! . . .

There was more than enough! All of the people got to eat as much as they wanted. *Matthew 14:19-20*

MURIEL LOVES TO go to her mother's bakery after school each day, because it smells of freshly baked bread. Her mother gives each customer a slice of fresh, hot bread, and Muriel gets some too. Each day there is a different kind of bread for customers to try. Sometimes there's seven-grain bread. Sometimes there's rye. Sometimes there's a special kind, like cranberry-orange loaf. Muriel's favorite is honey wheat.

All over the world, people eat more bread than any other food. Bread is sometimes called the "staff of life." That means most people use it to get life and health.

But just as our bodies depend on food to be healthy physically, so our spirits depend on Jesus to be healthy spiritually. In this way, Jesus is truly the Bread of our lives. Jesus said, "My purpose is to give life in all its fullness" (John 10:10, NLT). That's just what everybody wants: a life full of love and peace and joy. And that's what Jesus came to give us. Jesus is *Life.*

Dear God, thank you for sending Jesus to bring us a life full of love and peace and joy.

Wednesday

Read "Going Fishing," page 629 in the *Day by Day Kid's Bible*. Or read this part of the story:

"I think I'll go fishing," said Peter.

"We'll go with you," said the others. . . .

But that night they didn't catch anything.

At last the sun began to come up. There was Jesus, standing on the shore. But his friends couldn't tell it was Jesus. . . .

"Throw your net into the water."

Lots of fish got caught in the net. . . .

A camp fire was going when they got near the shore. Fish were cooking on it. There was bread, too. . . .

"Come have some breakfast," said Jesus. *John 21:3-4, 6, 9, 12*

A MISSIONARY in Kenya, Africa, was in charge of a Bible college. He had an office and held meetings and even taught some classes. One day there was a lot of cleanup work that needed to be done at the college. So this missionary got a bucket and some cleaning supplies and began to clean the toilets. The students were shocked. "You should not be cleaning the toilets," they said. "You are the leader of the college!" But he not only cleaned toilets, he did other cleanup jobs as well. This leader became a servant.

Before Jesus came to earth, he lived in God's perfect heaven. But the Lord Jesus, the greatest leader of all, became a servant. He even made breakfast for his friends. Jesus showed us the way to live, the way to serve, the way to love. And when he died for our sins so we could be forgiven, he showed us the way to heaven. Jesus is the *Way*.

Dear God, thank you for loving us enough to send Jesus to lead and serve. Thank you for showing us the way to live, now and forever.

Thursday

Read "Like the Sun at Noon," page 193 in the *Day by Day Kid's Bible.* Or read this part of the story:

> *Trust in God, and do what's good.*
> *Live and enjoy being safe.*
> *Be glad in God.*
> *Then he will give you what your heart really wants.*
>
> *Choose to always follow God.*
> *Trust him, and he will help you.* Psalm 37:3-5

ONE SATURDAY Anna and her family went to visit her grandma. Anna and her sister Ashley were playing outside when they heard a kitten mewing. They looked and looked for the kitten and finally saw it on Grandma's roof. They ran into the house and got their dad. He got an old wooden ladder from Grandma's garage and stood it up next to the house. But the ladder was wobbly. Dad took one look at it and said, "I don't trust that ladder to hold me up." He put it back and borrowed a sturdy metal ladder from the neighbors. Then he climbed up and rescued the kitten. Dad trusted the second ladder to hold his weight, so he climbed the ladder. He did something to show he trusted.

Trust is not just something you believe or think or say. Trust is something you do. It's easy to say that Jesus is the *Way,* the *Truth,* and the *Life.* But if he really is all of those things, we have to trust him enough to let him be in charge of our lives.

Dear God, thank you for being the Way, the Truth, and the Life. I will put my trust in you.

Friday

Read "Tricks," page 601 in the *Day by Day Kid's Bible.* Or read this part of the story:

The Jewish leaders sent some people to trick Jesus. They said, "We know you tell the truth. You teach about God. You don't follow people's ideas. So tell us something. Should we pay taxes to the king?"

Jesus knew what they were trying to do. He said, "Why are you trying to trick me? Show me the money you pay your taxes with."

They showed him the money.

"Whose picture is on it?" asked Jesus. "Whose name is on it?"

"The king's," they said.

"Then give the king what belongs to him," said Jesus. "And give God what belongs to God." *Matthew 22:16-21*

THE LAMP FELL to the den floor with a crash. It was an accident. But Mark and his little brother Brian had been running in the house, and Mark had bumped the lamp table. When Mom came in asking, "What happened?" Mark could have blamed Brian for chasing him. But Mark knew it was his own fault, because he had chosen to run in the house. Mark told the truth.

Jesus told the truth too. And Jesus' truth was very important, because Jesus told the truth about God. In fact, Jesus said that he *is* the truth. When Jesus lived on earth, anyone who watched and listened to him could find out what God was like.

When we want to know the truth about how to act or speak, or when we want to know the truth about God, we can always read about Jesus in the Bible. Jesus is *Truth*.

Dear God, thank you that Jesus tells the truth about you. Thank you that he is the Way, the Truth, and the Life.

☀ SOME THINGS YOU CAN DO THIS WEEK ☾

☀ **Write backward.** To make new words, write these words backward, putting the last letter first: lap, star, mug, stop, doom, reed, trap, rat, won, pin, net, not, spot, tap, nap. Now spell this word backward: live. Spelling *live* backward reminds us that life lived backward (the wrong way) is evil. Life lived the right way is full of joy and peace, even in times of trouble. Remember that Jesus said he is *Life*.

☾ **Write LIFE** in letters about two inches tall, spread out on a piece of paper. Then with one color of crayon or marker, outline the word. With another color, outline the first outline. Keep outlining each outline with a different color until you've filled the page. Read John 10:10. Jesus is the Lord, so he has the right and the power to give us life. Jesus is *Life*.

☀ **Get a carrot** that still has some of its leaves at the top. Ask an adult to cut off the green leaves and then cut off about one-half inch of the carrot top. Place the top in a bowl, and add enough water to cover it halfway. Place the bowl near a sunny window, but not directly in the sunlight. Make sure there's always enough water in the bowl. The carrot top may seem dead. But it will sprout in about a week. Our lives are a bit like that. Even if our bodies die, Jesus has given us eternal life, so he will raise us to live forever with him. He is *Life*.

☾ **Set up a treasure hunt.** Choose a treasure: a small toy, a candy bar in a zip-lock plastic bag, or a coin. Hide this somewhere in your yard or house. Then choose a starting point for your hunt. On an index card, write the place you want the hunter to go first, like PINE TREE. At the pine tree, put an index card that says where you want the person to go next, like GARAGE DOOR. At the garage door, put a card that says where to go next, like SLIDE. Lay out the cards wherever you want the hunter to go next until the last card says where the treasure is. You are showing the hunter the way. Remember how Jesus shows us the way to live now and forever, because Jesus is the *Way*.

THE WAY LIFE WORKS

I have set before you life and death, blessings and curses. Now choose life.
Deuteronomy 30:19, NIV

This week you will learn
· about the idea that God put in everyone's heart;
· how to find out the way life works best;
· why there is only One who can do everything to make life work best.

Monday

Read "When Time Began," page 3 in the *Day by Day Kid's Bible.* Or read this part of the story:

Then God said, "Let's make people to be like us. They can be in charge of the fish and birds and cows. They can take care of the earth and all the animals."

So God made people like himself. First he made a man from dust. Then God breathed life into Adam, and he came alive.
Genesis 1:26-27; 2:7

MOLLY'S GRANDMOTHER came to visit for Molly's eleventh birthday. Her grandmother said, "You look just like your mom did when she was your age." But Molly knew that even though she might look like her mother had looked, she was not exactly like her mother. Her mother liked parties and having lots of friends around. Molly liked reading, writing, drawing, and doing things alone or with one or two good friends.

How are you like your parents? How are you different? How are you different from God?

Even though we are different from God, we are like him in some ways. We were created in his image, in his likeness. We imagine, because he first imagined. We think and plan, because he first thought and planned. We make music and other things of beauty, because he first made music and all that's beautiful. Most important, we love, because he first loved us. All people in the world know that love is the greatest idea. Love is a "knowing," an idea placed in all people's hearts because of God's image in them.

Dear God, thank you for making all people in your image. Thank you for putting the idea of love in each person's heart.

Tuesday

Read "Moses' Song," page 94 in the *Day by Day Kid's Bible.* Or read this part of the story:

Moses said to God's people, "All of this isn't too hard for you. God's word is very close to you. It's in your mouth. It's in your heart. You can obey it.

"Today I'm showing you what to choose from. Choose between life and death. Choose between the good and the bad. Choose life. Then you and your children can live. You can love God. Listen to him. Stay with him, because God is your life."
Deuteronomy 30:11, 14-20

KEN WAS A MISSIONARY. He went to China and talked to people who had never read the Bible or heard about Jesus. He asked them, "Would it be right for me to steal from you or beat you up or kill you?" They said, "No. That would not be right." How did they know?

Ken went to Thailand. He talked to children who had never seen a Bible or heard about Jesus. He asked, "Would it be right for me to steal from you or beat you up or kill you?" They said, "No. That would not be right." Ken asked, "If I loved you, would I steal from you or beat you up or kill you?" They said, "No." Ken asked, "If everyone loved perfectly, what kind of world would it be?" They said, "It would be a beautiful, wonderful world."

How did the adults in China and the children in Thailand know these things? They knew because everybody in the world is made in God's image.

God's image of love in each of us shows us that love is the greatest idea in the world. As Moses said, "All of this isn't too hard for you. God's word is very close to you. It's in your mouth. It's in your heart." What kinds of things does God's love tell you to do?

Dear God, thank you for putting yourself so close to us. Thank you for putting your idea of love in everyone's heart.

Wednesday

Read "Good Fruit and Bad Fruit," page 536 in the *Day by Day Kid's Bible.* Or read this part of the story:

"People don't pick grapes from weeds," said Jesus. "They don't pick figs from weeds. Good trees make good fruit. Bad trees make bad fruit. A good tree can't make bad fruit. A bad tree can't make good fruit.

"Trees get cut down if they don't make good fruit. They get burned up." *Matthew 7:16-19*

PUT A DROP OF WATER at one end of a pan. Then lift that end of the pan slowly, higher and higher. What happens to the water? You just proved the law that says water goes to the lowest level. You saw another law too. The steeper the pan got, the faster the water flowed down. These are *natural laws,* or laws of nature. Here's one you know: Can you grow an apple from a carrot seed?

You see, the whole world works by laws of nature that God put in place. People discover God's natural laws. That's how we know we can use electricity to make light; we can use medicine to treat sickness; and we can use eggs, sugar, and flour to make cookies. Natural laws are the way things work on our earth.

Just as there are laws of nature, there are also moral laws. These laws have to do with right and wrong ways for humans to act toward each other. They are not really rules, just as laws of electricity or water aren't really rules. Instead, like natural laws, moral laws are the way life works best. Can you think of ways to treat others so everyone's life will have more joy and peace, so life will work best?

Dear God, thank you for giving the world natural laws so we can depend on how things work. Thank you for giving us moral laws and telling us in your Word how life works best.

Thursday

Read "Big Letters," page 662 in the *Day by Day Kid's Bible.* Or read this part of the story:

A farmer will get the kind of plant he planted. It's the same with you. The person who sins will get trouble. But let's say the person lives to please God's Spirit. Then he will get life from the Spirit. It will be life that lasts forever.

Don't get tired of doing good things. Someday we'll get paid back for doing good. But we must not give up. Let's do good whenever we can. *Galatians 6:7-10*

ANDREW'S LITTLE BROTHER KYLE got a super-city construction set. The box top showed what the pieces could make when they were hooked together. Kyle dumped out all the pieces and started building. In a few minutes, he yelled, "Stupid set!" What he had made looked nothing like the picture on the box. "Did you look at the instructions?" asked Andrew. Kyle shook his head. Andrew pulled the directions out of the box. Then he helped Kyle follow the directions to build the city the way it looked in the picture. The people who made the super-city set knew how it worked. They put directions in each box, so people could build the set just right.

God made the world. He gave us directions on how life works. If all people followed God's directions, life would work just right. Where can we find God's directions? God's image in us tells us that if we do the loving thing, we will be following God's directions about how life works best.

Dear God, thank you for letting us know how life works best. Help us to choose to do what's loving.

Friday

Read "Doing What I Don't Want to Do," page 707 in the *Day by Day Kid's Bible.* Or read this part of the story:

I want to do good, but I can't. Instead, I do things I don't want to do. Sin must be living in me. It's right beside me. But inside me, I love God's law. But another law works in me. It fights me. I feel like I'm in sin's jail. This is terrible! Who will save me? Thank God through Jesus! He will save me. *Romans 7:21-25*

GOD IS LOVE. If everybody loved the way God loves, there would be only good in the world. How would people act if they were loving the way God loves? Does anyone love perfectly like God? No matter how hard we try, we don't always act in loving ways. We don't always say loving things. We don't always think loving thoughts. No one does. Why not? It's because we are not God. Only God is perfectly loving and right and good. He is our Maker. We are the ones he made.

God sent Jesus to help us. Jesus came to do for us what we could not do for ourselves. Jesus came to be perfectly loving for us. He loved the way God loves. He even loved us enough to take the punishment for the wrong things we do. He makes us right with God. That's perfect love!

Dear God, thank you for loving us. Thank you for sending Jesus to do for us what we cannot do for ourselves.

☀ Some Things You Can Do This Week ☾

☀ **Make a string picture.** What do you think God looks like? How would you know? In the *Day by Day Kid's Bible,* read the first two paragraphs of "A Burning Coal," page 337 (Isaiah 6:1); the last two paragraphs of "In the Wind Storm," page 402 (Ezekiel 1:26–28); and the first three paragraphs of "An Open Door," page 803 (Revelation 4:1-3). On a piece of paper, write GOD with glue. Lay string on the lines of glue. Let the paper dry. Then lay another piece of paper on top of the string word and color over the paper with crayon, choosing colors that you thought of when you read the verses about God. Remember that God is love. He made life to work best when we act and speak in loving ways.

☾ **See some natural laws for yourself.** Get a spoon and a clear plastic measuring cup or drinking cup. Pour about one-fourth cup cooking oil into the cup. Add about one-fourth cup water. Stir to mix the oil and water. Watch what happens. This always happens with oil and water. What is this law of oil and water? Now that you know this law, you can see how it works in nature: When ducks dip under water, their feathers stay dry because they are oily, so the water can't soak in. Can you think of other natural laws? Hints: What happens to water when the temperature goes below freezing? Would a bike roll faster down a hill or on a flat street? Remember that God made the world with moral laws for people too.

☀ **Make a "Way" collage.** Go through some magazines and newspapers looking for the word *way.* Every time you find *way,* cut it out. On a piece of colored paper, write JESUS in the center. Glue the cutout words around the sides. If you do this with friends or family, talk about ways to act and speak that are how life works best. Are these ways Jesus would have acted or spoken? Read John 14:6.

☾ **Try making a cookie without any directions.** Without looking at a recipe, write down what you think you could mix together to make a good cookie. Then, in a cereal bowl, put a spoonful of each ingredient on your list. Stir. Put the dough on a cookie sheet and bake at 350 degrees for 10 minutes. Try your cookie. Then look at a recipe. The recipe shows the way. Follow this way to make another batch of cookies. Are recipes rules? Recipes show the way cooking works best, just as God has shown us how life works best.

GETTING RIGHT WITH GOD

It's your sins that keep you from God. Isaiah 59:2, DBD

This week you will learn
· *what the word* sin *really means;*
· *how most people try to get right with God;*
· *the only way we can get right with God.*

Monday

Read "The Snake's Trick," page 5 in the *Day by Day Kid's Bible.* Or read this part of the story:

Now the snake was tricky. He talked to the woman. "Did God say not to eat fruit from the trees?"

"No," she said. "We may eat fruit. Just not from the tree in the middle of the Garden. God said we can't even touch that tree. We'll die if we do."

"You won't die," said the snake. "God knows that the fruit will make you wise. Just like God. You will know good and bad."

The woman looked at the fruit. . . . Since she thought it would make her wise, she ate some. Adam was with her. So she gave some to Adam, too. And he ate it. *Genesis 3:1-6*

A PRESENT WAS on the table when Natasha got home from school. She knew it was a birthday gift from her mom. Friends would come for pizza later, and there would be a cake and more gifts. But Natasha wanted to know what this gift was. She turned it over and gently pulled up the edge of the paper. It was the T-shirt she wanted. A few minutes later, Mom came into the room. "Happy Birthday!" she said. "There's a surprise for you on the table." Natasha tried to act excited. But she felt bad. And she could tell that her mom saw what she had done.

Adam and Eve felt bad after they ate the fruit. They felt guilty. Natasha's mom loved her before and after Natasha peeked at her present. God loved Adam and Eve before and after they ate the fruit. God's love did not change. But Adam and Eve had changed. Now they knew that they were able to choose to do wrong. They knew they were not as good as God. God loves us even when we choose wrong. But he's sad, because he knows life won't work best when we do wrong.

Dear God, I'm sorry I make you sad by doing wrong things. But I thank you for loving me no matter what I do. Help me remember to choose to do things your way.

Tuesday

Read "Like a Spider's Web," page 371 in the *Day by Day Kid's Bible.* Or read this part of the story:

> *God's arm is not too short to save you.*
>   *His ear is not too stopped up to hear you.*
>   *It's your sins that keep you from God.*
> *You are to blame for what you did.*
> Isaiah 59:1-3

DILLON FITTED AN ARROW into the bow and aimed at the center of the target, the bull's-eye. The archery coach had shown him how to hold the bow, fit the arrow onto it, pull the arrow back, and let it fly. But this was Dillon's first time to shoot by himself. He pulled hard, got the arrow into position, then let it go. The arrow shot out. But it didn't reach the target, much less the bull's-eye. None of the students got the arrow to the bull's-eye the first day. They all missed the mark. They knew they would have to keep practicing.

Sin means missing the mark in the way we act and talk. Our target, our goal, is to love the way God loves. But we are not God. We often miss the mark. Then it's easy to feel like God is far away and to feel like we'll never be good enough to be with him. But God sent Jesus to be our way to get back to God. Now when we sin, we are free to try again, knowing God still loves us.

Dear God, I want to do right, but I often miss the mark. I sin. When I sin, help me remember that you still love me. Help me to do better next time.

Wednesday

Read "Even If Every Person Lies," page 704 in the *Day by Day Kid's Bible.* Or read this part of the story:

Now God is showing us how to be right with him. It has nothing to do with the Law. It's being right with God by believing in Jesus. . . .
     So how can we brag? We can't. Did we obey all the rules? No. We believed. People are cleaned from sin by believing in Jesus. It has nothing to do with obeying God's laws.
Romans 3:21-22, 27-28

THE STAR JAR sat on the kitchen counter at Kai's house. It was full of star stickers. When Kai remembered to do his jobs around the house, he got to put a sticker on the calendar. Kai's jobs each day were to make his bed, feed the dog, and put his dirty clothes in the clothes hamper. Anytime Kai got a whole week of stars on the calendar, he got an extra dollar in his allowance. Most of the time, Kai got his stars. But sometimes he forgot to make his bed or feed the dog. Or he hurried to go out and play and left his dirty clothes on the floor.

Rules and laws are good. They keep our lives in order. They remind us how to act to show respect for each other. But if we break a law, the law won't forgive us. It punishes us instead. If Kai forgets to make his bed, the rule doesn't say, "I forgive you." The rule is that Kai doesn't get a star on his calendar, and he doesn't get an extra dollar that week.

Laws and rules are not a good way to get to God. They show us that we need a better way. We need Jesus. He takes our punishment for us. God forgives us. When we believe in Jesus, he makes us right with God.

Dear God, thank you for sending Jesus to take our punishment. Thank you that we can be right with you.

Thursday

Read "Believing What You Heard," page 659 in the *Day by Day Kid's Bible*. Or read this part of the story:

Nobody is made right with God by the Law. . . . The Law has nothing to do with believing.

What if you choose to live by the Law? Then you have to keep it up. If you don't, you've sinned. Then you get in trouble.

But Jesus kept us from getting in trouble. He got in trouble for us when he died on a cross. He saved us. Now everyone can believe in Jesus. We can trust in God and get the Spirit he promised. . . .

You are all God's children. That's because you believe in Jesus.
Galatians 3:11-14, 26

Hayley: Why should I try to do good? I can be right with God just by believing in Jesus.

Angelica: But if cheating was the way to live, everybody should cheat, right?

Hayley: Right. I would copy your test paper and get good grades.

Angelica: Then the teacher could cheat too and ask questions about things she never taught us.

Hayley: The whole class would be mad at her then.

Angelica: See? We try to do good, because that's the way life works best. It just doesn't work for people to do the wrong things.

The good news is that we can be right with God just by believing in Jesus. But there's more good news: Jesus gives us his Holy Spirit to help us choose what's right. Then, day by day, we grow to be more like Jesus. We grow to love God more.

Dear God, thank you for giving me your Holy Spirit to help me choose what's right. Help me to grow to love you more.

Friday

Read "A Good Tree Growing Good Fruit," page 661 in the *Day by Day Kid's Bible.* Or read this part of the story:

Let God's Spirit lead you. Then the Law won't be in charge of you.
　　It's easy to see what sin is. . . .
　　God's Spirit helps you act a different way. You can be like a good tree growing good fruit. Loving. Showing joy. Having peace. Waiting quietly. Being kind. Being good. Keeping promises. Treating people with care. Having control of yourself. There is no law against these things. *Galatians 5:18-19, 22-23*

"THERE'S NO RULE that says you have to invite the new girl to sit with us at lunch," said DeeAnn.

"I know," said Marly. "But I think she might be lonely and need some friends."

DeeAnn is thinking about following rules. Marly is thinking about following God's Spirit. The reason we do what's right is not just to follow rules and make ourselves right with God. We become right with God by believing in Jesus. But then we want to do what's right, because God has shown us that's the way life works best. God is *Love*. We are made in his image, to give love and to want love in return. So life works best when people treat each other in loving ways. Jesus speaks to our spirit through his Holy Spirit, who is our Helper. He whispers to our heart and tells us how to act in loving ways.

Dear God, thank you for sending your Holy Spirit to be our Helper. Thank you for showing us how to act in loving ways.

Some Things You Can Do This Week

Make a target. Draw a target on a piece of paper, and color the middle circle (the bull's-eye) red. Hang this on a wall or a door or even on a tree trunk. Now wad up a piece of newspaper and throw it at the target. How far away can you stand and still hit the bull's-eye? If you do this outside, away from anything that might break, try throwing a ball at your target. Think about how the word *sin* means "missing the mark."

Play a board game or a card game with family or friends. What are the rules? Why do you need rules for the game? Why do we need rules for our lives? What happens if you just follow the rules because you have to, but you're angry about it, and you aren't kind and loving to the others who are playing the game?

Play a jumping game. Indoors or outdoors, mark a starting line by placing a penny or other object on the floor or on the ground. Stand with your toes at the starting line and see how far you can jump. Place another penny at the place where you land. If you do this alone, jump again and see if you can jump farther. If you do this with friends, see who can jump farthest. With a tape measure or yardstick, measure how far you jump. Sometimes we say we try to "measure up" in how we act. That means we try to behave in a way that is right. We try to "measure up" to certain rules or to the behavior someone expects from us. Can you always "measure up" to loving the same way that God loves? If no one can "measure up," how can we get right with God?

Make a fruit mobile. Draw and cut out nine pieces of fruit from construction paper. Write one of the fruits listed in Friday's reading on each paper fruit. Then cut out nine pieces of string, each a different length. For each piece of fruit, tie one end of a string to the bottom of a clothes hanger. Tape the other end of each string to the back of a piece of fruit to make a mobile that you can hang in your room.

THE HELPER

I will ask the Father, and he will give you another Counselor,
who will never leave you. He is the Holy Spirit. John 14:16-17, NLT

This week you will learn
· *about a teacher you can't see;*
· *about a gift that came with wind and fire;*
· *how a shaking room made someone brave;*
· *how to pray when you don't know what to say.*

Monday

Read "Where Are You Going?" page 610 in the *Day by Day Kid's Bible.* Or read this part of the story:

"I'm going to ask the Father to give you another Helper. He will be with you forever. He is God's Spirit of truth. The world can't believe that this Spirit is real," said Jesus. "They don't see the Spirit. They don't know the Spirit. But you know the Spirit. He lives with you, and he will be in you. . . .

"He will help you," said Jesus. "He will teach you everything. He will help you remember everything I've told you."
John 14:16-17, 26

BRETT WENT TO the country of Russia with his mother and father. They couldn't speak the Russian language. So a Russian friend named Katya traveled with them. Katya told Brett's family the meaning of the words that the Russian people said to them. She told them to try an Easter bread called *Kulich.* She pointed out some people to stay away from, people who would try to steal from them. She told them the best places to buy things. She was a good helper.

We have a helper who is always with us, although we can't see him. He is God's Holy Spirit. He knows more than we know. He teaches us. He counsels us by giving us good advice. He helps us remember what Jesus said. He helps us make the right choices. And he lives with us always.

Dear God, thank you for sending us your Holy Spirit to help us and teach us.

Tuesday

Read "Wind, Fire, and Different Languages," page 633 in the *Day by Day Kid's Bible.* Or read this part of the story:

Then God's Holy Spirit filled them. They started talking in different languages. God's Spirit made them able to do this. . . .

"Jesus is beside God now," said Peter. "His Father gave him the Holy Spirit as he promised. And Jesus has now given us that Spirit. That's what you are seeing and hearing now. . . .

"Be sorry," said Peter. "Change your ways. . . . Then [Jesus] will forgive your sins. Then you'll get the gift of the Holy Spirit. That's a promise." *Acts 2:4, 33, 38-39*

SKYLA'S MOM PROMISED to bring her a gift from England, where she was going on a business trip for a week. Skyla knew her mom would keep that promise. Still, it was hard to wait. Have you ever had to wait to get a gift someone promised to bring you?

Jesus told his friends to wait for the gift God would give them. So they waited and waited. When the gift came, Jesus' friends did not have to wonder if this was what God had promised. They knew. Peter told everyone that the wind, fire, and languages meant God had kept his promise to send his Spirit. It also proved that Jesus had not left them alone. It was important for Jesus' friends to be able to speak in different languages so the people from different countries could understand them. In the different languages, Jesus' friends told the people that Jesus is the path to get to God.

God promises to give us his Holy Spirit too. The Holy Spirit helps us tell others about Jesus.

Dear God, thank you for sending us your Holy Spirit. Help us to tell others about Jesus.

Wednesday

Read "Plain Men and Proud Leaders," page 636 in the *Day by Day Kid's Bible*. Or read this part of the story:

The leaders told Peter and John to leave for a few minutes. Then they had a talk. . . . "We must stop these men from saying Jesus is alive." . . .

Peter and John went back to their friends. . . . Then everyone prayed. . . .

"Now look at what our leaders are saying," they prayed. "Make us brave. Then we can say what you want us to say. . . ."

When they finished praying, the room shook. God's Holy Spirit filled all of them. So they became brave and talked about God.
Acts 4:15, 17, 23-24, 29, 31

IN THE MIDDLE OF THE NIGHT, the bedroom door rattled. "Did you hear that?" asked Micah. He was visiting his cousin in California.

Jordan said, "It was an earthquake." He was used to the little shaking of earthquakes. Most of the time, the shaking didn't last very long. Sometimes the only way he could tell if the earth had really shaken was to look at a light or a plant pot hanging from the ceiling. If it was swinging back and forth, he knew there had been a little earthquake.

When Peter and John and their friends finished praying, their room shook. And the gift of God's Holy Spirit grew strong in them. That made them brave so they could teach about Jesus without being afraid.

God's Holy Spirit can make us brave too. He can give us love for others. And remember: No matter what happens, God's love always wins.

Dear God, thank you for your Holy Spirit. Make me brave and help me say what you want me to say.

Thursday

Read "More than Winners," page 708 in the *Day by Day Kid's Bible.* Or read this part of the story:

God's Spirit helps us. We don't know what we should pray for. But the Spirit does. So he prays for us. He tells God things we don't know how to say. God looks into our hearts. He knows what the Spirit has in mind. The Spirit prays for what God wants for us. *Romans 8:26-27*

GRACIE WAS SO EXCITED, she could hardly stand still. Her mom had just had a new baby, a new sister for Gracie. When Gracie prayed that night, she thanked God for her new sister. But there were lots of new, good feelings that Gracie couldn't put into words. So she just closed her eyes and shared her feelings with God without saying a word.

Benton was sad and angry, because his grandfather had died. He prayed, but he couldn't find words to say what he was feeling. So he just closed his eyes and felt his feelings, knowing that God was hearing his feelings, even if he didn't say any words.

God's Holy Spirit knows the feelings and thoughts that we can't put into words. The Holy Spirit prays those feelings and thoughts to God for us. This means that even when we don't know the words to say, we can still pray, and God will still hear and understand.

Dear God, thank you for hearing and understanding me even when I don't know what words to use to say what I want to tell you. Thank you for your Holy Spirit, who prays for me.

Friday

Read "No Eye Has Seen It," page 676 in the *Day by Day Kid's Bible.* Or read this part of the story:

Only a person's spirit knows that person's thoughts. It's the same with God. No one knows what God is thinking. Only God's Spirit knows his thoughts.

We didn't get the spirit of the world. We got God's Spirit. Now we can understand what God freely gave us. *1 Corinthians 2:11-12*

DAD WAS SITTING in the big chair in the living room, his elbows on his knees, his chin resting on his folded hands. He was staring straight ahead, not smiling or frowning. Shane wondered what Dad was thinking. He wanted to ask Dad to play catch in the backyard. He tiptoed into the room and said what Dad often said to him: "A penny for your thoughts." Dad looked up and smiled. "Don't tell," said Dad, "but I was wondering what to get Mom for her birthday."

We don't know what people are thinking until they tell us. And only God's Spirit knows what God is thinking. So only God's Spirit can tell us God's thoughts.

Long ago, God's Spirit told people God's thoughts, and they wrote them down. You can read them in the Bible. And when you have a good and loving thought, you can be sure that thought comes from God at work in you.

Dear God, thank you for telling us your thoughts through the Bible. And thank you for the good thoughts you put in my heart.

SOME THINGS YOU CAN DO THIS WEEK

* **Get a couple of Ping-Pong balls** and a hair dryer with a round nozzle. Aim the nozzle up and set a Ping-Pong ball on top of it. Then turn the hair dryer on to the low setting. What happens? You can't see the air that's making the ball float, but you know it's there. You can feel it coming from the blow dryer and you can see what it does to the ball. This is like the Holy Spirit. We can't see him, but he is here. He is as loving and good as Jesus is. He is the Helper that Jesus sent to guide us in God's ways.

* **Learn different languages** to use when you say "hello." If you need help, ask an adult to help read the words. Remember how the Holy Spirit helped Jesus' friends speak in different languages so they could tell people about Jesus.

    Bonjour (bone-ZHOOR) French

    Hola (OH-lah) Spanish

    Yassoo (YAH-soo) Greek

    Halloj (hah-LOZH) Danish

    Zdrastvuytye (zdrahs-VOO-tyah) Russian

    Shalom (shah-LOHM) Hebrew

    Jambo (ZHAHM-boh) Swahili (swah-HE-lee) (Kenya)

    Ohayo (oh-hah-yoh) *gozaimasu* (go-zah-ee-mah-su) Japanese

    Haere-mai (hah-eh-reh-MAH-ee) Maori (New Zealand)

* **Try feeling a prayer to God** instead of praying in words. Close your eyes. Think about God. Start your prayer the way you normally do, like "Dear God," and then think of opening your heart to God and letting him look at the feelings you have there. Sit for a few minutes with your feelings open to him. Then you can tell him anything you want.

Remember that the Holy Spirit is helping show God your feelings and the thoughts you have no words for.

Write words in color. Red with anger, green with envy, blue with sadness. People sometimes think of colors that help tell how they feel. Take a box of crayons and write words like *sad, happy, angry, bored, wishful, excited, worried,* and other feelings, each with a color that you think goes with that feeling. Remember that the Holy Spirit talks to God for you about all of your feelings.

A MANAGER OF GOD'S WORLD

For we are God's masterpiece. He has created us anew in Christ Jesus,
so that we can do the good things he planned for us long ago. Ephesians 2:10, NLT

This week you will learn
· who God chose to take care of everything he made;
· how to be a time traveler;
· what it means to be wealthy.

Monday

Read "Adam's Helper," page 4 in the *Day by Day Kid's Bible.* Or read this part of the story:

Now God had planted a garden in Eden. It was in the East. God had put beautiful fruit trees in the Garden. . . .

God put Adam in the Garden of Eden. Adam could work there and take care of the Garden. *Genesis 2:8-9, 15*

KRISTI'S DAD OWNS three food stores in her city. He pays for the buildings that the stores are in. He pays the workers at the stores. He pays to buy the food on the shelves. He makes money when people shop at his stores. For each store, there is a manager. The managers make sure the stores open and close at the right time. They make sure the stores are clean and that the workers help the people who come to shop.

God owns our world. But he has made us managers of his world. Part of what we manage is the rest of God's creation: land and sea, plants and animals. We take care of nature. When we cut down trees for wood, we plant more trees. We recycle everything we can. We protect endangered animals. We try not to waste water. Can you think of other ways we care for God's creation?

Dear God, thank you for all you made. Help me to do a good job of caring for your creation.

Tuesday

Read "A Time for Everything," page 262 in the *Day by Day Kid's Bible.* Or read this part of the story:

There's a time for everything.
There's a season for everything people do.

A time to be born, and a time to die.
A time to plant, and a time to pull plants up.
A time to kill, and a time to heal.
A time to break, and a time to build.
A time to cry, and a time to laugh.
A time to throw stones, and a time to gather them.
A time to hug, and a time not to hug. Ecclesiastes 3:1-5

WE ARE ALL TIME TRAVELERS! Think about when you went to bed last night and when you woke up this morning. You travel about eight hours through time every night. Even when you are completely still, you are traveling through time, because time is always going, and we go with it. We travel through time at the speed of 24 hours a day.

God made us managers of time. He wants us to use time wisely. If we don't let God control our time, our time controls us: We hurry and worry. But if we let God control our time, he will give us all the time we need.

Dear God, thank you for giving me 24 hours every day. Help me to use my time wisely, letting you be in control.

Wednesday

Read "Being Rich and Poor," page 248 in the *Day by Day Kid's Bible*. Or read this part of the story:

Use your riches to show God he is the most important to you.
Give him the first part of everything you earn. . . .

Don't get all tired out trying to get rich.
Be wise. Control yourself.
Riches don't last.
They seem to grow wings.
They seem to fly into the sky like birds. . . .

Be happy to be poor and right.
That's better than being rich and wrong.
Proverbs 3:9; 23:4-5; 28:6

WEALTH IS HAVING MORE THAN WE NEED for living. Many families in the world don't have even one car. Many don't have enough food for the rest of the day. Some don't have more than one pair of shoes; many don't have shoes at all. If your family has one or more cars, if you have food in your refrigerator and pantry, if you have more than one pair of shoes, then you are wealthy.

God made us to be managers of money and possessions (the things we own), and he wants us to use them wisely. How can you use your money wisely?

Dear God, thank you for the money you give us. Thank you for making us wealthy. Help me to use my money and possessions wisely.

Thursday

Read "Rich Gifts and Hard Work," page 73 in the *Day by Day Kid's Bible.* Or read this part of the story:

Moses said that God chose one man to be a special worker. "God filled him with his Spirit. God made him good at art. He knows how to work with gold and silver. He knows how to cut and set stones. He knows how to work with wood. God has made him to be a good teacher." *Exodus 35:30-34*

ARMANDO LIKES TO WORK PUZZLES. It's easy for him to see how all the pieces fit together. Jazmine loves to read and work with words. Steven is good at soccer and baseball. Bethany loves animals. She has a cat and a dog and a fish, and her favorite place to go is the zoo. Trevor enjoys music. He can sing right in tune, and he plays piano every day just because he wants to.

Things we do well and enjoy are called *talents.* God made us managers of our talents. How can we use our talents wisely? We can use them to help and bless others. We can become excellent in using our talents. And we can help others become excellent too.

Dear God, thank you for the talents you gave me. Help me to use my talents to help and bless others. And help me teach others to become excellent too.

Friday

Read "Friends," page 253 in the *Day by Day Kid's Bible*. Or read this part of the story:

> *A friend will love you all the time.*
> *Brothers and sisters help you through hard times.*
>
> *Some people think they have many friends.*
> *But the real friend is the one who stays closer than a brother. . . .*
>
> *Sweet smelling perfume makes you feel happy.*
> *Friends make you happy too.*
> *They tell you what's right.*   Proverbs 17:17; 18:24; 27:9

HAVE YOU EVER SEEN a family tree? That's a drawing of all the people in your family. The trunk is you. The main branch on one side is your mother. The main branch on the other side is your father. Branches coming from your mother's side show who her father and mother were. Branches coming from your father's side show who his father and mother were. All of your family members are connected.

People connections are called *relationships*. You not only have a connection with family, but also with friends, old and new. You have many relationships. God made us managers of our relationships. He wants us to treat other people with respect.

Dear God, thank you for my relationships with my family and friends. Help me to treat my family and friends with respect.

SOME THINGS YOU CAN DO THIS WEEK

Sprout bird seed. Fill a plant pot almost full with potting soil. Sprinkle bird seed over it. Then cover the seeds with a shallow layer of soil. Water it and place it in a sunny spot. Keep the soil damp. In a few days these seeds should sprout. Read "Earth, Sea, and Moon," page 206 in the *Day by Day Kid's Bible* (Psalm 104). What does it tell about the One who owns the earth? What are some ways you can be a good manager of God's plants?

Put God in control. Draw a circle in the center of a paper plate. Write GOD inside the circle. Now, like spokes on a wheel, draw a line from the center circle to the top edge of the plate, a line from the center to the right edge, a line to the left edge, and a line to the bottom edge. You have divided the plate into four parts. In one part, write "Keep praying." In another, write "Seek God first." In another, write "Don't worry. Trust." And in the last, write "Do what God gives you to do." When you look at this plate, let it remind you of a steering wheel on a car. It tells you how to put God in control of your life. Your life is like the car, and God is the driver.

Make a neck pillow. Place two or three handfuls of fiberfill or cotton along one edge of a bandanna or handkerchief. Roll the bandanna up as if making a tube. Tie the ends of the bandanna with fabric ribbon. You have made a neck pillow. Think about how you manage time. There is a time to work and a time to rest. When it's time to rest, you can use this neck pillow.

Make a handprint wreath. Draw around your hands on a piece of paper. Draw around the hands of people who are your friends and family. Write each person's name on his or her handprints. Cut these handprints out and arrange them in a circle like a wreath. Some of them can overlap. Tape them together. You can color or paint your wreath and hang it up to remind you of the relationships over which God has made you manager.

GIFTS FROM GOD

We all have different gifts. Each gift came because
of the grace that God gave us. Romans 12:6, ICB

This week you will learn
· about some very important gifts;
· how we are like clay;
· how gifts can show up when something spills;
· the difference between speaking gifts and doing gifts.

Monday

Read "In Trouble for Following Jesus," page 773 in the *Day by Day Kid's Bible*. Or read this part of the story:

God has given each of you a gift in your spirit. Use your gift to help people. Show God's kindness in different ways.

Some people teach about God. They should teach as if they're saying God's own words. People who serve should let God make them strong. *1 Peter 4:10-11*

DO YOU KNOW THE STORY of *The Lion, the Witch and the Wardrobe* by C. S. Lewis? In that book, Father Christmas gives Peter, Susan, and Lucy different gifts. To Peter, he gives a shield and sword. He gives a bow and arrows and a small ivory horn to Susan. He gives Lucy a small bottle of healing liquid. He knows they will need these gifts to help others as they go on their journey.

Life on earth is like a journey. God has a purpose for every person. But he doesn't want to send us through life by ourselves. God wants to help us. He wants us to let him go with us to guide us on our journey. And he gives each of us gifts that we can use to help others.

Dear God, I want you to go with me and guide me in my journey through life. Show me the gifts you have given me to help others.

Tuesday

Read "Making a Fuss with the Maker," page 364 in the *Day by Day Kid's Bible.* Or read this part of the story:

Does clay talk to the person who makes it a pot?
       Does it say, "What are you making?"
Does the thing you make tell you that you don't have hands?

Here's what I, your Maker, say.
       Are you telling me what to do with what I made?
Isaiah 45:9, 11

NATHAN TOOK A SUMMER CLASS in pottery at the art center. The teacher showed how to roll and flatten the clay and how to mold it into different forms. Nathan made a vase for his mother to put flowers in. He made a pencil holder for his big sister and a bowl to hold his father's coins. He read Isaiah 45:9 and thought it was funny. He could picture his clay standing up to him and saying, "I don't want to be a bowl. I want to be a vase."

We are like clay for God. He makes us and gives us the gifts he chooses for us. It would be silly for clay to argue with the potter about what the potter was going to do with the clay. It would also be silly for us to argue with God about the talents and skills he has chosen to give us.

Dear God, thank you for giving me talents and skills that are just right for me. Help me to use my talents and skills in ways that please you.

Wednesday

Read "What If Your Whole Body Were an Eye?" page 685 in the *Day by Day Kid's Bible*. Or read this part of the story:

There are different kinds of gifts. But they all come from the same Spirit. There are different ways to help. But it's all for the same Lord. There are different kinds of work. But the same God does the work through everyone.

A gift from God's Spirit can be seen in each person. It's for everybody's good. *1 Corinthians 12:4-7*

KENDRA'S TEACHER SPILLED a box of supplies. Scissors, pencils, erasers, and crayons scattered all over the floor. James has the gift of serving and started picking things up. Yoko, with the gift of leadership, said, "Marcy, you get the pencils. I'll get the erasers." Benjamin told the teacher, "That's okay. Everybody spills sometimes." He has the gift of kindness. Jacob has the gift of teaching and said, "They spilled because the heavy things were all at one end of the tray." Quinn said, "Cheer up. You're still a good teacher. A few spilled pencils won't hurt." She has the gift of encouraging. And when there was still one pencil missing, Peter said, "Here, you can use mine." He has the gift of giving.

Which of these students would you have been?

Dear God, thank you for the gifts you give each one of us. Help us work together to use our gifts for everybody's good.

Thursday

Read "We Won't Be Babies," page 741 in the *Day by Day Kid's Bible.* Or read this part of the story:

God is kind to all of us. The psalm says, "He gave gifts to people."
. . .

God gave these gifts to make his people ready to serve. These gifts build up Jesus' followers, his "body." God gave gifts to help us all agree about what we believe. The gifts help us really know Jesus. They help us grow up in how we think and act. Now we can grow until we are filled to the top with Jesus. *Ephesians 4:7-8, 11-13*

SOME OF THE GIFTS God gives are *speaking* gifts: teaching, cheering others up (encouraging), and saying clearly what's right and wrong (prophecy). Other gifts are *doing* gifts: giving and serving. Some gifts are for both speaking and doing: leading and kindness. Leaders must do what they say others are to do. Kindness shows both in what we do and what we say. All of the gifts are important. And even though we might have one or more special gifts, that doesn't mean they are the only ones we have. For example, giving and helping and being kind come naturally to some people, because they have those gifts. But all of us can give and help and try to be kind, even if those things might not come naturally to us.

Dear God, thank you for the gifts you have given me. Help me to bless others with my gifts.

Friday

Read "A New Self," page 735 in the *Day by Day Kid's Bible.* Or read this part of the story:

Do everything in Jesus' name. It may be what you say. It may be what you do. But do it in Jesus' name, giving thanks to God. . . .

Whatever you do, do it with your whole heart. Do it as if you were working for Jesus. He has good things planned for you. It's really Jesus you're serving. *Colossians 3:17, 23-24*

ERIC'S AUNT AND UNCLE bought a new house. It was called a fixer-upper, because it needed lots of repairs. So one morning Eric went with his dad and his uncle to help fix the house. When Eric got there, he didn't know how to paint and clean a window. But he watched his uncle tape around the edge of the window, then paint, and then scrape dried paint off the glass. Eric's uncle let him try it. By the end of the day, Eric could do it by himself.

We can learn by watching Jesus. And we can do that by reading what the Bible says about Jesus' life on this earth. He showed us how to serve each other. He reminded worried people to trust in God. He visited the sick. He was kind to little children. He encouraged people who were afraid. He told rich people how to have true treasure in heaven. What can we learn about serving people by watching Jesus?

Dear God, help me to remember that when I am serving other people, I'm really serving your Son, Jesus. Thank you for sending Jesus to show me how to serve with love.

☀ SOME THINGS YOU CAN DO THIS WEEK 🌙

Make play dough. Mix one-third cup of salt, one-third cup of water, and one cup of flour. Work on a paper plate or a piece of wax paper. Make a vase or bowl and set it aside to dry. Remember how God is our Potter and makes us just the way he wants us to be, with gifts he chooses to give us.

Make a napkin holder. Cut off the top part of a cereal box until it is just tall enough to hold napkins with part of the napkins sticking out. Paint the napkin holder box, and when it dries, put napkins in it. The napkin holder is a reminder of the "doing" gifts, because you can give it to someone in your family, and the napkins in it can be used to clean and serve.

Make an apron out of a dish towel. Cut four holes across one of the short ends of the towel. Two holes should be close to the center of the short edge, one hole should be near the right side and one near the left side. The holes should be big enough to thread a fabric ribbon through. Measure the ribbon so that it will go around your waist twice. Cut that much ribbon. Then thread it through the holes on the towel to make an apron. It will help to keep you clean when you serve in the kitchen.

Collect for the poor. If your church or other group has a way of giving food or clothes to people who are poor, gather clothing or food this week and give it to that group. They might even tell you about a family you could take the food or clothes to.

GETTING ALONG WITH OTHERS

Do your part to live in peace with everyone,
as much as possible. Romans 12:18, NLT

This week you will learn
· what God plans for us to carry wherever we go;
· what is like a cobra in the heart;
· ten ways to control your anger;
· how to do one-heart forgiving and two-heart forgiving.

Monday

Read "Choosing the Next King," page 137 in the *Day by Day Kid's Bible.* Or read this part of the story:

God's Spirit had left Saul. A bad spirit had come on Saul instead. . . .

So Saul sent a message to Jesse. "Send David here." . . .
David played his harp when the bad spirit bothered Saul. Then Saul would feel better. The bad spirit would leave.
1 Samuel 16:14, 22-23

DAVID KNEW THE PEACE of being in the fields watching sheep. David's life was not always peaceful, but David was at peace with God. David carried that peace with him wherever he went. He was able to help King Saul find peace too.

God plans for each of us to carry inside us a peace that's greater than we can understand. It's a peace in our spirits that can be with us wherever we go. In this peaceful place within us, we can meet God anytime we like, even if our surroundings are not so peaceful.

Dear God, thank you for your plan for us to have peace inside us wherever we go. Help me to feel this peace.

Tuesday

Read "Keep On Running," page 789 in the *Day by Day Kid's Bible*. Or read this part of the story:

Try your best to live at peace with everyone. Try not to sin. People who live in sin won't see God.

Make sure nobody misses God's kind love. Don't let anger grow and get you in trouble. It can hurt many people.
Hebrews 12:14-15

WHEN FRANK WAS A BABY, his father left his mother and married somebody else. Frank didn't see his father much after that. He felt like his father never loved him. Frank was angry. Years went by. Frank grew up and grew old. When Frank was 80 years old, he went to a family reunion. All he could talk about was how his father had left his mother 80 years ago. Frank couldn't smile or enjoy the party. And no one enjoyed him. His anger had turned into bitterness.

Bitterness is anger that has grown deep into someone's heart and has made the person miserable. Bitterness grows in a heart that won't forgive. Someone once said that if you hold anger in your heart, it becomes a cobra. What is a cobra? What do you think that saying means?

Dear God, help me never to stay angry or get bitter. Help me to do what I can to live at peace with everyone.

Wednesday

Read "Anger, Waiting, and Selfishness," page 241 in the *Day by Day Kid's Bible*. Or read this part of the story:

Be happy to control your anger.
That's better than controlling a whole city.

People who get angry too fast will get in trouble.
You might get them out of trouble.
But you'll have to do it again.

Don't make friends with people who get angry too fast.
You might learn to act like them.
Then you'll be trapped. Proverbs 16:32; 19:19; 22:24-25

THOMAS JEFFERSON, who was president of the United States long ago, once said, "When angry, count ten before you speak; if very angry, [a] hundred." Sometimes that's a good idea.

Here are ten more ways to handle anger: Tell someone that you are angry. Get away to cool off. Pray. Exercise. Take deep breaths. Listen to calm music. Focus on finding out how to solve the problem. Put your energy into something else. Draw a picture that shows your anger. Write a letter, poem, or story that tells about your anger. (But don't send the letter.) Do you have another idea about how to control anger?

In the Bible, Paul wrote, "Don't sin by letting anger gain control over you" (Ephesians 4:26, NLT).

Dear God, help me not to get angry too fast. When I do get angry, help me to control my anger.

Thursday

Read "Fighting and Hurting," page 246 in the *Day by Day Kid's Bible*. Or read this part of the story:

Some people are angry at what others did to them.
Their hearts are harder than the walls of a fort.
Fussing keeps friends apart like a gate with iron bars. . . .

Don't say, "I'll get even with you for being mean to me."
Wait for God. He will take care of things.
Proverbs 18:19; 20:22

"WHEN THE ELEPHANTS FIGHT, the grass gets hurt." That's an African saying. We all want to get back at the people who hurt us or make us angry. But if we try to get back at people, they get hurt and angry. Then they get back at us. Then we get back at them. There is no end. People get hurt over and over again.

Once there was a pilot who hated everyone. A man asked him, "Would you like to get rid of your enemies?" "I sure would!" said the pilot. The man said, "Love them, and you won't have any enemies."

God forgives us for all the wrong we do. So we can forgive others and let God deal with them however he wants. Forgiving is something we choose. We choose not to hate or get revenge. We choose not to gossip or mention it to others. When we remember the wrong, we choose to think about something else. We choose to be friendly to the person who wronged us. We let God take care of things.

Dear God, thank you for forgiving me for the wrong I do. Help me to forgive others when they do wrong. I will let you take care of things.

Friday
Read "The Words We Say," page 244 in the *Day by Day Kid's Bible*. Or read this part of the story:

A kind word will take away anger. . . .
But a mean word will bring anger.

A fire goes out if there's no wood to burn.
Fussing stops when nobody says bad things about others.
Proverbs 15:1; 26:20

ONE NIGHT WHEN KAYLA was helping her mom cook, a skillet of grease got too hot, and a fire started in the pan. Right away, Kayla's mom put a flat cookie pan on top of the skillet, and she turned off the burner. The fire went out, because it couldn't get any air. Fire needs fuel and air if it is going to burn.

Fights and quarrels need anger to keep going. Forgiving takes away the fuel. There are two kinds of forgiving. *One-heart forgiving* is when you forgive someone even though the other person is not sorry or at least doesn't say so. *Two-heart forgiving* is when someone else is sorry and you forgive that person. But you can forgive either way. Then at least your heart will be at peace.

Dear God, help me to take away the fuel of fights and quarrels by forgiving others. Give me peace in my heart.

☀ Some Things You Can Do This Week ☾

☀ **See an afterimage.** Draw and cut out a heart shape from a piece of green paper. Glue it onto a piece of white paper. Now stare at the middle of the green heart and count "One heart, two hearts, three hearts," all the way through "fifteen hearts." Then turn the paper over and stare at the middle of the white paper. What do you see? What color is it? This is an afterimage. Sometimes when someone is angry, they say they are "seeing red." Bitterness is like the afterimage. If we focus on the wrong someone did to us, we keep being angry long after what happened is over. How can we stop being angry?

☾ **Make lemonade.** Set out some lemon juice. Taste it. Mix one cup of the lemon juice with one cup of sugar and five cups of cold water to make lemonade. Now taste the lemonade. How is the flavor different from the flavor of plain lemon juice? There is a saying, "If life hands you a lemon, make lemonade." It means: Try to turn the "sour" times of your life into something good. So instead of getting sour and bitter when someone treats you wrong, you can try to see how to make something good out of it.

☀ **Make anger disappear on paper.** Write "anger" on a piece of paper with a yellow pencil. Now place a piece of red cellophane or a see-through, red plastic report cover over the writing. The words disappear. When we forgive someone, we let our anger disappear.

☾ **Pop some popcorn.** Do you know what makes the corn pop? A bit of moisture inside each kernel of corn turns into steam when it gets hot. The steam pushes against the sides of the corn kernel and makes it explode. Anger inside us can explode like moisture inside popcorn. How can we get rid of anger without exploding?

MAKING PEACE

Jesus said, "Father, forgive these people,
because they don't know what they are doing." Luke 23:34, NLT

This week you will learn
· *how you can be like an oyster;*
· *some ways to bring peace;*
· *what is the most important kind of peace.*

Monday

Read "A Silver Cup" and "Telling the Secret," pages 40 and 41 in the *Day by Day Kid's Bible.* Or read this part of the story:

"Is my father still alive?" Joseph asked.

Joseph's brothers could not say a word. They were afraid.

"I am Joseph, your brother!" he said. "You sold me to be a slave. I was taken to Egypt. But don't worry about it now. God sent me here so I could save many lives." *Genesis 45:3-5*

HAVE YOU EVER SEEN A PEARL? Pearls are round, whitish beads that cost a lot of money. They come from sea animals called oysters. A bit of shell, sand, or grit gets inside the oyster's shell. The oyster begins coating it with thin sheets of a pearly substance. Layer after layer, the oyster covers this bit of sand. After a while, that makes a pearl.

The way a pearl is made teaches us about our life. When we have a problem with people, it's like sand in the shell. We can let the trouble make us angry and bitter. Or we can forgive and trust God to turn our problem into something good, like the oyster turned the sand into a pearl.

Joseph had good reason to be angry and bitter toward his brothers. But he chose to forgive them. He told them, "You intended to harm me, but God intended it for good" (Genesis 50:20, NIV).

Dear God, when people treat me badly, help me to remember that you can turn it into something good. Help me to forgive.

Tuesday

Read "In Saul's Camp at Night," page 153 in the *Day by Day Kid's Bible.* Or read this part of the story:

"This is the day!" said the man with David. "God is giving your enemy to you. I can kill him with one blow. Let me pin him to the ground!"

"No," said David. "He is the one God chose to be king. If we kill him, we're to blame. God will get him." *1 Samuel 26:8-10*

THE WHOLE CLASS was in an uproar when Mrs. See walked into the room. "What's going on?" she asked.

"Sophie hit Ben," said Joe.

"Why did you do that, Sophie?" asked Mrs. See.

"Ben called Trina a birdbrain," said Sophie.

"Why did you do that, Ben?" asked Mrs. See.

"Because Trina called Caleb a toad," said Ben.

"Yeah, because Caleb kicked Maria's foot," said Trina.

"Why did you do that, Caleb?" asked Mrs. See.

"Because Maria tripped me," said Caleb.

"I didn't mean to. It was an accident," said Maria.

Who could have stopped this uproar before Mrs. See came in? Caleb or Trina or Ben or Sophie. Instead of fighting back, somebody could have said, "I forgive you."

In today's reading, David could have gotten back at Saul. Instead, he kept the peace. Normally, we want to get back at someone who hurts us or our friends. But to make peace, somebody has to forgive.

Dear God, thank you for showing me that I can keep the peace by forgiving. Help me to forgive.

Wednesday

Read "Like Sheep Going Where Wolves Are," page 554 in the *Day by Day Kid's Bible.* Or read this part of the story:

Jesus called his 12 special friends. He told them to go out two by two. He gave them power that was stronger than bad spirits. . . .

"Go into the towns," said Jesus. "Look for people who will help you. . . . Be friendly and pray for peace to come to them. . . .

"What if people won't listen to you?" said Jesus. "Then shake the dust off your feet when you leave that town." *Mark 6:7-11*

WHEN PEOPLE WERE RUDE to Jesus' friends, the friends had to choose what to do. They could be rude to those people. They could put them down and dis them (disrespect them). Or they could keep quiet but remember the people with anger and become bitter. What else could they do? What did Jesus tell them to do? He said, "Shake the dust off." In other words, "Forget about it."

Has there ever been a time when someone didn't welcome you? Or maybe someone didn't listen to you? Or your friends didn't choose you for their team? Or they mistreated you in some way? One thing you could choose to do is take Jesus' advice: "Shake it off." Refuse to get angry and bitter. Over-look it. Forget about it. Pray and forgive, and let God deal with them.

Dear God, when others mistreat me, help me to shake it off and let you deal with them.

Thursday

Read "Jesus' Home Town," page 520 in the *Day by Day Kid's Bible*. Or read this part of the story:

"When Elisha lived, many people had a skin sickness," said Jesus. "But Naaman was the only one God made well. He was not Jewish."

Everyone was angry when Jesus said this. The people all stood up. They pushed Jesus out of town.

The town was on a hill. The people pushed Jesus right to the edge of the hill. They were going to throw him over the edge. But Jesus passed right through the crowd. He walked away.
Luke 4:27-30

PEOPLE WERE OFTEN rude to Jesus. He could have said, "You're not so great yourselves!" Sometimes the leaders tried to get Jesus into a big argument with them so there would be a big uproar and they could blame Jesus. He could have gotten into an argument with them or laughed at them. He could have held anger in his heart and become bitter toward them. But he didn't. Sometimes he just talked calmly to them, telling them the truth. Other times he walked away.

Sometimes getting away from people who are causing trouble is enough to bring peace.

Dear God, thank you for the way Jesus shows me how to act when people mistreat me. Help me to know when to just walk away to bring peace.

Friday

Read "Like a New Green Plant," page 367 in the *Day by Day Kid's Bible*. Or read this part of the story:

God's servant grew up with him. . . .

But he was hurt because of our sins.
He was paid back for what we did wrong.
That brought us peace. But he paid for it. . . .

He had hard times. People hurt him.
But he didn't say a word. . . .
He gave his life. He died. . . .
He took the sins of many people.
He stood in their place.
Isaiah 53:2, 5, 7-8, 12

PRINCE OF PEACE is a name for Jesus. His death on the cross made peace between God and us. Here's the way it works: God loves perfectly. So he is always good and kind. If we could love perfectly, we would be always good and kind too. But we don't love perfectly. We miss the mark, because we are not God. Our sins keep us away from him. So God came to earth in the form of a man: his Son, Jesus, who loved perfectly. He was always good and kind. Then he took the blame for the times we miss the mark and sin. He was punished for us on the cross when he died. But there was no sin in him, so death could not hold him. He came back to life and now sits beside God to speak up for us. Now we can be at peace with God. That's the most important peace of all.

Dear God, thank you for sending your Son to die for me and make peace between you and me. Thank you for sending the Prince of Peace.

Some Things You Can Do This Week

Write disappearing words. Wet a piece of paper and lay it on the kitchen counter. Put a dry piece of paper on top of it and write the verse for this week on the top paper. Now take the dry paper off. You will see where the writing has been pressed onto the wet paper. Lift the wet paper carefully off the counter. Let it dry. The words disappear. If you want to see the words again, just wet the paper. The disappearing words are like our sins that disappear when we are forgiven.

Make a cross. Glue two Popsicle sticks or craft sticks together to make a cross. Write the word FORGIVE on it. Remember that Jesus' death forgives your sins.

Draw a hand-shaped dove. Place your left hand on the left side of a piece of white paper, with your fingers pointed to the left edge and your thumb pointing up at about the center of the paper. Trace around it. Place your right hand on the right side of the paper, with your right fingers pointing to the right edge of the paper and your right thumb on top of the tracing of your left thumb. Trace around your right hand. Now look at the drawing. The place where your thumbs overlapped makes the head of a dove. Your fingers are the dove's wings. You may draw a beak on the head and color around your white dove. Sometimes doves are used as a symbol for peace. Let this one remind you of how Jesus made peace between us and God.

Make an oyster shell. Fold a plain paper plate in half. Inside the folded plate, on the bottom half, drop a big blob of plain white glue. Let it dry. It can remind you of the pearl an oyster makes from a grain of sand or grit. It can help you remember to trust God to turn the troubles of your life into something beautiful and good.

HARMONY

Finally, all of you, live in harmony with one another; be sympathetic, love as brothers, be compassionate and humble. 1 Peter 3:8, NIV

This week you will learn
· *what harmony means;*
· *some advice from a man who had 700 wives;*
· *what it means to confront and repent;*
· *how to clean a dirty heart.*

Monday

Read "All about People," page 251 in the *Day by Day Kid's Bible*. Or read this part of the story:

> Be happy to live on the corner of the roof.
> That's better than living with someone who makes a fuss.
>
> Be happy to live in the desert.
> That's better than living with someone who gets angry a lot.
> Proverbs 21:9, 19

KING SOLOMON'S NAME is famous because he was so wise. He lived long ago, but even today you might hear someone say that another person is "as wise as Solomon."

Solomon wrote 3,000 wise sayings called proverbs. Many of them are about how people should treat each other. But how did Solomon know the best way to treat others?

First of all, being king, Solomon had to learn to get along with other leaders and the people in his court. Second, he had 700 wives! This was not God's best for him, and his wives ended up bringing him trouble. But having 700 wives must have taught Solomon many things about how to get along with other people. And third, can you imagine how many children Solomon must have had? So we can trust that Solomon knew what he was talking about when he wrote wise sayings about how to get along with each other.

Another way to say "getting along with each other" is "living in harmony."

Dear God, thank you that Solomon's wise sayings are in the Bible. Help me to learn how to get along with others and live in harmony.

Tuesday

Read "What Makes You Beautiful," page 771 in the *Day by Day Kid's Bible*. Or read this part of the story:

All of you, live peacefully with each other. Try to understand each other's feelings. Love each other as if you were family. Be kind. . . .
    The psalm says it this way.

    ". . . Look for the way of peace, and follow it." 1 Peter 3:8, 11

PETER, UNLIKE SOLOMON, had only one wife. But he had to learn to get along with the eleven other friends who lived and worked with Jesus just like he did. They all had to learn to live in harmony.

Have you ever heard a little child bang on a piano or strum all the strings of a guitar at once? Notes that are all scrambled up and don't sound good together are not in harmony. But if a piano player or a guitar player plays a song, you will hear harmony. There may be different notes, but they all go together.

That's the way God wants people to be: in harmony. Each person may be different, they may like different things, but they can learn to get along together and live in harmony.

Dear God, thank you for the different people who are my friends and family. Help us to get along together and live in harmony.

Wednesday

Read "A Little Child and a Little Sheep," page 567 in the *Day by Day Kid's Bible.* Or read this part of the story:

"Someone may do something wrong to you," said Jesus. "Then you should go to see him. Show him what he did wrong. Keep it just between the two of you. If he listens, then you have won a friend.

"If he won't listen, go back later," said Jesus. "Take one or two people with you. Maybe he will listen to them." *Matthew 18:15-16*

AMBER WORKED HARD at school and made good grades. Brooke was jealous and told everyone that Amber made good grades because she cheated. When Amber found out what Brooke was saying, she was very angry. Amber decided she needed to confront Brooke if they were going to have a chance to live in harmony. She needed to tell Brooke she was angry and ask Brooke to stop saying bad things about her.

How do we confront someone? First we pray about it. Then we make sure we didn't do something mean or rude to that person. If we did, we first have to tell our friend we are sorry, even if he or she did something worse to us. We may need to take someone with us. And we always need to speak kindly. "A gentle answer turns away wrath, but harsh words stir up anger," said Solomon (Proverbs 15:1, NLT).

Dear God, when someone does something unkind to me, help me to know if I need to confront the person. If I do, please help me to speak kindly.

Thursday

Read "The Poor Man's Sheep," page 168 in the *Day by Day Kid's Bible.* Or read this part of the story:

Then Nathan told David what God said. "I chose you to be my people's king. . . . Why have you done this terrible wrong? . . ."

"I've sinned against God," said David.

David wrote,

Be kind to me, God.
Show me your love that never stops.
Erase my sins because you are so kind. . . .
You are the one who has really been hurt by this terrible sin.
I did wrong. . . .
Save me, God. . . .
The gift you want is a heart that's sorry about doing wrong.
You won't turn away a sorry heart.

"God has taken away your sin," said Nathan.
2 Samuel 12:7, 9, 13; Psalm 51:1, 4, 14, 17

NATHAN CONFRONTED DAVID because David had done wrong. David could have said, "I didn't do it." Or "So what?" Or "Other people do that all the time. It's not so bad." But David apologized. He told God he was sorry. And he repented. That means he wasn't just sorry he got caught. *Repent* means to change directions. David changed his ways so he would not do that wrong again.

Have you ever been in a car or van when the driver went the wrong direction? The driver had to turn around to get to where he wanted to go. Repenting is like that. We find out we're going the wrong direction in life because we said or did something wrong. So we apologize to God and to any people we may have hurt. Then we change the way we act and speak. It's not easy to repent and apologize. But it helps us live in harmony with others. That's the way life works best.

Dear God, help me to be like David, to repent and apologize quickly when I've done wrong. Thank you for forgiving me.

Friday

Read "Not like a Horse," page 216 in the *Day by Day Kid's Bible.* Or read this part of the story:

When I kept quiet about my sins, I felt terrible.
I cried all day.
Day and night, God, you tried to get me to listen.
My strength melted away like it does on a hot summer day.
Then I told you about my sins.
I didn't hide them.
I said, "I will tell God about my sins."
Then you forgave me. Psalm 32:3-5

WE FEEL DIRTY in our heart when we do something we know is wrong. That feeling is called *guilt.* When our hands are dirty, we can just wash our hands to get clean. But when the dirty feeling is in our heart, we have to admit to someone that we did wrong. We say we are sorry. We ask the people we hurt to forgive us. And we ask God to forgive us. We may have to replace something that was lost or damaged. But God promises to forgive us when we tell him we're sorry and we mean it. Then the dirty, guilty feeling should go away. We are clean again in our heart.

Dear God, help me to be quick to tell you and others that I'm sorry when I've done wrong. Then clean the dirty feeling out of my heart.

☀ Some Things You Can Do This Week ☾

☀ **Gather some old pennies** and clean them with copper cleaner and old, soft rags. Think of the dirt and grime on the pennies as being the dirty feeling of guilt we have when we do wrong. Think of cleaning the penny as God forgiving our sin. Think of the shiny penny as the way we are after God forgives us.

☾ **Make pretzels.** Mix one package of yeast and one and one-half cups of warm water. Let this stand for five minutes. Mix one teaspoon of salt, one tablespoon of sugar, and four cups of flour in a big bowl. Add the yeast mixture and stir, adding more flour if the dough is too sticky. Make a one-inch ball of dough. Roll it into a rope and twist it into a pretzel shape by making the rope into a circle, crossing the ends of the rope, and pulling the ends back toward the side they came from. Bake at 425 degrees for 12–15 minutes. Pretzels were first made in southern Europe. They were shaped to look like the crossed arms of a child praying and repenting.

☀ **Learn about bending and breaking.** Get a drinking straw and a piece of uncooked spaghetti. Bend the straw quickly and let it go. What happens? Bend the piece of spaghetti. What happens? When someone sins against us, we can choose to be like the straw or the spaghetti. We can forgive (bend like the straw) and keep growing with God's peace in our hearts. Or we can choose not to forgive (break like the spaghetti) and live with a hurting heart.

☾ **Play "Repent Ball."** Everyone stands in a circle. When you say "Go," pass the ball around the circle. When you call "Repent," the ball should change directions. Keep saying "Repent" every time you want the ball to go the other way. You can make the game harder by throwing the ball to someone, who throws it to someone else. But when you call "Repent," the ball has to go back to the person who threw it. This game helps everyone remember that repent means to turn around and go the other way.

FIGHTING TEMPTATION

I have hidden your word in my heart so I won't sin against you. Psalm 119:11, DBD

This week you will learn
· *a way to fight temptation;*
· *what is the most dangerous trap;*
· *how to hide God's Word in your heart.*

Monday

Read "Trying to Make Jesus Do Wrong," page 513 in the *Day by Day Kid's Bible.* Or read this part of the story:

The Spirit led Jesus into the desert. That's where Satan tried to make Jesus do wrong. . . .

Satan took Jesus to a high mountain. He showed Jesus the riches of all the world's kingdoms. "I'll give all this to you," Satan said. "Just bow down and worship me."

"Get away from me, Satan!" said Jesus. "God's Word says to worship only the Lord your God. Serve only him."
Matthew 4:1, 8-11

JEROD'S MOM TOLD HIM to clean his room before going to his friend's house. But Jerod was in a hurry. He was tempted to shove everything under his bed. *Tempt* means "to draw someone toward sin by causing that person to believe that he or she will get something good or pleasant out of it."

In our reading for today, Satan wanted Jesus to believe that he could own all the world's riches right then and there. That would have been a pleasant outcome. But Jesus fought temptation by saying a verse from God's Word, the Scriptures. Since Jesus came to show us how to live, we can fight temptation the same way he did.

So if Jerod wanted to fight temptation like Jesus did, he could say to himself, "I will clean my room, because God's Word says, 'Children, obey your parents'" (Colossians 3:20, NIV).

Dear Father God, when I am tempted to make the wrong choice, help me to remember that Jesus fought temptation. Help me fight temptation too.

Tuesday

Read "The First Children," page 6 in the *Day by Day Kid's Bible.* Or read this part of the story:

God said that what Abel gave him was right. But what Cain gave him was not. Cain got mad, and he frowned.

"Why are you mad?" asked God. "Why are you frowning? Do the right thing. Then I'll like what you bring me. But what if you don't do the right thing? Then sin will wait at your door. Sin wants to catch you. But you must not let it get to you." *Genesis 4:4-7*

MICE GOT INTO Mr. Barrett's storage room. They chewed through the corner of a box and even nibbled on the important papers inside. So Mr. Barrett bought a mousetrap. He put a piece of cheese on it and set the trap. Late that night, he heard a loud snap. The cheese had tempted the mouse. And when the mouse ate the cheese, he got caught in the trap.

For us, temptation is like that cheese. It looks good to us. But it's a dangerous trap. If we do the wrong we are tempted to do, we often find ourselves trapped in sin. Sooner or later, we get hurt or someone else gets hurt. If we hide God's Word in our heart, we can fight temptation like Jesus did. We can say, "I will not sin, because God's Word says, 'Do what is right and good'" (Deuteronomy 6:18, NIV).

Dear God, help me to resist temptation and stay out of sin's trap.

Wednesday

Read "Rest," page 781 in the *Day by Day Kid's Bible*. Or read this part of the story:

Jesus understands us. He faced every sin that looks good to us. But he said no every time. He did not sin.

So let's go to the kind, loving King in heaven. We can be sure he will understand. He will be kind and loving to us. He will help us when we need him. *Hebrews 4:15-16*

JACKSON WAS TEMPTED to cheat at school during a test. He didn't know the answer to one of the questions. Sarah's paper was where he could see her answer clearly if he looked. What was the good or pleasant thing that he thought might happen if he cheated? What could he do to resist temptation?

Sometimes when people are tempted, they forget to think about what might happen that would be bad. Things that are wrong, like cheating, are not wrong just because God said not to do it. Things are wrong because they cause anger and fear. They hurt us or others. God made the world, and he knows how it works. He has told us how to live so that life will work for us, bringing peace and joy. That's why we should choose to do what's right.

Dear God, thank you for making a way for me to fight temptation. Help me to make the right choices.

Thursday

Read "A Way to Say No," page 683 in the *Day by Day Kid's Bible*. Or read this part of the story:

The only sins that come to your mind are sins everyone has problems with. God won't let a sin come to your mind unless he knows you can say no to it. . . . Then God gives you a way to say no. That way, you can win over sin. *1 Corinthians 10:13*

THE WORD *tempt* also means "to test." When Satan tempted Jesus, that tested Jesus. It showed whether Jesus trusted God to take care of him. It showed whether Jesus would do things God's way or Satan's way. When Jesus resisted temptation, he passed the test. He showed that he trusted God.

When you are tempted, it's a test that shows if you trust God or not. What kinds of "temptation tests" have you been going through lately? When you learn Bible verses, you hide God's Word in your heart. Then you can say those verses when you are tempted, just like Jesus did.

Dear God, when I am tempted, help me to make the right choice, trusting you to take care of me.

Friday

Read "Angels in Sodom," page 14 i the *Day by Day Kid's Bible.* Or read this part of the story:

When morning came, the angels told Lot, "Hurry and leave. Or you'll be in the city when God wipes it away! . . ."

But Lot did not go. So the angels took him by the hand. They took his wife's hand and his daughters' hands. The angels led them out of the city. God was being good to them.

They got out of the city. Then one of the angels said, "Run for your lives! Don't look behind you. Don't stop until you get to the mountains!" . . .

But Lot's wife looked back. She turned into a post made of salt. *Genesis 19:15-17, 26*

SOMETIMES IT'S EASIER to resist temptation if a friend helps us. Lot was tempted to stay in the city of Sodom. But the angels took his hand and led him and his family out.

What temptations are hard for you to resist? If something is easy to resist, it's not much of a temptation. Has a friend ever helped you resist temptation? It's important to choose the right friends. Some friends tempt us. They are not helpful friends. Other friends help us resist temptation. They are the best kind of friends. Maybe you can be the kind of friend who helps others resist temptation.

Something else can help you resist temptation: family rules. Sometimes it's easier to say no to someone who is tempting you if you can say, "My dad and mom won't let me do that."

Dear God, thank you for friends and family who help me resist temptation. Help me be the kind of friend who will help others resist temptation.

SOME THINGS YOU CAN DO THIS WEEK

Line up dominoes, one in back of the other, standing them on their ends. Tap the first one to see all of them tumble. Sin affects all of our life, just like the first domino affects the others. What are some of the effects of sin?

Bake biscuits. Mix one cup of flour, one-half teaspoon of salt, one-fourth teaspoon of baking soda, one and one-half teaspoons of baking powder, and two tablespoons of shortening. Slowly stir in one-half cup of buttermilk. Drop tablespoonfuls of this batter onto a greased pan. Bake for 10 to 12 minutes at 450 degrees. Think about how Jesus was tempted to turn stones into bread. How did Jesus resist? What else was Jesus tempted to do?

Make a sword. Cut a sword shape out of poster board or cardboard. Cover the blade with aluminum foil. Decorate the handle by coloring, painting, or gluing on construction paper symbols that have meanings. A cross stands for Jesus. A sun means light. A lion means courage. A crown means authority. A dove represents the Holy Spirit. An olive leaf means peace. What symbol would you choose to represent yourself? Jesus resisted temptation by quoting God's Word. Read Ephesians 6:17 to find out what the word of God is called. When you fight temptation by quoting God's Word like Jesus did, it's like sword fighting!

Play "Trap the Ball." Turn a box upside down and cut two or three arched "doors" in one side. Make one door just large enough for a Ping-Pong ball (or other small ball you have chosen) to roll through. Make the next door a bit larger, and make the third door the largest. Now set the box on the floor some distance away and try to roll the ball through the smallest door. Give yourself more points for rolling the ball through the small door and fewer points for rolling it through the larger doors. When the ball is in the box, it's trapped. What makes sin a trap for us?

PAYING ATTENTION

Pay attention and listen to the sayings of the wise. Proverbs 22:17, NIV

This week you will learn
· *the difference between hearing and listening;*
· *what it means to be distracted;*
· *when pointing isn't a good thing to do;*
· *who's paying attention to you.*

Monday

Read "Listen and Learn," page 230 in the *Day by Day Kid's Bible.* Or read this part of the story:

> *These sayings will teach people the wise way to think.*
> *They'll help you do what's right and fair.*
> *They'll make fools become wise.*
> *They'll help young people know and choose what's good.*
> *So if you're wise, listen and learn even more.*
> Proverbs 1:1-5

CARS ZOOMING PAST, phones ringing, timers beeping, radios playing, people's voices shouting, dogs barking, airplanes flying overhead. We hear lots of sounds every day. Our minds block out most of the sounds we don't want to pay attention to. We only hear them in the background. That's the difference between hearing and listening. If we are really going to listen, we have to pay attention.

Have you ever heard someone talking, but you didn't really listen? Sometimes looking at the person who is talking will help you to pay attention. When you are tempted not to pay attention, you can fight that temptation like Jesus did. You can say, "I will pay attention because God's Word says, 'Pay attention and listen to the sayings of the wise'" (Proverbs 22:17, NIV).

Dear God, help me to pay attention when I need to.

Tuesday

Read "As White As Light," page 564 in the *Day by Day Kid's Bible.* Or read this part of the story:

Jesus took Peter, James, and John . . . up on a high mountain.

All of a sudden . . . Jesus' face started shining. It was as bright as the sun. His clothes turned as white as light.

Then Moses and Elijah showed up. They talked with Jesus.

"Lord!" said Peter. "It's wonderful to be here. If you want, I can make three tents here. I'll make one for you. I'll make one for Moses. I'll make one for Elijah!"

Then a bright cloud came down around them. A voice came from the cloud. It said, "This is my Son. He is the Son I love. I'm happy with him. Listen to him." *Matthew 17:1-5*

KIMBERLY RAN DOWNSTAIRS because her mom had called to her. "I'm going to the corner store," said Mom. "Then I need to drop by the post office. . . ." Kimberly looked toward the TV and began thinking about the cartoon her little brother was watching. "Kimberly?" said Mom. "Are you listening?" Kimberly moved so she could not see the TV screen. Then she asked Mom to tell her again.

Sometimes it's hard to listen because we are *distracted.* That means other things take our attention away from what we are supposed to be doing. What are some things that distract you (take your attention away) from things you need to listen to?

Sometimes we need to be reminded to pay attention. Peter was distracted when he started thinking about Moses and Elijah. When God spoke, Peter knew he needed to just settle down and pay attention to Jesus.

Dear God, help me to know when I'm getting distracted, and help me to pay attention to what's most important.

Wednesday

Read "Being Trained to Do What's Right," page 234 in the *Day by Day Kid's Bible.* Or read this part of the story:

> *Listen when someone shows you what's right.*
> *That shows you how to live.*
> *People who don't listen lead others to do wrong. . . .*
>
> *Some people don't listen when they're told they're wrong.*
> *They grow poor and feel like nothing.*
> *Some people listen when they're told they're wrong.*
> *Others treat them like they're important.*
> Proverbs 10:17; 13:18

SAMMY'S PIANO TEACHER kept reminding him to play the keys with the tips of his fingers. She sometimes gently lifted his wrists when he was playing a song. When he did it wrong, she would tell him and show him the right way to do it. Sammy was so eager to play the songs that he didn't like to be told he was doing it wrong. But he paid attention to his teacher, and he practiced. It wasn't long before he was playing the songs better than ever, and his teacher didn't have to remind him anymore.

No one likes to be told they are wrong. We all want to be right. But everyone is wrong sometimes. So if we pay attention when someone tells us we're wrong, we can learn and grow and try again. That's the smart thing to do.

Dear God, help me to pay attention when someone tells me I'm wrong. Help me to learn and try again.

Thursday

Read "The Dust and the Log," page 535 in the *Day by Day Kid's Bible*. Or read this part of the story:

"Why point at a bit of dust in someone's eye? You don't even see the big log in your own eye. How can you say, 'Let's get that dust out'? You have a log in your own eye," said Jesus. "First get rid of the log in your eye. Then you'll see clearly. You'll be able to get rid of the other person's dust." *Matthew 7:3-5*

"JOSH LEFT HIS soccer socks on the bathroom floor!" said Rebekah, pointing at her brother, who was lying on the floor, reading a book.

Grandma put her hands on her hips and said, "When you point your finger, look at your hand. Three fingers point back at you. Who left a glass half full of milk on the table?"

"Oops," said Rebekah. "It was me." Rebekah put the glass of milk in the refrigerator and didn't say anything else about Josh's socks.

What Grandma told Rebekah was the same thing Jesus said in today's reading. Pointing at another person's fault isn't fair, because you have faults too. Jesus' story means that we should not pay so much attention to the wrongs that *other* people do. Instead, we should pay more attention to the wrongs that *we* do. We can't change other people. But we can change ourselves with God's help.

Dear God, help me not to pay so much attention to what other people do wrong. Instead, help me pay attention to you and to how I can please you.

Friday

Read "All This Work," page 579 in the *Day by Day Kid's Bible.* Or read this part of the story:

Martha had a sister named Mary. She sat down at Jesus' feet. She listened to what he said. . . .

At last, Martha came to Jesus. "Lord," she said. "My sister left me to do all the work by myself. Don't you care? Tell Mary to help me."

"Martha, Martha," said Jesus. "You're upset. You're worried about so many things. There is only one thing that's important right now. That's what Mary chose to do." *Luke 10:39-42*

NOT ONLY WAS MARY paying attention to Jesus, but Jesus was paying attention to both Mary and Martha. Part of loving others or respecting them is paying attention to them. Jesus paid attention to people, because Jesus loves people. He paid attention to Zacchaeus. He paid attention to sick people and poor people. He paid attention to children. And he pays attention to you, because he loves you.

Jesus' friend John wrote that we love God and others because God loved us first. We pay attention to others because God first paid attention to us. That fits God's plan: God blesses us, and we bless others.

How can you pay attention to God? How can you pay attention to others?

Dear God, thank you for paying attention to me. Show me how to pay attention to you and others.

SOME THINGS YOU CAN DO THIS WEEK

Make a sound drawing. Sit where you can hear many sounds. Have some crayons or markers and paper. When you hear a sound, draw what made that sound. Listen carefully. Sometimes there are sounds we don't hear at first, like the hum of the refrigerator or air conditioner. What might distract you from paying attention to some of these sounds? What might distract you from paying attention to God?

Help your ears. Face something that is making a sound. Cup your hands behind your ears. The sound should be louder. Turn your back to the sound. Where should you place your cupped hands to better hear the sound that is now behind you? If you have a cat, watch your cat's ears when you make a sound behind the cat. The cat turns its ears. Some animals have large ears so they can catch sound better. Rabbits, for example, need to pay attention to the sounds around them so they can stay safe. Can you think of some sounds that might alert you so that you can stay safe? Why would it be important to pay attention to those sounds?

Play a spy game. Paying attention can mean looking and seeing carefully as well as listening. Sit in the middle of a room with a friend. Choose a shape. Set a timer for three minutes. Without talking, both of you look around the room and count the number of things you see that are that shape. For example, if you choose a rectangle, you could count window panes, books, pillows, and other items. When the timer rings, tell each other how many items you counted. Choose another shape and count again. Think about how Jesus paid attention to the people who were around them. He watched them and listened to them to find out what they needed and how he could help them.

Make a tin-can phone. Ask an adult to help you punch a hole in the bottom of each of two tin cans by hammering a nail in the center of the bottom. Then cut a piece of string long enough to go across your yard or through one room of your house. Push each end of the string from the outside bottom of one can to the inside. Tie each end to a paper clip so it won't pull out. Let a friend take one can, you take the other, and stretch the string tight. As one of you talks into a can, the other will listen by putting one ear to the opening of the other can. Sound travels in waves down the string, just as sound normally travels in waves through the air. The waves go into our ears, hit our ear drum, and we hear the sound. Think about the difference between hearing and listening.

DEPENDABILITY

Do what is right and good. Deuteronomy 6:18, NIV

This week you will learn
· *what it means to be dependable;*
· *who sent a message with a bow and arrow;*
· *whose hand locked around his sword;*
· *what it means to let someone down.*

Monday

Read "At the Captain's House," page 34 in the *Day by Day Kid's Bible.* Or read this part of the story:

God took care of Joseph. He lived in the captain's house. The captain saw that God helped Joseph. Good things happened when Joseph was around. So the captain put Joseph in charge of everything in his house. With Joseph in charge, the captain didn't worry about anything. *Genesis 39:1-6*

"WHICH CAR will we take, Grandpa?" asked Riley, grabbing the fishing poles.

"The new Camry," said Grandpa. "It's dependable. The other car is so old it sometimes doesn't start. I don't want to get to the lake and not be able to get back home." Grandpa wanted to drive a car that would start when it was supposed to, a car that was dependable.

Being *dependable* means doing what you're supposed to do, when you're supposed to do it. When a person is dependable, others can trust that person to get the job done right. Joseph was dependable.

But it's not always easy to be dependable. When we are tempted to not do what we're supposed to do, we can fight temptation like Jesus did. We can say, "I will be dependable, because God's Word says, 'Do what is right and good'" (Deuteronomy 6:18, NIV).

Dear God, I want to be a person others can depend on. Help me to do what I'm supposed to do, when I'm supposed to do it.

Tuesday

Read "Two Sons and a Grape Garden," page 599 in the *Day by Day Kid's Bible.* Or read this part of the story:

There once was a man who had two sons. The man talked to his first son. "Go work in the grape garden today," he said.

His first son said no. Later, he changed his mind. He did go.

The man talked to his other son. "Go work in the grape garden today," he said.

His other son said, "Yes, sir. I will." But he didn't go.
Matthew 21:28-30

SEAN LIVED IN KENYA, Africa, in a small town. Most of the time, the city workers pumped water into water tanks. The water was stored there and used as people needed it at their houses. But sometimes the city stopped pumping water. When water in the tanks ran out, Sean and his family couldn't take regular showers. They couldn't water plants. Many African women had to walk to the river with big jars to get water. The water supply was not dependable. That made a lot of problems.

It makes a lot of problems when people are not dependable. In today's reading, both sons were tempted to not be dependable. Which son fell for the temptation? Which son won over the temptation? What kind of problems do you think it caused when the dad could not depend on his sons to work in the garden?

We want to be able to depend on people. So we try to act in ways that let them know they can depend on us.

Dear God, thank you for people I can depend on. Help me to be dependable.

Wednesday

Read "The Arrow," page 143 in the *Day by Day Kid's Bible.* Or read this part of the story:

Jonathan shot an arrow into the field. The boy ran to where it landed. Jonathan called, "The arrow is far away. It is past you." Then he called, "Hurry and go fast! Don't stop!"

The boy picked up the arrow and ran back to Jonathan. . . . This was a message for David. *1 Samuel 20:36-39*

THE SUN COMES UP every day. Wind blows a windmill that pumps water out of the ground so the cows on a ranch can drink. Soap loosens the dirt on our hands so we can wash up. We can depend on these things to work for us. What would life be like if the sun did not come up every day? Or if the wind didn't always turn the windmill? Or if soap worked sometimes, but not other times?

It's the same with people. We depend on people like the postal worker, who brings the mail. We would get angry if we never knew whether the mail would come or not.

David depended on Jonathan to send him a message. And Jonathan was dependable. He sent the message. Jonathan depended on the boy to bring back his arrow. Do you think Jonathan would have chosen that boy to help him if the boy had not been dependable? What might have happened if Jonathan had not been dependable?

Remember God's plan: God blesses us so we can bless others. God blesses us by being dependable. Now we can bless others by being dependable.

Dear God, I choose to be dependable. Thank you for showing me how.

Thursday

Read "Brave, Strong Men," page 170 in the *Day by Day Kid's Bible.* Or read this part of the story:

There were three strong men who led David's battles. One of them killed 800 men in one fight.

Then there was a second man. . . . He kept fighting until his hand got tired. His hand locked around his sword. God's people won the battle that day.

Then there was a third man. Once the enemy army came together in a field. David's army ran away. But this third man stayed right in the middle of the field. He kept fighting the enemy. God helped his people win. *2 Samuel 23:8-12*

The coach chose Lauren for the soccer team, even though Kara was a better player. But there were lots of times when Kara didn't come to practice. She was not dependable. Lauren always came. The coach said he would rather have on his team a good, dependable player than a great, undependable player.

When we choose people to help us, we want them to be dependable. David could trust his three strong fighters to do what they were supposed to do, when they were supposed to do it. They were dependable.

Are we dependable because a rule says we have to be dependable? No. We are dependable because God has shown us that's the way life works best.

Dear God, help me to be dependable and show others how life works best.

Friday

Read "A Colt," page 596 in the *Day by Day Kid's Bible.* Or read this part of the story:

Jesus asked two of his 12 special friends . . . to go into the next town. "You'll see a donkey with her colt just as you go into town. . . . Untie it, and bring it to me. . . ."

Jesus' two friends went to town. They found the colt. . . . Jesus' friends took the colt to Jesus. *Matthew 21:1-7*

"WE BROUGHT YOU A HORSE to ride, because it was nearby, and we were too tired to walk to the next town." What if Jesus' two friends had said that? Would you think they were dependable? They could have brought him the donkey instead of its colt. Or they could have brought him a camel. Or they could have spent the night in the town and brought the colt later, whenever they felt like it. But that would not have been dependable. They did just what Jesus asked them to do, when he asked them to do it.

But is there anyone who is dependable all the time? No. We all let people down sometimes. That's why we need Jesus. He did for us what we could not do for ourselves. Jesus was always dependable. And he died to take the punishment for all those times we are not dependable. Now we can feel free to try again. Because the way God made it, life works best when we are dependable.

Dear God, I'm sorry for times when I am not dependable. Thank you for sending Jesus to take my punishment. Help me learn to be dependable and more like Jesus.

☀ Some Things You Can Do This Week 🌙

Make an arrow design. Cut two and one-half inches off the bottom of a piece of printer paper to make it square. Draw a diagonal line across each corner as if making arrowheads, with the corner of the paper being the tip of each arrow. Now use a ruler to make the shafts (the bodies or stems) of these arrows, drawing two lines from the arrowhead in one corner to the arrowhead in the opposite corner. Do the same thing with the remaining two arrowheads. What other shapes are formed when you do this? Color this design. What weapons do you think David's mighty men used?

Draw a maze. Give it to a friend and see if your friend can solve the maze. Ask several friends or family members to draw a maze. Then trade mazes and try to work the maze you have been given. David's travels took him and his men in many different directions. How did he and his men show they were dependable?

Make COLT salad. The *C* is for one 12-ounce container of cottage cheese. The *O* is for one small can of oranges (mandarin oranges). The *L* is for one 3-ounce package of lime Jell-O. The *T* is for topping (4 to 5 ounces of frozen whipped topping that has been thawed). Mix the cottage cheese and dry Jell-O in a big bowl. Drain the oranges and mix them in. Stir in the whipped topping gently. Chill this in the refrigerator for at least one hour before you eat it. Remember how Jesus' friends were dependable and brought him the colt he asked for.

Make a money bank out of a margarine tub. Cut a slit in the middle of the lid so a quarter will fit through it. Cut different colors of Con-Tact paper into small triangles, circles, rectangles, and squares. Stick these or other kinds of stickers onto the lid and sides of the margarine tub. If you have a job and earn money or if you have an allowance, why do you need to be dependable? How can you show that you are dependable with your money?

FAILURE

Though a righteous man falls seven times, he rises again. Proverbs 24:16, NIV

This week you will learn
· what failure means;
· what we are tempted to do when we fail;
· how failing is like climbing a ladder.

Monday

Read "Afraid in the Desert," page 283 in the *Day by Day Kid's Bible.* Or read this part of the story:

At last Elijah got to Horeb Mountain. That was the mountain of God. Elijah spent the night in a cave there.

Then God spoke to Elijah. "Why are you here, Elijah?"

"I have worked hard for you, God," said Elijah. "But your people have turned away from you. They broke your altars. They killed your prophets. I'm the only prophet left. Now they're trying to kill me." . . .

Then God said, "I have saved 7,000 people for myself in Israel. They do not worship Baal or follow him." *1 Kings 19:8-9, 13-14, 18*

HAVE YOU EVER READ stories about Winnie-the-Pooh? One of Pooh's friends is the gloomy donkey Eeyore. He always thinks things are going to turn out bad. But Christopher Robin always tells Pooh not to worry, because everything is going to be all right.

Some people are like Eeyore, gloomy about life. They expect the worst to come from whatever happens. Other people look for what's good in everything that happens.

In most books and movies, something goes wrong, and we keep reading, hoping that everything will turn out all right. In real life, things go wrong too. We sometimes wonder if they will ever really be all right.

That's what Elijah wondered. He had worked hard and thought he had failed. *Failure* means "trying something but not being able to do it." Elijah was gloomy. But God knew that things would turn out all right, if Elijah kept following him.

Dear God, sometimes I get gloomy. Help me to remember that you will work everything out for good.

Tuesday

Read "On Top of the Water," page 557 in the *Day by Day Kid's Bible.* Or read this part of the story:

About three o'clock in the morning, Jesus went out to [his friends]. He walked right on top of the water. . . .

    Peter got out of the boat. He stepped onto the water. He began to walk to Jesus. Then he saw the waves. He got scared, and he started going down into the water.

    "Lord! Save me!" Peter cried.

    Right away, Jesus reached out to Peter. He lifted Peter up. *Matthew 14:25, 29-31*

IF YOU HAD BEEN IN THE BOAT with Jesus' friends, would you have expected Peter to be able to walk to Jesus, or would you have expected him to fail? We know that Peter didn't think he would fail, because he really stepped out of the boat onto the water. But when he saw the waves all around him, he failed and started sinking.

When we fail, we are often tempted to get mad at ourselves or lose courage or give up. We are tempted not to try again.

Peter learned that Jesus was not going to let him drown. As soon as Peter asked Jesus for help, Jesus pulled him up, and they both walked on the water back to the boat.

When we fail, we don't have to be mad at ourselves or lose courage or give up. We can ask for God's help, and we can try again. Even if we fail again, we know all things will work out for the best, because God is in control. God is love. God and his love always win.

Dear God, when I fail, help me not to be mad at myself or lose courage or give up. Help me to try again and know that whatever happens, you will work everything out for the best.

Wednesday

Read "A Sharp Ax," page 267 in the *Day by Day Kid's Bible.* Or read this part of the story:

> *If your boss gets angry at you, don't give up.*
> *Be full of peace. That can make up for mistakes.*
>
> *If you dig a pit, you may fall in.*
> *If you break down a wall, a snake might bite you.*
> *If you cut stones from hills, you might get hurt.*
> *If you chop wood, you might be in danger. . . .*
>
> *Being wise is like having a sharp ax. It helps you do your job well.*
> Ecclesiastes 10:4, 8-10

HERE'S A RIDDLE: A person who never makes a mistake never makes anything. What does that mean? Think of it this way. Aunt Carla tried to get Savannah to learn how to bake biscuits. But Savannah was afraid she would do it wrong, so she didn't even try.

It's like not running the race because you're afraid you might trip and fall. Or not writing a poem because you're afraid you might not spell the words right. If you're afraid to make a mistake, you'll never make anything.

Making mistakes and failing are part of life. Every time you fail at something you try, you get closer to doing it right. God knows we will fail, because he's the only one who does everything right. He loves us and wants us to do something very important when we fail: ask for his help.

Jesus said that without him we "can do nothing" (John 15:5, NIV). Paul wrote that we can do everything through Jesus, because he makes us strong (Philippians 4:13).

Dear God, thank you for understanding that I will make mistakes. Thank you for helping me try again.

Thursday

Read "Hiding Places," page 148 in the *Day by Day Kid's Bible*. Or read this part of the story:

David was staying in the Ziph Desert. He found out that Saul was coming after him.

But Jonathan went to see David there. He said, "Don't be scared. Saul won't hurt you. You'll be the king of God's people." *1 Samuel 23:15-17*

THE TREE HOUSE was in the tallest tree of Corbin's yard. "Come on up," he called to his cousin Austin. When Austin looked up, the tree house seemed far away. And the thought of climbing the ladder made Austin's knees feel mushy. He wished he could just snap his fingers and be up there. He took a deep breath and started climbing, one rung at a time. Each rung brought him closer to the top. At last he was there.

Failure is like a rung on a ladder. Each time we fail, it brings us closer to the time when we can do it right.

In our reading today, Jonathan was telling David to cheer up. God had chosen David when he was just a boy to be king after Saul. But King Saul had chased David out of the land. David must have been tempted to think he had failed or God had failed. But every time Saul came to try and kill David, David was getting closer to being the king. God loved David, And David loved him. God and his love always win.

Dear God, help me to remember that whenever I fail, I am getting closer to the time when I'll do things right. Thank you that I can trust you to love me and help me.

Friday
Read "Good and Bad Days," page 264 in the *Day by Day Kid's Bible*. Or read this part of the story:

Be happy when days are good.
But think when days are bad.
God made both good and bad days. . . .

Try to be wise without being too hard on yourself.
But don't do too many wrong things. Don't be a fool. . . .

There's nobody on earth who always does right.
There's not one person who never sins. Ecclesiastes 7:14, 16-17, 20

REMEMBER WHAT SIN IS? It's missing the mark. It's not like making a mistake in spelling or playing the wrong note on the piano or not washing your hands before you eat. A sin is choosing to do something that hurts you or someone else. It might hurt someone's body or it might hurt a person's feelings. It is choosing not to act in a loving way.

But is there anyone who always does the loving thing, who never sins? No. Everybody fails by sinning sometimes. That's why we need Jesus.

Jesus did for us what we could not do for ourselves. He never failed to do the loving thing. And he died to take our punishment for the times we sin so that we can be free to try again to do what's right. That shows just how much God loves us.

Dear God, I'm sorry for the times when I have not acted in loving ways. Thank you for showing how much you love me by sending Jesus.

SOME THINGS YOU CAN DO THIS WEEK

Make a trick picture. Fold an index card in half, with the short edges together. Open it up again. On the left half, draw a cave with a big opening. On the right half, near the fold line, draw Elijah's face. Now hold the card with your arm stretched out in front of you, and look at the center fold line. Keep looking at it as you bring the card closer to your eyes. As you get closer, you will have to unfocus your eyes, but keep looking at the line. All at once, you will see Elijah in the cave. Remember that Elijah thought he had failed, but he hadn't. God can make things turn out all right.

Draw a desert scene on sandpaper with crayons. Then place it on some old newspaper on top of an ironing board. Lay a piece of waxed paper on top of the picture. Ask an adult to help you carefully place a hot iron over the waxed paper to melt the crayon onto the sandpaper. Remember that both Elijah and David hid in the desert, and it seemed like they had failed. But God had a plan for each of them, and they trusted God to make things right.

Make "heartwiches." Cut a flat square of cheese into a heart shape. (Use a heart-shaped cookie cutter if you have one.) Place this on top of a piece of bread and heat it under the broiler in your oven until the cheese starts to melt and bubble. As you eat your "heartwich," think about how much God loves you. He sent Jesus to die for your sins. Remember: God will never stop loving you.

Make an orange globe. Using a permanent marker with a sharp tip, draw the general shapes of the earth's land on a large orange. Then stick whole cloves into the orange to cover the inside of each shape that forms the land. The orange rind that still shows is where the oceans are. Let this dry to make an air freshener. It can remind you that as long as you stick with God, nothing in the world can make your life a failure. That's because God loves you, and his love always wins.

SUCCESS

It is not that we think we can do anything of lasting value by ourselves. Our only power and success come from God. 2 Corinthians 3:5, NLT

This week you will learn
· *what success is;*
· *what it means to be humble;*
· *who thought some men were gods;*
· *who was invited to have dinner with a queen.*

Monday

Read "A Friend, a Spear, and a Wife," page 140 in the *Day by Day Kid's Bible.* Or read this part of the story:

The army came back home after Goliath was killed. Women came out of all the towns on the way. They met King Saul and his men. They danced and sang happy songs. They played music and shook tambourines. "Saul killed thousands," they sang. "But David killed tens of thousands." *1 Samuel 18:6-7*

JESSICA WAS THE PITCHER on the girls' softball team. She pitched so well that she helped her team win most of their games. She was a success at pitching.

Success is doing something well. It is the opposite of failing. You're a success if you try something, and you do a great job of it. People may tell you how well you did. They may even clap for you or give you a prize.

In today's reading, David was a success. But success can be as hard to deal with as failure. When we succeed, we are tempted to think we are the best. We are tempted to brag and be boastful or prideful. But the truth is that

God has made us who we are. He has made us able to do what we do well. When we are tempted to feel prideful, we can fight temptation like Jesus did. We can say, "I will not be prideful, because God's Word says, 'Our only power and success come from God'" (2 Corinthians 3:5, NLT).

Dear God, whenever I do something well, I know it's you who made me able to do it. Help me to be humble and not prideful.

Tuesday

Read "The Groom," page 517 in the *Day by Day Kid's Bible.* Or read this part of the story:

John's followers went to John. "Remember the man you told us about? . . . Now everybody is going to him."

"A person has only what God gives him," said John. "I told you I'm not the Promised One. I was sent to make things ready for him. . . . Jesus has to become more and more important. I have to become less and less important." *John 3:26-28, 30*

JOHN WAS A BIG SUCCESS. Lots of people went to hear him teach and to be baptized by him. Then Jesus came along. John could have been tempted to be prideful, because he was there first. But John chose to be humble. He chose to admit that Jesus was the important one. Being *humble* is knowing that we are not the greatest. God is. And it's God who makes us able to do things well.

Did you know that Jesus is humble? Jesus, God's Son, left his place as king in heaven to become a human being, born into a poor family. He didn't strut around bragging about being God's Son and saying he was better than everyone else. Instead, he was a friend to poor people, sick people, and sinners. He did everything well. He was a success. But he showed us how to be humble.

Dear God, thank you for loving us enough to send your Son to the earth as a man. Thank you, Jesus, for not bragging, but for letting yourself be one of us. Help me to be humble like you.

Wednesday

Read "The Proud Prayer," page 587 in the *Day by Day Kid's Bible.* Or read this part of the story:

"Once there were two men," said Jesus. . . . "The leader stood up tall. He prayed about himself. 'God, thank you that I'm not like other men. . . . I don't sin. . . .'

"The tax man stood a little way off. He wouldn't even look up. . . . 'God, be kind to me,' he said. 'I'm a sinful person.'

"God forgave the tax man," said Jesus. . . .

"Some people think they're great. God will make those people feel like they're not important." *Luke 18:9-14*

ANTHONY WENT TO BASKETBALL CAMP. There were two coaches who worked with the boys. One coach told the boys he had played on a team that had won all its games. His team's game had been on television. He had been voted the best player. He showed the boys what they were doing wrong. Anthony felt clumsy next to that coach. He felt like a failure. But when the other coach worked with the boys, he told them what they were doing right. He smiled a lot and cheered them on when they made a mistake. With him, Anthony felt like a success. Later, Anthony found out that the second coach had been on the same winning team as the first coach. He just didn't brag about it.

People who brag about their success make themselves feel important. But they make others feel small. People who are humble about their success make others feel important.

Dear God, when I have success, help me to be humble and make others feel important.

Thursday

Read "People Who Wanted to Worship Paul," page 654 in the *Day by Day Kid's Bible.* Or read this part of the story:

A man in Lystra could not walk. . . .

Paul knew that the man believed he could get well. So Paul said, "Stand up on your feet!"

The man jumped up. He started walking!

The crowd saw this. They shouted, "The gods are here! They are in human bodies!" . . .

The people wanted to offer worship gifts to Paul and Barnabas.

Paul and Barnabas heard about this. They ran out to the crowd. "What are you doing?" they asked. "We are just people like you. . . . Worship the living God." *Acts 14:8-11, 13-15*

A GOD OF SUNLIGHT, a god of the sea, a god of love. The people Paul and Barnabas visited did not know there is just one God. They thought there were many gods. When Paul healed the man through Jesus' power, the people thought Paul was their main god. And because Barnabas was doing most of the talking, they thought he was their messenger god.

Paul and Barnabas could have taken the gifts and let the people worship them. They would have been famous and would have looked successful. But Paul and Barnabas knew that would not be right. They chose to be humble. They told the people that it is God who is important.

God wants us to be humble when we have success. But are we humble because it's a rule? No. We are humble because God has shown us that's the way life works best.

Dear God, I choose to be humble. Thank you for showing me how.

Friday

Read "Haman Brags" and "The King's Book," pages 479 and 480 in the *Day by Day Kid's Bible*. Or read this part of the story and find the rest of the story about Haman in your Bible (Esther 5:13–7:10):

Then Haman called his friends and his wife. He bragged about his riches. He bragged about how many sons he had. He bragged about how the king had made him great. He bragged about how important he was.

"That's not all," said Haman. "The queen asked the king to come to dinner. I'm the only other person she invited." *Esther 5:10-*

ANNA DIDN'T HAVE to go to school on Friday, even though everyone else did. Anna had made a clay map of her state and had won a state geography prize. So she got to go with her parents to a lunch for the prize-winning students. Television cameras were there, and that night Anna saw herself with her clay map on the TV news.

All her classmates had made history projects. Only Anna had won. Did that mean that everyone else failed? No. Just to finish a project is a success. Anna told her classmates that she wished everyone could have won. Anna was humble.

Is there anyone who is humble all the time? No. Everyone gets prideful sometimes. That's why we need Jesus. Jesus did for us what we could not do for ourselves. He was humble. And he died to take the punishment for all those times when we are prideful. Now we can feel free to try again and grow to be like Jesus.

Dear God, I'm sorry for times when I am prideful. Thank you for sending Jesus to take my punishment. Help me learn to be humble and more like Jesus.

SOME THINGS YOU CAN DO THIS WEEK

- **Make a photo frame.** On top of a plastic lid from a large margarine tub, and toward one side, draw a rectangle. Make it one inch wide and about three inches long. Cut along all the sides of the rectangle EXCEPT the line near the center of the lid. Fold the rectangle out along the uncut fold line. The lid is the photo frame and the rectangle is the stand that it leans on. On the other side of the lid, glue a photograph of yourself. You can decorate around the photo by gluing sequins or glitter to the frame, placing stickers on it, or coloring designs on it with permanent markers. Remember that it's God who makes you who you are and helps you have success.

- **Make a place mat** out of a large piece of paper or a piece of cloth. Color it with markers or crayons. Write across it, "Queen for a Day" or "King for a Day." Then use it as someone's place mat at dinnertime. Serve your special guest and clean up this person's dishes. You can put the place mat at someone else's place the next night or use it one night a week, if you want. Think about the man Queen Esther invited to dinner, and about how his bragging got him into trouble.

- **Make a hand puppet.** Hold your forearm up straight and bend your hand forward at the wrist, fingers and thumb straight out and together. Now place your thumb underneath your fingers. Move your thumb up and down so that it looks like a mouth opening and closing. This is the head of your puppet. Your arm is its neck. Show what position his head should be in if he were a proud person. Show what position his head would be in if he were a humble person. Remember how different the prayers of the proud man and the humble man were.

- **Make a blue ribbon.** At fairs, there are contests with judges who decide who made the best pie, who painted the best picture, which cow is the best, and so on. The winner is often given a blue ribbon. Get a small blue or white picnic plate. In the center, write "God's love wins." If the plate is white, color it blue. Cut two strips of white or blue paper to hang down from the lower edge of the plate when it is hung on a wall or door. If the paper is white, color it blue. Let this blue ribbon remind you that no matter what happens, you win if you stick with God, because he loves you, and God's love always wins.

SYMPATHY

Rejoice with those who rejoice; mourn with those who mourn. Romans 12:15, NIV

This week you will learn
· *what sympathy means;*
· *what it means to mourn and to rejoice;*
· *why a family got yelled at;*
· *how Jesus felt about some people who followed him for three days.*

Monday

Read "Getting a Son Back," page 537 in the *Day by Day Kid's Bible*. Or read this part of the story:

Jesus saw the dead man's mother. "Don't cry," he said. His heart was very sad for her.

Jesus touched the long box that held the body. The people who were carrying it stood still.

Jesus said, "Young man, get up."

The man who had been dead sat up. He began to talk. So Jesus gave him back to his mother. He was alive! *Luke 7:12-15*

SYMPATHY IS SHARING another person's feelings. People who don't share the feelings of others could be called uncaring. They don't care about how other people feel.

In today's reading, Jesus showed sympathy for the mother whose son had died. His heart was sad for her. He did what the verse for this week says. He mourned with the mother who mourned.

To *mourn* means to show your sadness. To *rejoice* means to show your joy. Both mourning and rejoicing happened in today's reading.

When we are tempted not to care about other people's feelings, we can fight temptation like Jesus did. We can say, "I will have sympathy, because God's Word says, 'Rejoice with those who rejoice; mourn with those who mourn'" (Romans 12:15, NIV).

Dear God, sometimes I don't care about other people's feelings. Help me to care. Help me to have sympathy.

Tuesday

Read "A Wedding Party," page 515 in the *Day by Day Kid's Bible.* Or read this part of the story:

Two days later, there was a wedding in Galilee. . . .

But the people who were having the party ran out of wine. So Jesus' mother went to him. "They're out of wine!" she said. . . .

"Fill those jars with water," Jesus told the servants. . . .

The servants did just what Jesus said.

The man in charge took a drink. He didn't know it had been water. That's because it had turned into wine! *John 2:1-3, 7-9*

LINDSEY WENT TO her aunt's wedding. Afterward there was a party with singing and dancing and laughing. One table was full of fancy food. Another table had plates of cake. And a long table held lots of coffee pots and tea pots and two big punch bowls. When there wasn't much punch left, the ladies who were serving went to the kitchen and brought out more. What if they had run out of drinks? The ladies would have been upset, just like Jesus' mother, Mary, was.

Mary had sympathy. It was not her wedding party, but she felt bad for the people who had run out of wine. Jesus had sympathy too. He not only felt bad for them, but he also did something about it.

It's not always possible for us to solve other people's problems, but we can let them know that we feel what they feel. People like to know that we're trying to understand their feelings.

Dear God, thank you for having sympathy for me. Help me to have sympathy for others and show them what you are like.

Wednesday

Read "Things to Do," page 234 in the *Day by Day Kid's Bible*. Or read this part of the story:

> *Some people make fun of others.*
> *If you tell them they're wrong, they'll make fun of you. . . .*
>
> *A wise child listens to what his father says.*
> *But a person who laughs at others doesn't listen. . . .*
>
> *Don't talk to foolish people. They'll make fun of the wise things*
>   *you say.*
> Proverbs 9:7; 13:1; 23:9

HAS ANYONE EVER made fun of you, not caring about your feelings? How did that make you feel? Have you ever made fun of someone else, not caring about their feelings?

Plenty of people have had their feelings hurt when others made fun of them. Life does not work best that way. That's why God wants us to have sympathy, to be happy for people who are happy and to be sad for people who are sad. When we do that, everyone works together better and plays together better. We can be at peace with each other.

Does anyone have sympathy all the time? No. All of us have times when we stop caring about others' feelings. That's why we need Jesus. Jesus did for us what we could not do for ourselves. He always cared about other people's feelings. And he died to take our punishment for the times when we don't care about others. That shows just how much God loves us.

Dear God, I'm sorry for times when I don't care about others' feelings. Thank you for showing how much you love me by sending Jesus to forgive me. Help me to have sympathy.

Thursday

Read "Seven Rolls," page 562 in the *Day by Day Kid's Bible.* Or read this part of the story:

The crowd around Jesus hadn't had anything to eat. So Jesus called his friends to him.

"I feel sorry for these people," said Jesus. "They've been with me for three days. They don't have anything left to eat. Many of them came a long way to get here. They'll get hungry if I send them home. They might be too weak to get home." *Matthew 15:32*

A FAMILY MOVED to the United States from another country, where they were in danger. They came to America to be safe and find jobs. They had to go to a special office to get green cards so they could work here. Since they could not speak English very well, an American friend went with them. But the clerks at the office would not let the family be helped together at one window. Then the clerks yelled at the family. The clerks even yelled at the American friend who was there to help.

The clerks were uncaring. They did not have sympathy. Many people went home sad and angry that day. Life does not work well when people are uncaring.

Jesus had sympathy for people. He shows us how to rejoice when others rejoice and mourn when others mourn. He wants to help us understand how other people are feeling.

Dear God, thank you for showing me how life works best. Help me to have sympathy.

Friday

Read "Jesus' Brothers and Sisters," page 780 in the *Day by Day Kid's Bible*. Or read this part of the story:

Jesus had to become human like us. That's so he could understand us. Now he can tell God what it's like to be human.

It hurt Jesus to have sins come to his mind. He had to say no to sin. Sins come to our minds too. But Jesus knows what that's like, so he can help us. *Hebrews 2:17-18*

JUAN WAS TRYING to tell his friend Matt why Jesus came from heaven to become a man on earth. Juan pointed to some ants crawling in a line down the sidewalk. "What if you wanted to give a message to those ants?" said Juan. "How could you do it?" Matt got down on his hands and knees and watched the ants crawl toward an anthill. "I guess I would have to turn into an ant and talk ant language," said Matt.

God had a very important message to give us: "I love you and want to be with you so much that I will become like you. I will live like you. I'll keep all the moral laws for you. And I'll show you just how much I love you by dying for your sins. I'll trade places with you, taking your sins and giving you my sinless life." God knows what it's like to be human, because his Son, Jesus, came to earth as a man. God is sympathetic with us.

Dear God, thank you for your understanding and sympathy. Help me to be sympathetic with others.

SOME THINGS YOU CAN DO THIS WEEK

● **Make chocolate sugar cookies.** Mix two-thirds cup brown sugar, one-third cup of white sugar, four tablespoons of softened margarine, one teaspoon of vanilla, and two eggs. In another bowl, mix three-fourths cup of cocoa, three-fourths cup of flour, and a pinch of salt. Mix this into the sugar mixture. Chill the dough for one hour. Roll dough into one-inch balls, place on a baking sheet, and bake for 14 to 15 minutes at 350 degrees. After you take the cookies out of the oven, while they are still soft and hot, gently press small colored candies (like Red Hots or M&M's) onto each cookie to make two eyes and a smile. Think about people you can rejoice with and people you can mourn with.

● **Make balloon heads.** Inflate balloons. Mix flour and water until it looks and feels like thick paste. Tear old newspapers into strips. Dip the strips, one at a time, into the flour paste. Gently pull the strip between your thumb and forefinger. Some of the paste will drip off. Lay the strip across the balloon. Keep adding strips of dipped paper onto the balloon until the whole balloon is covered. You can even mold a nose, eyebrows, eyes, and ears onto it. Let the covered balloon dry completely. Then stick a straight pin into the bottom to pop the balloon. The popped balloon doesn't need to come out, but you can pull it out the bottom if you want. Make several balloon heads and paint them to show different feelings. Have you ever felt these ways? Who has sympathy with you?

● **Make smiling and frowning "masks."** Draw a large *U* shape on a piece of construction paper. Draw a line across the top of the *U* to close the shape in. Do the same thing on another large piece of construction paper. Then cut these shapes out. Fold the shapes down the middle from top to bottom. About one-half inch from the fold and about halfway down from the top, place a quarter and trace around it. Halfway between this circle and the bottom rounded edge of the folded *U* shape, make a curved line for half of a smile, starting at the fold and going up toward the circle. This is the top lip. About one-half inch below that, make the bottom lip curving up to meet the top one at the corner. Cut through the fold and through both layers of paper to make the mouth. Cut the circle through both layers to make the eyes. Then open the "mask." For the other mask, make the eye a half circle with a line straight across the bottom, and curve the mouth lines down to make a frown. These "masks" can help you remember to rejoice with those who rejoice and mourn with those who mourn.

Make an ant farm. Put a rock or block of wood in the middle of a jar. Put dirt around it. Find an anthill or ant hole. Sometimes these are under rocks or leaves or wood. Dig into it, looking for ants and their eggs (tiny and white) and the queen ant, which is larger than the rest. Put these into the jar and cover the jar with a square of nylon cut from your mom's old hose. Put a rubber band around this to keep the cover on. Put the jar in a dark place and leave it for a few days. Then look to see if the ants have made tunnels. You can then set your ants free outdoors. If you want to keep them, you'll need to feed them with bits of food. If you didn't get the queen ant, you'll need to let them go, because they'll die if they go too long without her. As you watch the ants, remember how you'd have to become one of them to talk to them. God became one of us when his Son, Jesus, came to earth to let us know how much he loves us.

BEING THOUGHTFUL

Each of you should look not only to your own interests,
but also to the interests of others. Philippians 2:4, NIV

This week you will learn
· what thoughtful means;
· what happened to a lost ax;
· what a king did for a lame man;
· who always thinks about you.

Monday

Read "An Ax on the Water," page 298 in the *Day by Day Kid's Bible*. Or read this part of the story:

The sharp iron top of one man's ax fell off. It fell into the river. "Oh no!" cried the man. "That's not my ax! It belongs to someone else!"

"Where did it go?" asked Elisha.

The man showed Elisha where it fell into the water.

Elisha cut a stick. He threw the stick into the water. . . .

Then the heavy iron top of the ax came up. *2 Kings 6:5-6*

TWO PEOPLE WERE thoughtful in today's reading. A thought is something you think. So being *thoughtful* means taking the time to think about what other people need and about what they are interested in.

The man who lost the top of his ax was thoughtful. He didn't just say, "Oh well, the ax wasn't mine anyway, so it doesn't matter." He wanted to give it back to the person it belonged to.

Elisha was thoughtful. He didn't say, "It's not my problem." Elisha knew the man was interested in getting the ax back. He knew he could do something about that problem, and he did.

When we are tempted to not be thoughtful, we can fight temptation like Jesus did. We can say, "I will be thoughtful, because God's Word says, 'Each of you should look not only to your own interests, but also to the interests of others'" (Philippians 2:4, NIV).

Dear God, help me to be thoughtful toward others.

Tuesday

Read "Jonathan's Son," page 164 in the *Day by Day Kid's Bible.* Or read this part of the story:

"Is anybody from Saul's family still alive?" asked David. "Is there someone I can be kind to because of Jonathan?"

"There is Jonathan's son," the servant [from Saul's family] said. "He can't walk." . . .

So David sent for Jonathan's son. . . .

"Your father, Jonathan, was my best friend. I'll give you all the land that Saul, your grandfather, owned. I'll always let you eat at my table." *2 Samuel 9:2-3, 5, 7*

DAVID HAD A GOOD REASON not to be thoughtful to anyone from Saul's family. Do you remember why? Saul had tried to kill David. Saul had chased David and hunted him down. Anyone in Saul's family might say, "I should be king, not David." But David chose to be thoughtful and looked "to the interests of others." He knew that life works best that way. And when David was kind to Jonathan's son, he helped bring peace.

Remember that God's plan is to bless us so we can bless others. One way God blesses us is by being thoughtful toward us. God is thoughtful about what we need and what we are interested in. So we can be thoughtful toward others too. We can be thoughtful about what they need and about what they are interested in. When we are thoughtful toward others, we show them what God is like.

Dear God, thank you for being thoughtful toward me. Show me how to be thoughtful to others.

Wednesday

Read "A Camel and a Needle," page 591 in the *Day by Day Kid's Bible*. Or read this part of the story:

People started bringing little children to Jesus. They wanted Jesus to touch them and pray for them. But Jesus' friends got mad at the people.

Jesus saw this, and he was upset. He said, "Let the little children come to me. Don't stop them." *Mark 10:13-14*

) ✳) ✳) ✳) ✳) ✳

AT THE MALL, there was one store where Anika didn't feel welcome. It was a store that had fancy plates and glass figures and pottery dishes. The sales lady at that store always frowned when Anika came in, as if she thought Anika might break something. But there was another store where Anika felt welcome. It was a place that sold gifts, but there was a corner that had a child-sized couch and chair and some books and games on a shelf. That store owner was thoughtful toward children. He thought about what they need and what they are interested in.

Today's reading shows us that Jesus was thoughtful to children. He still is. He thinks about what you need and what you are interested in. He doesn't say, "Wait until you're grown up, and then you'll be important to me." You are important to Jesus right now.

Is it easy for you to be thoughtful to children who are younger than you are? Think of some ways you can be thoughtful to younger children, to children your age, and to adults.

Dear God, I choose to be thoughtful. Show me how.

Thursday

Read "The Neighbor," page 578 in the *Day by Day Kid's Bible*. Or read this part of the story:

There once was a man who was on a trip. He was going from Jerusalem to Jericho. But robbers jumped out at him. They took his clothes. They beat him. Then they left. There the man was, lying by the road. He was half dead.

Soon a priest came down the road. He saw the hurt man. But he moved to the other side of the road. He just passed by. *Luke 10:30-*

ALEC, EMILY, AND PAIGE lived next door to Mrs. Camp, who was 90 years old. Most of the time another lady spent the day with Mrs. Camp. But one afternoon, Mrs. Camp phoned saying that the other lady couldn't come that day. She wondered if Alec or Emily or Paige might walk out to her mailbox and bring in her mail. When Mom asked who would get the mail for Mrs. Camp, Alec said, "I can't. I'm supposed to be at Ryan's house in five minutes to play ball."

Emily said, "I can't. I'm in the middle of my math homework."

Paige had her arms full of dirty clothes she was taking to the washing machine. "I'll go," said Paige. She set the clothes on the washer and ran out to get Mrs. Camp's mail.

Who was most thoughtful to Mrs. Camp? Paige thought about what Mrs. Camp needed and was interested in.

Are we thoughtful because it's a rule? No. We are thoughtful because God has shown us that's the way life works best.

Dear God, thank you for showing us how life works best. Help me to be thoughtful.

Friday

Read "You're Out of Your Mind!" page 727 in the *Day by Day Kid's Bible*. Or read this part of the story:

Then Festus shouted, "You're out of your mind, Paul! You've learned so much, your mind is gone!"

"I'm not out of my mind," said Paul. "I'm telling the truth. It makes sense." *Acts 26:24-25*

FESTUS CHOSE to speak rudely to Paul. But when Paul answered, he was thoughtful. He chose to speak kindly. What would have happened if Paul had spoken rudely back to Festus? Maybe they would have gotten into a big argument or a fight. Festus would have been even more angry at Paul. But when Paul was thoughtful about what he said, he helped make things more peaceful.

King Solomon once wrote, "A kind word will take away anger. But a mean word will bring anger" (Proverbs 15:1, DBD). It's not easy to be thoughtful toward people who are being rude to you. But that's what Paul did.

Is there anyone who is thoughtful all the time? No. We all have times when we are not thoughtful. That's why we need Jesus. Jesus did for us what we could not do for ourselves. He was always thoughtful. And he died to take our punishment for the times when we are not thoughtful. That shows just how much God loves us. Now we can feel free to try again and grow to be like Jesus.

Dear God, I'm sorry for times when I have not been thoughtful. Thank you for showing how much you love me by sending Jesus to forgive me. Help me to be thoughtful.

SOME THINGS YOU CAN DO THIS WEEK

* **Learn about first aid.** Find out how to help if someone gets cut or has a nosebleed or gets hurt in other ways. Read about first aid in a book, look up "First Aid" in an encyclopedia, or check it out on the Internet. Think about the story Jesus told of the traveler who was hurt by robbers. The man who finally helped him gave him first aid.

* **Go for a "trash walk."** Walk around your neighborhood with a friend. Take a trash bag with you and pick up any trash you find on your walk. Why is this a thoughtful thing to do?

* **Make a card to send to someone.** Think of a person who needs to be cheered up or someone who would be interested in hearing from you. Fold a piece of paper in half and write on the front, "Thinking of You." Draw a picture on the card and write a note inside. Mail it to the person you thought of.

* **Make a strawberry-banana smoothie.** Serve it to a friend or family member. For each serving of this drink, you will need six ounces of pineapple juice, one eight-ounce container of strawberry yogurt, and one sliced ripe banana. Mix these in a blender and pour into a glass. Serve it to someone. Is it easier to be thoughtful to someone you think deserves it or to someone you think doesn't deserve it? Why?

WILLINGNESS

Make me willing to obey you. Psalm 51:12, NLT

This week you will learn
· *what it means to be willing and what it means to be stubborn;*
· *how to fight the temptation to be stubborn;*
· *how a person can be like play dough;*
· *how a person can be like a mule.*

Monday

Read "The Angel at the Barn," page 182 in the *Day by Day Kid's Bible.* Or read this part of the story:

The angel was standing at a farmer's work place. David looked up and saw the angel. . . .

The farmer was working. His four sons were with him. He turned around. He and his sons saw the angel too. . . .

David said, "Sell me your work place. I want to build an altar to God here. . . ."

"Take my barn for free," said the farmer. . . .

"No," said King David. "I'll pay you for it. I won't take something that's yours and give it to God. I won't give God something that cost me nothing." *1 Chronicles 21:15-16, 20-24*

WILLINGNESS IS BEING READY and willing to do something if you are asked to do it or if you need to do it. It's saying, "I will." *Stubbornness* is choosing not to do something no matter how many times you are asked and no matter how much you need to do it.

The farmer was willing to give his barn to David for free. David ended up paying for it, but the farmer was willing to give it to him.

In a family, people need to be willing and ready to do many things. What are some things you are willing to do in your family if you need to?

When we are tempted to be stubborn, we can fight that temptation like Jesus did by saying, "I will not be stubborn, because it is written, 'Make me willing to obey you'" (Psalm 51:12, NLT).

Dear God, sometimes I am stubborn. I'm sorry, God. Please help me to be willing to do what's right.

Tuesday

Read "The Big Gift," page 699 in the *Day by Day Kid's Bible*. Or read this part of the story:

You're ready to help. I've been bragging about it to the people in Macedonia. I told them you've been ready to give for a year. They know you want to give, so most of them are giving too. . . .

People should give because they want to, not because they have to. God loves people who are happy to give. *2 Corinthians 9:2, 7*

A WILLING HEART is a heart that is open to God. A stubborn heart is a heart that is closed to God. The people in the reading today were willing to give money to people who needed it. When other people saw that they were willing to give, the others decided to give too.

If you are willing to follow God, other people may be willing to follow God too. That can happen in a family where there are younger brothers and sisters. Sometimes when you say, "I'll help set the table," your younger brother or sister copies you. That child becomes willing to help too.

Dear God, give me a willing heart.

Wednesday

Read "On the Worship Day," page 528 in the *Day by Day Kid's Bible.* Or read this part of the story:

There was a man in the worship house. His right hand was small and twisted. . . .

"Stand up in front of everyone," said Jesus. Then Jesus turned to the people. "Should we do good or bad on the worship day? . . ."

Nobody answered. The people were all quiet.

Jesus looked around. He was very upset because their hearts were hard. They didn't care about God. *Mark 3:1, 3-5*

STEVEN POPPED THE RED COVER off the can of play dough and tried to pull it out. He groaned.

"What's wrong?" asked Will.

"The play dough is dried out. It's hard. We can't make anything out of this old dough," said Steven.

Stubborn people are like hard play dough. They are not easy to work with. They are not ready to do what God wants. That's why we might say a stubborn person's heart is hard. Jesus could tell that the people at the worship house had hard hearts. They didn't want Jesus to heal the sick man on a worship day. But a willing person is like soft play dough. God can do a lot with willing people, because they are ready to do what God wants. That's the way life works best.

Dear God, thank you for showing us how life works best. Help me to be willing to do right.

Thursday

Read "A Judge and a New Jewish Teacher," page 673 in the *Day by Day Kid's Bible*. Or read this part of the story:

While Paul was traveling, a man named Apollos went to Ephesus. He was Jewish. He was very smart. He knew God's Word well. Apollos told people about Jesus. But he only knew about baptizing like John did.

Apollos talked in the town's worship house. Aquila and Priscilla heard him. They asked him to come home with them. They taught him more about Jesus. *Acts 18:23-26*

AS STUBBORN AS A MULE. That's what people used to call someone who was not willing to cooperate. When a mule doesn't want to move, he sits down and pulls away from the person who is trying to pull him forward. He won't budge. King David wrote, "Do not be like the horse or the mule, which have no understanding but must be controlled by bit and bridle or they will not come to you" (Psalm 32:9, NIV).

Sometimes it's hard for smart people to be willing to learn. But Apollos was willing to let Aquila and Priscilla teach him. And that's just what Aquila and Priscilla were willing to do. It is not always easy to be willing to do what's right. When is it hardest for you to be willing?

Dear God, I choose to be willing to learn. And I choose to be willing to do what's right.

Friday

Read "People from Everywhere," page 523 in the *Day by Day Kid's Bible.* Or read this part of the story:

One day a man with a skin sickness came to Jesus. "You can make me well if you want to," he said.

Jesus felt kind and caring toward this man. So Jesus touched him. "I do want to," said Jesus. "Be well."

Right away the sickness went away. The man was well.
Mark 1:40-42

IS ANYONE WILLING to do right all the time? No. We all have times when we are stubborn. That's why we need Jesus. Jesus did for us what we could not do for ourselves. He was willing to do right.

"If you want to, you can heal me," said the sick man. That meant, "If you are willing." What did Jesus answer? "I do want to." That meant, "I am willing."

Jesus was willing to come to earth and be a human being. He was willing to die to take our punishment for the times when we are stubborn, not willing to do right. That shows just how much God loves us. Now we can feel free to try again and grow to be like Jesus.

Dear God, I'm sorry for the times when I have been stubborn. Thank you for showing how much you love me by sending Jesus to forgive me. Help me to be willing to do what's right.

SOME THINGS YOU CAN DO THIS WEEK

* **Make a heart necklace.** Use homemade or canned play dough to make the shape of a heart. (To make play dough, mix one part salt, one part water, and three parts flour.) After you make the heart shape, use a drinking straw to poke a hole through the top center of the heart. Let the heart dry. Then thread a string or ribbon through the hole to make a necklace. Let it remind you to have a willing heart, ready to obey God.

* **Do without your thumb.** Ask someone to tape the thumb of your right hand to your right palm with bandage tape. Or ask this person to tie a bandanna around your hand to keep your thumb close to your palm. If you are left-handed, do this with your left hand. Now try to go through your normal activities without using your thumb. What is it like? Remember the man whose hand was twisted. The rulers were not willing to let Jesus heal him. But Jesus was willing.

* **Make a pencil holder.** Use an empty vegetable can. Cut pages out of a magazine. Cut the pages up so that they are about six inches wide. Roll each page into a small roll around a pencil. Tape the end of the paper to keep it rolled. Slide the pencil out. Ask an adult to supervise as you hot glue the roll of paper vertically to the outside of the can. Keep making and gluing rolls of paper to the can, side by side, until it's covered with these colorful columns and ready to hold your pencils. What other supplies do you use when you learn? Willing people are ready to learn whatever they need to learn.

* **Mark up a paper.** Take a piece of black construction paper outdoors. Gather some rocks and try to make marks on the paper with each rock. Can you find any rocks that make marks? The softer the stone is, the easier it marks. You can also make marks on white paper with pencils. Soft lead makes dark, thick lines. Have you ever heard people call a stubborn person "hardheaded"? Remember that the softer and more willing you are, the easier it is for God to use you to help do his work.

SELFLESSNESS

Don't be selfish; don't live to make a good impression on others.
Philippians 2:3, NLT

This week you will learn
· what it means to be selfless;
· how to fight the temptation to be selfish;
· about a selfless young lady who left almost everything behind;
· about the greatest, most selfless king ever.

Monday

Read "Lazarus and the Rich Man," page 585 in the *Day by Day Kid's Bible.* Or read this part of the story:

"Once there was a rich man," said Jesus. . . . A beggar man named Lazarus sat at his gate. . . . Little bits of food fell off the rich man's table. Lazarus would have loved to eat those bits. One day, Lazarus died. Angels came and got him. . . .

"Sometime later, the rich man also died. But he went to hell. He felt terrible there. He hurt all over. The rich man . . . cried. '. . . All this fire is too much for me!'

"But Abraham said, 'Remember the way you lived? You got your good things on earth. Lazarus got bad things. But now he is feeling good and you're not.'" *Luke 16:19-25*

"I GET TO SIT way in the back!" called Whitney, running past her sister. She climbed into the van and made her way to the backseat. Pepper, Aunt Jo's big shaggy dog, jumped in beside her. Then her cousins piled in, and her sister ended up in the front seat. It was a hot day, and they were going across town to the swimming pool. Whitney began to get hot. Pepper lay his head in her lap and made her hotter. But Whitney's sister was sitting in the front seat with the cold air blowing on her. Aunt Jo called back, "I'm sorry, but the air conditioning doesn't reach all the way to the back." Whitney had thought she was getting the best seat. She knew in her heart that she had been selfish.

The opposite of being selfish is being *selfless.* That's doing what is best for others, even if it's not what you really want to do. When we are tempted to be selfish, we can fight temptation like Jesus did by saying, "I will not be self-ish, because God's Word says, 'Don't be selfish; don't live to make a good impression on others'" (Philippians 2:3, NLT).

Dear God, sometimes I am selfish. Help me to be selfless instead.

Tuesday

Read "The Man Whose Name Means 'Fool,'" page 151 in the *Day by Day Kid's Bible.* Or read this part of the story:

[David] sent 10 young men to Nabal. David said, "Tell Nabal hello for me. Tell him we pray for good things for him and his family. Then tell him that his shepherds were with us for a while. We were good to them. He can ask them about it. Then ask Nabal to give us whatever he can."

So David's men went to Nabal. They told him what David had said.

"Who is David?" said Nabal. ". . . Why should I give bread and water to him?" *1 Samuel 25:5-11*

DAVID'S MEN HAD BEEN selfless. They had kept Nabal's men safe. Now David's men needed food. But Nabal was not selfless. He was selfish. Do you think it would be easy for David to be kind to Nabal now?

Is it easier or harder to be selfless toward a person who has been selfish to you? Most of the time, we want to treat people the way they treat us. But the Bible says, "If your enemy is hungry, feed him; if he is thirsty, give him something to drink" (Romans 12:20, NIV). That's doing what Jesus said to do: He said we should love our enemies and do good things for those who treat us badly. (See Luke 6:27.) So being selfless, even to people who are selfish toward us, is part of loving the way that God loves. And remember: God's love always wins.

Dear God, help me to be selfless toward others, even if they have been selfish toward me.

Wednesday

Read "Who Is the Greatest?" page 567 in the *Day by Day Kid's Bible.* Or read this part of the story:

Jesus and his friends were walking down the road. His friends began fussing with each other . . . over who was the greatest.

Jesus sat down. "Do you want to be first?" he asked. "Then make yourself last. Serve others." *Mark 9:33-35*

"TOMORROW IS THE BIRTHDAY of the most important person in our school," said the third-grade teacher, Mrs. Carr. Rose said she would bring balloons, and Mei Ling promised to bring cake. Jacob said everyone should make cards for the principal.

"But it's not the principal's birthday," said Mrs. Carr. Bradley wondered if it was the coach, and Philip asked if it was the art teacher. Mrs. Carr shook her head. "It's Mr. Peebles, the janitor," she said. "He unlocks the school doors in the morning. He cleans the classrooms and halls and restrooms. He makes sure the lights and heater and water fountains work. What would we do without him?" Mei Ling and her friends thought about what their teacher said and decided that Mr. Peebles really was the most important.

Can you think of people you know who serve others? They are selfless. They work to help other people, even though few people notice them. What could you do to let a selfless person know you are thankful for what he or she does?

Dear God, thank you for people who are selfless. Help me to learn to be self-less and serve others.

Thursday

Read "Going Home," page 111 in the *Day by Day Kid's Bible.* Or read this part of the story:

When Naomi's sons were old enough, they got married. One married a young woman named Orpah. One married a young woman named Ruth. But about 10 years later, both of Naomi's sons died. . . .

One day Naomi heard there was food in Judah. . . .

Naomi kissed Orpah and Ruth good-bye. . . .

Orpah kissed Naomi . . . and went home. . . .

"Don't tell me to leave you," said Ruth. "I'll go where you go. I'll stay where you stay. Your people will become my people. Your God will be my God. . . . I won't leave you as long as I live." *Ruth 1:4-6, 9, 14, 16-17*

FRIDAY NIGHT WAS FUN NIGHT in Carter's family. Each week a different person chose what to do for the night. Dad asked Carter, "What do you want to do this Friday?" Carter thought a minute. He wanted to go see a movie. He knew, though, that his dad had forgotten it was little Mike's turn to choose. But Mike always chose putt-putt golf. Carter thought he would pretend he forgot that it was Mike's turn too. Then they could go to the movie anyway. Carter scratched his head. Finally he said, "It's Mike's turn. We'd better ask him." Carter had a choice, and he made the selfless choice.

What choices did Ruth have? Ruth was selfless to leave her people and go with Naomi. You can read more in the book of Ruth to find out how Ruth served Naomi.

Are we selfless because it's a rule? No. We are selfless because God has shown us that's the way life works best.

Dear God, thank you for showing us how life works best. Help me to be selfless.

Friday

Read "To Sit at Your Right Hand," page 592 in the *Day by Day Kid's Bible.* Or read this part of the story:

"You know, the world's rulers boss everyone around. They tell everyone what to do. But you're not supposed to act like that. Instead, if you want to be great, you'll serve people," said Jesus. "Anybody wanting to be first has to be a servant. Even I didn't come to earth to be served. I came to serve. I came to give up my life. Then I can set people free from sin." *Matthew 20:25-28*

BEFORE A KING EVER RULED over God's people, the prophet Samuel told them what a king would be like. He said a king would have servants to take care of his chariots and horses. Servants would plow the king's ground and gather his harvest, make his swords, make perfume, and cook his meals. A king's servants would clean his palace, play music for him, and fan him when he got hot.

Jesus is the King of kings. He is the Son of God, the great King who sits on the throne in heaven. God could have been selfish and said, "There's no way I'm going to send my Son to the earth to be laughed at and beaten and killed." Jesus could have said, "I'm not going to go to earth just so people can make fun of me and hurt me." But Jesus was selfless. He did for us what we could not do for ourselves: He lived a life of selfless, perfect love. Then he died to take our punishment for the times when we are selfish. Now we can feel free to try again and grow to be like Jesus. That shows just how much God loves us.

Dear God, I'm sorry for times when I am selfish. Thank you for showing how much you love me by sending your Son, Jesus, to forgive me. Help me to be selfless.

SOME THINGS YOU CAN DO THIS WEEK

- **Make raisin cakes.** With the help of an adult, heat one-fourth cup of sugar, one tablespoon of cornstarch, one cup of water, and two cups of raisins in a pan on the stove. When this mixture is thick, take it off the stove and let it cool. Now mix one-half cup of softened margarine and one cup of brown sugar. In another bowl, mix one and a half cups of flour, one-half teaspoon of baking soda, and one-half teaspoon of salt. Add this flour mixture to the margarine mixture. Now stir in one and a half cup of oats and one tablespoon of water. Press half of this dough into a 13-inch by 9-inch baking pan. Spread the raisin mixture over it. Then spread the other half of the dough on top. Bake it at 350 degrees for 35 minutes. Read the whole story of David and Naboth to find out why raisin cakes showed that someone was selfless.

- **Play "Pack My Bag."** Ask friends or family to sit in a circle with you. Choose one person to start by saying, "I'm going to (a place that starts with the letter *A*) and I'm going to pack an (a thing that starts with the letter *A*)." The next person says the same, except she names a place and thing that start with *B*. Continue this way with each person naming a place and thing that starts with the next letter of the alphabet. If you, like Ruth, were moving to a new place, what is the one thing you would want to take with you?

- **Play balloon volleyball.** You'll need to play with at least one other person. Stretch a string or clothesline across a room or yard, about five feet off the ground. You can make it higher or lower if you wish. And you may use a volleyball net or badminton net instead. Blow up a large balloon. Bat it back and forth across the string or net, playing volleyball with the balloon. You may want to have some extra balloons handy in case the first one pops. Is it possible to be selfless in sports? If so, how? If not, why not?

◗ **Make hand shadows.** Shine a bright light onto a wall and try to make a king. One hand can be the king's head. Use the fingers on the other hand to make the crown. Try a paper plate shadow to make the king's head. What other objects could you try? If a friend is with you, use your friend's hands to help you. Remember how the greatest King came to earth to be a selfless servant and to die for your sins. He never stopped being King. He sits on a throne in heaven even now.

ACCEPTING THOSE WHO ARE DIFFERENT

Accept one another, then, just as Christ accepted you,
in order to bring praise to God. Romans 15:7, NIV

This week you will learn

· *how to fight the temptation to reject someone who is different;*
· *about someone who tried to accept all people;*
· *about someone who felt like an outsider;*
· *about a man who didn't eat for three days and three nights.*

Monday

Read "Making People Well," page 561 in the *Day by Day Kid's Bible.* Or read this part of the story:

Jesus went to a town called Tyre. . . .

A woman who was not Jewish lived near there. She came to Jesus. She cried, "Lord, be kind to me! Bad spirits control my daughter!" . . .

Then Jesus said, "You have a lot of faith. I'll give you what you asked for."

At that very moment, her daughter got well. . . .

Big crowds of people came to Jesus. . . . Jesus made them well.
Matthew 15:21-22, 28, 30

ACCEPTING OTHERS MEANS being kind to others, treating them as important people. Rejecting others means ignoring them or making fun of them.

In Bible times, Jewish people rejected people who were not Jewish. But Jesus healed the daughter of the woman from Tyre, even though she was not Jewish.

Some people are tempted to reject a person who is blind or who has another handicap. Why? If you are handicapped, are you tempted to reject other people? Why or why not? When you are tempted to reject someone, you can fight temptation like Jesus did. You can say: "I will not reject others, because God's Word says, 'Accept one another, then, just as Christ accepted you, in order to bring praise to God'" (Romans 15:7, NIV). How can you make others feel accepted?

Dear God, sometimes I reject people. Help me to be like Jesus and accept others.

Tuesday

Read "Let the Ox Eat," page 682 in the *Day by Day Kid's Bible.* Or read this part of the story:

I [Paul] became like a Jew to help Jews believe in Jesus. I became like a person who follows the Law. I did it to help Law followers believe in Jesus. I became like a person who doesn't follow the Law. That way, I could help people who don't follow the Law. I could help them believe in Jesus. I became weak. I did it to help weak people believe in Jesus.

I have become all things to all people. That way, I have the best chance to save some people. *1 Corinthians 9:20-23*

DO YOU KNOW what a clique (CLICK) is? It's a group of people who are friends only with the people in their group. Maybe they are all on the soccer team. Or they all like to wear the same kind of clothes. Or they all like to listen to a certain kind of music. They don't want to let anyone else be in their group of friends. If a new student joins their class, the new student has a hard time making friends with anyone in the clique.

In the reading for today, Paul was saying that he was not in any clique. He was friends with weak people and strong people, Jewish people and people who were not Jews. He did not reject anyone, because Jesus does not reject anyone.

We love because God first loved us (see 1 John 4:19). Part of loving others is accepting them. We accept others because God first accepted us. When we accept others, we show what God is like.

Dear God, thank you for accepting me. Help me to accept others and show them what you are like.

Wednesday

Read "Animals in a Big Sheet," page 646 in the *Day by Day Kid's Bible.* Or read this part of the story:

There was a Roman army captain named Cornelius. . . .

Peter went to see Cornelius at his house. . . . Cornelius had asked his family and some good friends to come over.

Peter began to talk to them. "You know the law of Jewish people. We're not supposed to visit someone who is not Jewish. But God showed me that it's all right with him. . . . God doesn't love one person more than another. He loves people from every nation."
Acts 10:1, 24-28

"I'M AN OUTSIDER wherever I go," wrote Shen. "My grandparents moved from India to Africa, where I was born. But my first name is from Iran. My brother's name is German. In Africa, they say we're not Africans. In India, they say we are not Indians. The language I speak is part Gujarati, part Swahili, and part English, so none of the words sound right. Now my family lives in America. I don't know who I am, except that I am human."

Maybe you know kids at school who are from other nations. Maybe they feel like outsiders. Peter saw Cornelius as an outsider until he realized that God loves people from all countries.

How can you make others feel accepted? If you have a friend from another nation, list some of the blessings that having this friend has brought you.

Dear God, show me how to help others feel accepted. Help me to be a friend to people from other countries.

Thursday

Read "Your Friend's Faith," page 714 in the *Day by Day Kid's Bible.* Or read this part of the story:

Some people don't have much faith. But don't judge them. Some people believe they can eat everything. Other people eat only vegetables. The person who eats everything shouldn't think people who don't are silly. The person who doesn't eat everything shouldn't blame people who do. They belong to God too.
Romans 14:1-3

RENEE'S MOTHER SHOPS at a health food store. Her family doesn't eat meat. They don't eat or drink anything that comes in a can. They believe that's the way their family can stay healthy. Brooke's family eats lots of meat, but not very much bread. That's the way they try to be healthy. So when Renee and Brooke sit beside each other at lunch, their lunch boxes hold very different foods. Renee might be tempted to laugh at Brooke's lunch. Brooke might be tempted to laugh at Renee's lunch. How could you tell if Renee and Brooke have learned to accept each other?

Do we accept others because it's a rule? No. We accept others because God has shown us that's the way life works best.

Dear God, thank you for showing us how life works best. Help me to accept others.

Friday

Read "Saving Wives and Children," page 155 in the *Day by Day Kid's Bible*. Or read this part of the story:

David's men found a man from Egypt in a field. They took him to David. He hadn't eaten anything for three days and three nights. So they gave him part of a fig cake and two raisin cakes. They gave him some water to drink. . . .

"I'm from Egypt," he said. "I'm a slave. My master left me here because I got sick." *1 Samuel 30:11-13*

"I DON'T WANT TO GO," said Miranda. Her mom and dad were going to play the guitar and sing for children at the hospital. Miranda had never been in a hospital before. It sounded like a sad, strange place. But Miranda had to go. "You can sit in the back and watch," said Mom. They went to a colorful playroom that had games and crayons and clay and a television. Lots of children came, some walking, some in wheelchairs, some carried by a nurse or parent. They sat and listened to Miranda's mom and dad. One girl sat by Miranda and started working a puzzle. Soon Miranda was helping her. When it was time to go, Miranda wasn't ready. She was having fun. She had made lots of new friends. "When can we come back?" Miranda asked.

Why would someone be tempted to reject a sick person? Does anyone accept people all the time? No. Everybody rejects someone at some time. That's why we need Jesus. He did for us what we could not do for ourselves: He accepted all people. Then he died to take our punishment for the times when we reject people. Now we can feel free to try again and grow to be like Jesus. That shows just how much God loves us.

Dear God, I'm sorry for times when I reject others. Thank you for showing how much you love me by sending Jesus to forgive me. Help me to accept others.

SOME THINGS YOU CAN DO THIS WEEK

Adopt a nation. Choose a nation you want to pray for. Make a poster for this nation. At the top of the poster, write, "God loves people from every nation." Then write the name of the nation you chose. Look it up in the encyclopedia. Draw a map of it. List the climate and some of the customs, the main crops, the religions, and any other interesting information you find. Put this poster in a place where it will remind you to pray for this nation.

Learn how people are alike. Put your foot to your forearm with your heel at your elbow. Where do your toes come to? Ask friends or family to try this. What do you learn about the size of a person's foot compared to his forearm? Now place one of your hands on your face, with the base of your palm at your chin, fingers pointing upward, covering your nose. Where does the tip of your middle finger come to? Ask other people to try this. What do you find out about the size of a person's face compared to the size of his hand? Look carefully at people's faces from the front. Where are the tops of their ears compared to where their eyes are? Where are the bottoms of their ears compared to where their lips are? People are all different. But in many ways, people are alike. What are some other ways that we are alike? Why might a person reject someone who is different?

Discover how long your body is. Are you short-waisted, long-waisted, or neither? Stand straight with your arms by your sides. Now bend your forearms up, keeping your upper arms at your sides so that your elbows are pointing down. If your elbows come above your waist, you are long-waisted. If your elbows come below your waist, you are short-waisted. If your elbows come exactly to your waist, you are neither long-waisted nor short-waisted. You probably choose your friends without caring whether they are short-waisted or long-waisted. In what other ways are your friends different from you? Does that difference matter? Why? How can you show people you accept them?

🌙 **Make up a limerick** about figs, the fruit that David's men gave to the man from Egypt. A limerick is a poem written in a rhythm and rhyme like the following poem. You may use the opening line of this limerick to start your own. Eat some figs or fig cookies. Remember how God wants us to accept people.

> There once was a man who found figs
> In his garden among the tree twigs.
> But he sat down and said,
> "I like carrots instead."
> And he fed all the figs to his pigs.

RESPECT

In everything, do to others what you would have them do to you. Matthew 7:12, NIV

This week you will learn
· *what respect and disrespect are;*
· *who got a letter and laughed at it;*
· *what happened at a dinner party for sinful people;*
· *who Jesus was talking about when he said, "Leave her alone."*

Monday

Read "Wake Up!" page 713 in the *Day by Day Kid's Bible.* Or read this part of the story:

People should obey the leaders of their country. Leaders were put in charge by God. . . .

Are you supposed to treat them as important people? Then treat them as important people. . . .

If you love people, you've done what God wants.
Romans 13:1, 7, 9

YESENIA, JANEAL, AND MONICA ran down the hall to catch up with their class. Most of the kids were already on the playground. Miss Daly, the kindergarten teacher, stepped out of her room. "Slow down, girls. Walk," she said.

They slowed down. But when Miss Daly went back into her room, Monica began running again. "Come on," she said. "She's not our teacher. We don't have to obey her."

"Yes we do," said Janeal. She and Yesenia walked the rest of the way. Janeal had respect for Miss Daly just because she is a teacher. Some people, like teachers and police officers and parents, should be respected because of the jobs they have.

To *respect* someone is to treat that person as someone who is important to you, someone who is worth your time and attention. *Disrespect* is treating someone as if he or she is not important to you and not worth your time and attention.

Dear God, help me to be careful to respect other people.

Tuesday

Read "Rules for Treating People Right," page 93 in the *Day by Day Kid's Bible.* Or read this part of the story:

Be kind to your father and mother. . . .

Stand up when an old person is with you. Be kind to old people.

Be kind to women whose husbands have died. Be kind to children whose mother and father have died.

Someone from another land may choose to live with you. . . . Treat him like one of your own people. . . .

Don't say bad things about people who can't hear. Don't put something in the way of someone who can't see. . . .

Love your neighbor as you love yourself.
Exodus 22:22; Leviticus 19:3, 14, 18, 32-34

SETH'S FAMILY GOT A PUPPY and named him Biff. Biff was so excited that he jumped all over Seth and his sister. Biff chewed on Seth's shoes. Biff wet on the floor. Seth's family took Biff to dog classes. The trainer showed them how to give commands to Biff and train him so he would respect their rules. Now that Biff respects Seth and his family, he is more fun to be with.

Seth does not give Biff commands to spoil Biff's fun. Instead, he has rules for Biff so that life with his dog will work out best and everyone will enjoy Biff more.

In the same way, God does not give us commands to spoil our fun. Instead, he has rules for us because he knows if we follow the rules, life will work best. We will all enjoy life more. Today's Bible reading gives us some rules from God about treating people with respect. When we respect people, we enjoy each other more.

Dear God, thank you for teaching us how to respect each other.

Wednesday

Read "A Holiday," page 348 in the *Day by Day Kid's Bible.* Or read this part of the story:

Then King Hezekiah wrote letters to all the people of Judah. . . . He asked everyone to come for the Pass Over holiday. . . .

So the king's helpers took the letters all over the land. . . .

Many people laughed at the letters. They laughed at the people bringing the letters. But some people came to Jerusalem.
2 Chronicles 30:1, 10-11

HAS ANYONE EVER LAUGHED AT YOU or made fun of you? You probably felt embarrassed. Or dumb. Or angry. People who make fun of others are not being respectful.

The people who laughed at King Hezekiah's letters were not being respectful of him. King Hezekiah was a good king. But what if he had been a bad king and the people didn't like him? Would it have been all right for them to make fun of him or call him stupid or good-for-nothing?

A king has an important job. He should be respected, even if people don't like what he says or does. It's the same with a president or governor or other leader. We can respect our leaders even if we don't always agree with them. Life works best that way. Maybe someday you will be a leader. Then people should respect you, too.

Dear God, help me to respect my leaders.

Thursday

Read "A Party at Matthew's," page 525 in the *Day by Day Kid's Bible.* Or read this part of the story:

Matthew followed Jesus. He even gave a big dinner party for Jesus. It was at his own house. Tax workers and many other people came to his party.

Some of the Jewish leaders came to the party too. But they didn't like tax men. These men took more money than they should. The leaders talked to Jesus' friends about it. "Why are you eating and drinking with these tax workers? They are sinners." *Matthew 9:9-11*

WHEN YOU GO TO THE GROCERY STORE in some cities, you have to pay more than the food costs. The extra you pay is called a tax. In some places, the food is not taxed, but if you buy something that is not food, like a book or paper and crayons, you have to pay tax on those. Different states have different tax rules. The tax money goes to your city or your state to pay for fire fighters and police officers and road repairs. But nobody really likes to pay taxes.

In Bible times, lots of people hated the men who collected taxes, because they always took a little extra money for themselves. Some tax men got very rich this way. So the Jewish leaders were mad at Jesus for eating with the tax workers. But Jesus respected everybody. He thought everyone was worth his time and attention. If people are worth Jesus' time and attention, they are worth our time and attention too.

Dear God, thank you for respecting me, for thinking I'm worth your time and attention. Help me to respect others.

Friday

Read "A Jar of Perfume," page 595 in the *Day by Day Kid's Bible*. Or read this part of the story:

Mary took out a jar of nard. It was perfume that cost a lot of money. She tipped the jar over. She let perfume flow out onto Jesus' feet. . . .

Judas, one of Jesus' 12 helpers, said, "Why didn't Mary sell this perfume? . . . She could have given the money to poor people!" . . .

"Leave Mary alone," said Jesus. *John 12:3-7*

MEN AND BOYS WERE thought to be the most important people in Bible times. Women and girls could not go to school. Most men thought that women were not very smart. But Jesus respected women. He talked to them as if they were smart. He let them be his friends and travel with him just like his men friends did.

In today's reading, Jesus did not allow Judas to be disrespectful toward Mary. Jesus spoke up for Mary.

Did you know that Jesus speaks up for you, too? When you are trying to follow Jesus but you do something wrong, God's enemy, Satan, accuses you. He says, "See how bad this kid is? He's not worth your love."

Then Jesus says, "Leave this kid alone. He belongs to me."

That's why we need Jesus. To him you are worth his time and attention and even his whole life. He gave up his life and died for you to pay for the times when you do wrong. Now you belong to him. You can feel free to try again and grow to be like Jesus. That shows how much God loves you.

Dear God, thank you for showing how much you love me by sending Jesus to die for me. Thank you that he came back to life and that he speaks up for me.

SOME THINGS YOU CAN DO THIS WEEK

Make a perfume jar. First make salt dough by mixing one cup of flour, one-third cup of salt, and one-third cup of water. Make a jar out of this dough and let it dry. Then put a little bit of perfume or cologne in it. Set it in your room to make a sweet smell. When you smell it, remember how Jesus spoke up for Mary and how Jesus speaks up for you, too.

Turn letters into people. On a large piece of paper, draw very lightly the letters *D T O.* These stand for three words in this week's verse: "Do To Others." Now go back and make these letters into people. For example, the straight line in the letter *D* can be a tall thin person standing with his arms straight down by his sides. The curve on the letter *D* can be a person with feet touching the feet of the straight person, legs and body curving around, head halfway up the curve, and arms stretched over his head to form the top of the curve. His fingers touch the top of the head of the straight person. Make the other letters the same way. Keep this poster as a reminder of the verse.

Make thumbprints. Get an ink pad or make a paint pad by pouring a bit of paint onto a folded paper towel that you have set on a paper plate. Press your thumb onto this pad and then press it onto a piece of paper to make a thumbprint. You may have to press your thumb down in several spots to make a clear print. Ask friends and family to make their thumbprints too. Then get a magnifying glass and look carefully at each person's thumbprint to see how they are different. Remember that Jesus respected all kinds of people. Think about how you can show respect to the people who made thumbprints for you.

Make an "honored guest" place mat. Start by coloring a design onto a piece of poster board, which you have cut to the size of a place mat. Fold a small piece of paper or an index card to make a place card. Then invite a friend or grandparent over for dinner and let them sit at the place of honor. You are showing respect to your guest. Remember how Jesus respected others by eating with them and talking with them. He thought others were worth his time and attention.

BEING CAREFUL

Give careful thought to your ways. Haggai 1:5, NIV

This week you will learn
· about eating ants and grasshoppers;
· the difference between being careful and careless;
· how haste makes waste;
· what King David said he would be careful not to do.

Monday

Read "Rules about Sickness and Food," page 92 in the *Day by Day Kid's Bible.* Or read this part of the story:

A person might get a sickness that others could catch. Then that person should live by himself. . . .

You may eat the ox, sheep, goat, deer, and gazelle. . . . But don't eat camels or rock badgers or rabbits or pigs.

You may eat sea animals that have fins and scales. But if they don't have fins and scales, don't eat them.
Leviticus 13:1-8; Deuteronomy 14:4-10

"WE'RE HAVING ANTS AND grasshoppers for dinner tonight," calls your mom. "Yummy! I'm coming!" you say, licking your lips. Can you imagine such a dinner? In some parts of the world today, people still eat ants and grasshoppers, just like they did in Bible times.

God gave his people rules about what to eat, because they didn't know that if they ate the meat from some kinds of animals, they could get very sick and even die. God was teaching his people to be careful.

Being careful means paying attention so you can make wise choices. It means watching out for things that might cause trouble so you can stay away from them. Being careless means not taking care to see if something is good for you or not. When you are tempted to be careless, you can fight temptation like Jesus did by saying, "I will be careful, because God's Word says, 'Give careful thought to your ways'" (Haggai 1:5, NIV).

Dear God, sometimes I am careless. Help me to be careful.

Tuesday

Read "Other Rules," page 91 in the *Day by Day Kid's Bible.* Or read this part of the story:

Let's say someone digs a pit and doesn't cover it. What if an ox or a donkey falls into it? Then he has to pay for the animal that died.

Let's say someone starts a fire. It may get out of control and burn somebody's wheat. What if it burns the whole field? Then the person who started it pays for what burned.

What if somebody lets his animals eat from another person's field? He has to pay for what they ate. *Exodus 21:33-36; 22:5-6*

"BE CAREFUL WITH THAT BALL," called Jordan's mom. "You can play with it in the house only if you just roll it on the floor." So Jordan and his little brother, Ben, rolled the ball back and forth. Then they got excited. The ball sailed across the living room and *CRASH!* It knocked a tin pot of flowers onto the floor.

Jordan's mom came in with her hands on her hips. "Clean it up, and then go outside to play," she said.

"It was an accident," said Jordan.

"I know," said Mom. "But it happened because someone wasn't careful."

Being careful means thinking about how we can take care of ourselves and others and even the world around us. God cares about what happens to us. We can care about what happens to others.

Dear God, thank you for caring about what happens to me. Help me to be careful.

Wednesday

Read "The Day the Enemy Won," page 158 in the *Day by Day Kid's Bible.* Or read this part of the story:

Saul's son Jonathan had a son who was five years old. His name was Mephibosheth. The news came that Jonathan and Saul had been killed. So the woman who took care of the boy picked him up and ran. She was in such a hurry that she dropped the boy. He fell and hurt his feet very badly. From then on, he couldn't walk.
2 Samuel 4:4

THERE'S AN OLD SAYING: Haste makes waste. *Haste* is hurrying. So the saying means that when we're in a hurry, we don't take the time to think about making the best choices.

Tamika's grandmother always said, "Where's the fire? Slow down." She meant that Tamika was going so fast, she was like a fire truck zooming off to fight a fire.

Of course, there are times when we have to hurry. That's what happened to the woman who took care of Jonathan's son. She had to leave town fast. She would have been more careful if she'd had more time.

Sometimes we get angry too fast. Wise King Solomon wrote about that. He said, "People who get angry too fast will get in trouble" (Proverbs 19:19, DBD). It's hard to be careful about what we say and do when we get angry too fast.

Slowing down and thinking helps us be careful. That's the way the world works best.

Dear God, I want to be careful. Help me to slow down and think about what I do and say.

Thursday

Read "Yeast," page 563 in the *Day by Day Kid's Bible.* Or read this part of the story:

Jesus' friends had only one loaf of bread. . . .

"Be careful about the leaders' yeast," said Jesus.

His friends looked at each other. "Is it because we're running out of bread?" they whispered.

Jesus knew what they were saying. . . . "I wasn't talking to you about bread. Be careful about the leaders' yeast."

Then they understood. . . . He meant, "Be careful about what the leaders teach." *Matthew 16:5-8, 11-12; Mark 8:14-17*

WOULD A LEADER teach something wrong? Some of the leaders in Bible times did. They got mad at Jesus for healing someone. They taught people that it was not right to heal anyone on the worship day (see Mark 3:1-6). But Jesus knew they were wrong. He knew people are more important than days. If people need to be healed, it doesn't matter what day it is; they can be healed.

Sometimes in schools and other places today, teachers might teach things that are wrong. They might teach that there isn't any God. But you know that God is alive and loves all people—even the teacher who doesn't believe in him! That's why we are careful about what leaders say and about what teachers teach. God has told us how life works best. If teachers teach us something different from what God has said, we can still respect them, but we don't have to agree.

Dear God, thank you for showing us how life works best. Help me to be careful to believe what you teach in the Bible.

Friday

Read "Proud Eyes," page 217 in the *Day by Day Kid's Bible.* Or read this part of the story:

> *I will sing about your love, God.*
> *I will sing about how fair you are.*
> *I will be careful to live a life without sin.*
>
> *I will walk in my house with a sinless heart.*
> *I won't let my eyes see anything bad.*
> Psalm 101:1-3

LILY KATE WATCHED a scary show on TV at her friend's house. That night, she was scared to go to bed. She had a hard time sleeping, because when she closed her eyes, she remembered the scary movie.

King David wrote the reading for today. He said he would be careful not to let his eyes see anything bad. He had learned what Lily Kate found out: What we see goes into our minds and sometimes comes back to our thoughts when we don't want it to. David also said he would be careful to live without sin. That means David planned to be careful about the choices he would make.

But even if we are very careful, all of us still sin sometimes. That's why we need Jesus. Jesus did for us what we could not do for ourselves. He was always careful, so he never sinned. And he died to take our punishment for the times we are careless. That shows just how much God loves us. Now we can feel free to try again and grow to be like Jesus.

Dear God, I'm sorry for the times when I am careless. Thank you for showing how much you love me by sending Jesus to forgive me. Help me to be careful not to sin.

SOME THINGS YOU CAN DO THIS WEEK

- **Play Mix-Up.** Get six disposable picnic cups. Turn them upside down and line them up. On each one, write one word from the verse for this week. Now mix up the order of the cups and time yourself to see how long it takes you to put them in order again.

- **Make a Mexican pizza.** Spread canned refried beans on top of a flour tortilla. Put grated cheese on top. Put salsa on if you want. Then put it under the broiler and heat it until the cheese gets bubbly. Remember to be careful when you are cooking. Ask an adult to help. Why does a cook have to be careful?

- **Have a grape snack.** With a toothpick, dip grapes into vanilla yogurt. Then roll them in shelled sunflower seeds and eat them. Do we need to be careful about what we eat? Why or why not?

- **Have a three-legged race.** Ask at least three friends to help you with this, and do it in a gym or outdoors. Decide where the starting point and the finish line will be. Form two teams. You and another friend stand next to each other. With bandannas, tie your right leg to your friend's left leg. Your other two friends should do the same. Stand at the starting line and ask someone to say, "Go." Then both teams should run for the finish line to see who can get there first. Be careful not to get hurt. What are some things to remember that will help you be careful when playing active games and sports?

COOPERATION

How good and pleasant it is when brothers live together in unity! Psalm 133:1, NIV

This week you will learn
· *what unity means;*
· *how to fight the temptation to fuss and argue;*
· *when it might be good not to cooperate;*
· *what compromise is.*

Monday

Read "Two Are Better than One," page 263 in the *Day by Day Kid's Bible.* Or read this part of the story:

> Two are better than one.
> They can get a lot more for their work.
> When one falls down, the other picks him up.
> But it's sad if there's nobody to help him up. . . .
> An enemy can win over one.
> But two can fight back.
> It's like tying three strings together.
> Three together is not easy to break.
> Ecclesiastes 4:9-10, 12

IN SOCCER OR FOOTBALL or basketball, all the players on one team try to get the ball to the same goal. Having the same goal, the same purpose, is *unity.* If a team is in unity, the team members must work together. *Co* means "together." *Operate* means "work." So *co + operate* = cooperate, which means to work together.

People who follow Jesus have the same goal: to love God and to love others. So we can live in unity. We can cooperate. Together we can show the world

God's love. When you are tempted to fuss and argue, you can fight temptation like Jesus did by saying, "I will cooperate, because God's Word says,
'How good and pleasant it is when brothers live together in unity!'" (Psalm
133:1, NIV).

Dear God, sometimes I fuss and argue. Help me to cooperate instead.

Tuesday

Read "King Hiram Helps," page 224 in the *Day by Day Kid's Bible*. Or read this part of the story:

Solomon sent a message . . . to [King] Hiram. . . .

"Please send some cedar logs for building a worship house. . . .
Send someone who can work with gold and silver. . . ."

King Hiram wrote back . . . "I'm sending a good worker to
you. . . . We'll cut the logs you want." . . .

Every year Hiram sent wood to Solomon. Solomon sent wheat,
barley, oil, and wine to Hiram.

Solomon got 30,000 (thirty thousand) men. . . . They would
work on Hiram's land for a month. Then they would work at home
for two months. *1 Kings 5:2, 5-6, 8, 10-11, 13-14; 2 Chronicles 2:7-10*

KING SOLOMON AND King Hiram and their workers cooperated. Their
goal was to build the worship house. Even though they agreed about the
goal, they probably had times when they did not agree about how to get it
done.

Becca and her friend Ivy were cooperating. Their goal was to decorate a
wagon for their neighborhood's autumn parade. But they did not agree.
Besides covering the wagon with colorful streamers, Ivy wanted to fill the
wagon with balloons. Becca liked the streamer idea, but she wanted to fill
the wagon with her big dog, Barky.

Becca and Ivy knew that if they fussed and argued about it, they might never get the wagon decorated. So they did something to stay in unity. They came up with a *compromise*. That means each person lets the other have a little of her way. Ivy let Becca put her dog in the wagon. Becca let Ivy tie balloons all around the sides. That was a good way to cooperate.

Dear God, when I need to cooperate, help me not to fuss and argue. Make me willing to compromise.

Wednesday

Read "A Fair Trade," page 697 in the *Day by Day Kid's Bible*. Or read this part of the story:

Don't get tied down with people who don't believe in God. Can right and wrong fit together? Can light and darkness be together? Do Jesus and Satan agree? Does a believer agree with someone who doesn't believe?
2 Corinthians 6:14-15

PUT ON YOUR THINKING CAP. Here's something interesting to think about. Are there ever times when it might be a good idea not to cooperate? The Bible says, "Do not follow the crowd in doing wrong" (Exodus 23:2, NIV). That means we should not cooperate with other people who are trying to get us to do something wrong. Their goal and our goal would not be the same. We could not be in unity. We want to cooperate with people who have the same goal we do. Life works best when we cooperate with people who want to do what's right and when we don't cooperate with those who want to do wrong.

Dear God, help me to cooperate with people who are doing what's right.

Thursday

Read "One Heart," page 715 in the *Day by Day Kid's Bible*. Or read this part of the story:

We shouldn't try to make just ourselves happy. We should try to make others happy. We should try to do good for them and help them. Even Jesus didn't try to make himself happy. . . .

I pray that God will help you work together to follow Jesus. That way, it will seem like you have one heart. Together you can show God's greatness. *Romans 15:1-3, 5-6*

HOW CAN LOTS OF PEOPLE have just one heart? Having "one heart" means having the same goal.

When Noah watches his big sister, Jessie, play soccer, he sees everyone on her team working for the same goal. They all have the same hope to play well and win the game. So we say they all have "one heart." But when Jessie watches Noah's team, she can tell they are just beginners. They are very young, and they haven't learned to cooperate yet. Some of the little boys just want to kick the ball, and they don't care which goal they kick toward. Some want to run around. And others want to sit in the grass and look for bugs. Their team does not have "one heart" yet.

Being with other people who follow Jesus is kind of like being on a team. We are all working together to love God and others. We are working together to show how great God is. We are in unity. We cooperate. We have one heart.

Dear God, thank you for giving me friends who love and follow you. Give my friends and me "one heart."

Friday

Read "Camping under the Flags," page 75 in the *Day by Day Kid's Bible*. Or read this part of the story:

God said, "The people will camp around the worship tent. Each family group will camp under its own flag." . . .

That's the way they traveled. Each group camped under its flag. The people traveled with their own family group. *Numbers 2:1-2, 34*

WHEN GOD'S PEOPLE traveled together, there were so many of them that the families needed to travel in order. Two silver horns gave the signal to go. When one blow of the horn sounded, Judah's family would start out and lead everyone else. Then they marched out, one family after another. Naphtali's family came last. What if Naphtali's family had fussed and said, "We want to go first"? What if they had not cooperated? Then none of the people would have been able to travel. God told them what order to travel in so they could all go quickly and easily. Life worked best for them that way.

What groups are you a member of? (Maybe a band, choir, drama group, homeschool group, church group, family group, ball team?) Does your group have rules?

Does anyone cooperate all the time? No. All of us have times when we fuss and argue. That's why we need Jesus. He did for us what we could not do for ourselves. He did not fuss or argue. And he died to take our punishment for the times we do. That shows just how much God loves us. Now we can feel free to try again and grow to be like Jesus.

Dear God, I'm sorry for the times when I fuss and argue. Thank you for showing how much you love me by sending Jesus to forgive me. Help me to cooperate with people who do what's right.

SOME THINGS YOU CAN DO THIS WEEK

Carry different things. What can you carry on your head? Start with a pillow and walk across the room. Try a book. Try a basket. What kinds of things can you carry in your arms without help? What kinds of things can be carried with the help of just one other person? What kinds of things need to be carried by lots of people? Why would these people need to cooperate?

Use a flashlight. At night, turn a flashlight on in a brightly lit room. Walk into a dimmer room. Keep your flashlight on and walk into different rooms, trying to go into places that are darker and darker, until you come to a room that has no light in it. Go into this room with your flashlight and close the door. Does the darkness make your light go out? Can it be light and dark at the same time? Think of Wednesday's reading. What was Paul trying to say when he asked, "Can light and darkness be together?"

Be a wheelbarrow. You'll need one friend to help you. Kneel on the ground or the floor. Place your hands on the ground in front of you. Ask your friend to pick up your legs, holding your feet by the ankles. Keep your legs stiff. Now walk around on your hands as if you are the wheelbarrow. Trade places and let your friend be the wheelbarrow. Can you do this stunt without cooperating?

Make creature cards. Lay the narrow end of each of three index cards next to each other in a column: top, middle, and bottom. Draw a person's head on the top card, body on the middle card, and legs and feet on the bottom. Move these cards out of the way and do the same thing again, only this time, draw a very different person, an animal, or a pretend creature. Make at least two more different characters this same way. If a friend or your family is working with you, everyone can draw different characters. Then mix up all the head cards, all the body cards, and all the leg-feet cards. Turn them over and place them facedown in three piles. Pick up the top head card, the top body card, and the top leg-feet card, and lay these face up on a table to make a new character.

Go through all the piles this way and see what interesting characters you can make. All your body parts have to cooperate with each other to do anything. How can a family, a sports team, or children in a class at school cooperate to get things done?

MERCY

Make sure that nobody pays back wrong for wrong,
but always try to be kind to each other.
1 Thessalonians 5:15, NIV

This week you will learn
· how to fight the temptation to get back at someone;
· how anything we do and say can be like a boomerang;
· what happened when someone wrote in the dirt;
· why we're like a tree that got a second chance.

Monday

Read "Throwing Rocks at the King," page 175 in the *Day by Day Kid's Bible*. Or read this part of the story:

A man from Saul's family . . . yelled bad things about David. He threw rocks at David and the guards around him.

"Get out of here," called the man. "You're a killer! You're good for nothing!" . . .

One of David's army leaders spoke to David. ". . . Why let him talk to you like that? Let me go take off his head!"

"You and I don't think alike," said David. . . . "Leave him alone." *2 Samuel 16:5-7, 9-11*

NOBODY LIKES IT WHEN people yell at them and call them names. Nobody likes to have people throw rocks at them. Especially not the king.

What are some things that King David might have done to the man who yelled and threw rocks at him? Instead, King David had mercy on the man. *Mercy* is being kind to someone when you want to get back at the person or when the person deserves to be punished.

When you are tempted to get back at someone who has done something wrong to you, you can fight temptation like Jesus did. You can do it by saying, "I will have mercy, because God's Word says, 'Make sure that nobody pays back wrong for wrong, but always try to be kind to each other'" (1 Thessalonians 5:15, NIV).

Dear God, sometimes I try to get back at people who have done wrong to me. Help me to have mercy on them instead.

Tuesday

Read "Writing on the Ground," page 572 in the *Day by Day Kid's Bible.* Or read this part of the story:

The worship-house leaders pushed a woman in front of [Jesus]. They had found her sleeping with a man the way a wife would. This man wasn't her husband. . . .

Jesus stood up tall. "Is there anyone here who has never sinned?" he asked. "If you've never sinned, you can go first. You can be first to throw a rock at her."

Then Jesus bent down again. He wrote in the dirt some more. People started leaving, one at a time. *John 8:3, 7-9*

NO ONE REALLY KNOWS what Jesus wrote in the dirt. Perhaps he wrote, "Where is the man?" The law said that both the man and woman should die if they slept together without being married. No one brought the man. Still, Jesus knew that the woman deserved to be punished. He didn't say it was all right for her to sin, but he had mercy on her. He said, "I don't blame you, so you can go home. But stop sinning." The men who had blamed her were probably disappointed that she didn't get the punishment she deserved. They might have said, "It's not fair."

Have you ever heard those words when others didn't get the punishment they deserved? No one does right all the time. So all of us deserve to be punished. That's why we need Jesus. He did for us what we could not do for ourselves. Jesus had mercy on us by dying to take our punishment for the times when we do wrong. That shows just how much God loves us.

Dear God, thank you for having mercy on me. Help me to show mercy to others.

Wednesday

Read "An Eye for an Eye," page 532 in the *Day by Day Kid's Bible*. Or read this part of the story:

"You've heard that if somebody hurts you, then you can hurt that person. But I tell you not to fight a sinful person," said Jesus. . . .

"You've heard that you're to love your neighbor and hate your enemy," said Jesus. "I say, love your enemies. Pray for people who hurt you. Then you will be children of your Father in heaven. . . . God is kind to people who are not even thankful. He is kind to sinful people. So be kind like your Father."
Matthew 5:38-39, 43-45, 48

HAVE YOU EVER SEEN a boomerang? Most of the time, a boomerang is made of wood. It is flat and curved. Long ago, people in different parts of the world used boomerangs as tools for fighting or hunting. But one kind of boomerang was used for games or sports. That kind of boomerang could be thrown, and it would fly through the air, then whirl around and come back.

There is a saying that "what goes around comes around." This means that if we do good, we can be sure that good things will come back to us, like a boomerang. We like that. But if we do bad things, bad will come back to us. We don't like that.

Still, it's impossible for us to be good all the time. We end up doing bad things, even when we try to be good. That's a problem. But God made a way out of that problem. He sent Jesus to get "paid back" for the bad we have done. When we tell him we're sorry, he forgives us. That's mercy.

Since God gives us mercy, he expects us to have mercy on others. It's natural to feel that if someone treats us badly, that person deserves to be treated just as badly. That's what "an eye for an eye" means. But we should treat them kindly instead. We should give them mercy. That shows them how much God loves them.

Dear God, give me a heart of mercy so that I can show others your love.

Thursday

Read "Up the Mountain," page 530 in the *Day by Day Kid's Bible.* Or read this part of the story:

"God will bring good to people who know they need him. The kingdom of heaven belongs to them," said Jesus. . . .

"God will bring good to people who think others are more important. The earth will belong to them. . . .

"God will bring good to people who are kind. God will be kind to them. . . .

"God will bring good to people who make peace. They'll be called God's children." *Matthew 5:3, 5, 7, 9*

ON THE SIDE OF A MOUNTAIN, Jesus sat and taught the people. He talked about how God would bless, or bring good things, to people who are gentle, who want what's right, who work to bring peace, and who are kind to others, even when others don't deserve to be treated with kindness. That's mercy.

Was Jesus telling people rules? Was he saying that we must be gentle, want what's right, work for peace, have mercy on others? No. These are not rules. Jesus was just telling people how life works best.

If we make others feel important, we will be welcome anywhere in the world. If we make peace, others will say we are God's children, because peace is a work of God. If we are kind and have mercy, others will be more likely to treat us with mercy. All these are ways of showing God's love. And God's love always wins.

Dear God, thank you for showing us how life works best. Help me to show your love.

Friday

Read "Clouds from the West," page 545 in the *Day by Day Kid's Bible*. Or read this part of the story:

Jesus told a story. "A man planted a fig tree. . . . He was watching for fruit to grow on it. But there was no fruit.

"At last the man talked to his gardener about it. He said, 'I've been coming here for three years. I've been looking for fruit on this fig tree. But I haven't found any. So cut it down. . . .'

"But the gardener spoke up. 'Sir, leave the fig tree alone one more year. . . . I'll make the soil richer. Maybe it will give you fruit next year. If it doesn't, you can cut it down.'"
Luke 13:6-9

THIS STORY OF THE FIG TREE is really a lesson about people. The gardener wanted to give the fig tree a second chance to do the right thing: make figs. People who have done wrong often need a second chance. When we have mercy on people, when we don't treat them as badly as we think they deserve, we give them a second chance. Has anyone ever given you a second chance?

Does anyone show mercy to others all the time? No. All of us have times when we try to get back at someone who has done wrong to us. But God has mercy on us. He doesn't give us the punishment we deserve. He is sad when we do wrong, but he doesn't try to get back at us. Instead, he has mercy on us. That's why he sent Jesus to die for us. Now we can be free from our sins, and we can show mercy to others.

Dear God, I'm sorry for the times when I have tried to get back at someone for doing wrong. Thank you for having mercy on me by sending Jesus to forgive me. Help me to have mercy on others.

SOME THINGS YOU CAN DO THIS WEEK

Have a fig snack. Eat some dried figs or fresh figs or fig-filled cookies. In Bible times, people often made figs into dried fig patties in order to store them for a long time. Remember the story of the fig tree that was given a second chance.

Grow a vine. You can give a sweet potato a second chance. Try to find one with purplish buds close to the top, if you can. Put the longish end of the potato into a jar of water. At least a third of the potato needs to stick into the water. If you need to, push toothpicks into the sides of the potato to keep it from falling into the jar. Place it where it can get light, but not directly in the sun. Add water when you need to. Watch for roots and a vine to grow. In a couple of months, you can plant it in a pot of soil. Let it remind you of Jesus' story about the gardener who had mercy on the fig tree and gave it a second chance. God is like that gardener, and we are like the fig tree. God keeps having mercy on us.

Draw "Alphabet Feelings." Write the alphabet down the left side of some paper, skipping two lines between each letter. Now go down the alphabet and try to think of a feeling that starts with each letter. You can ask family or friends for help if you get stuck. Then draw a face that looks like each feeling beside each word. If someone said, "I feel merciful today," what would that mean? Do you have to feel merciful to show mercy? Why or why not?

Make a fruit salad. Ask an adult to supervise cutting and chopping. Scoop out sections from a fresh orange into a bowl. Squeeze the fresh juice into the bowl too. Scoop the rest of the orange out so the half orange rind is empty. Save these to be cups for your fruit salad. Add chopped apple and grapes and sliced bananas and any other fruit you like. Mix this up and spoon it into the orange halves. Serve it to family or friends. They don't always deserve to be served, but you serve them because of your kind love and your mercy.

EXCELLENCE

Whatever you do, work at it with all your heart
as working for the Lord, not for men. Colossians 3:23, NIV

This week you will learn
· how to fight the temptation not to do your best;
· the difference between being excellent and being perfect;
· what priests did with sick animals at one time.

Monday

Read "The End of the Race," page 748 in the *Day by Day Kid's Bible*. Or read this part of the story:

There is a reason Jesus took hold of me. I'm going for it. I want what Jesus planned for me. I don't think I have it yet.

But there is one thing I do. I forget what happened in the past. I push toward what's coming. I push on to get to the end of the race. God called me toward heaven. I want to win the gift he has for me.
Philippians 3:12-14

REMEMBER THE STORY of a race between a tortoise and a hare? The hare knew he was ahead, so he stopped for a nap. The tortoise plodded on down the road, passed the sleeping hare, and won the race. To win the race, the tortoise just had to keep going. That was the excellent thing for him to do, and that was the way he got the job done. Doing excellent work means doing the very best you can, "working with all your heart."

We like to watch good ball players or musicians or actors. We like to read well-written books and look at beautiful paintings and gardens. We like to eat food that tastes great. Excellent ball players, musicians, actors, gardeners, and cooks have practiced what they do over and over again, even when they did not feel like it. They knew that to be excellent, they had to keep going.

We can do each day's jobs, like keeping our rooms clean, with excellence, the best we can.

When you are tempted not to do your best, you can fight temptation like Jesus did. You can say, "I will do my best, because God's Word says, 'Whatever you do, work at it with all your heart, as working for the Lord, not for men'" (Colossians 3:23, NIV).

Dear God, help me to do my best. Help me to be excellent.

Tuesday

Read "Show Your Joy!" page 748 in the *Day by Day Kid's Bible.* Or read this part of the story:

Think about things that are true and good. Think about things that are right and clean. Think about beautiful things. Think about things you can look up to. If anything is the best, think about it. If it's something to cheer for, think about it. *Philippians 4:8*

THERE WAS ONCE A MAN who was so sick, he was about to die. He had tried everything he could think of to get well. Finally he found a man who told him, "You need to eat healthy foods." So he ate healthy foods. That helped. "Your body needs fresh air, sunshine, exercise, and lots of rest." So he exercised in the fresh air and sunshine. He went to bed earlier and got lots of rest. That helped. "You need to think good thoughts." So he decided to think only good thoughts. He felt much better. In fact, by doing all those things, he got well. He thanked God, because he knew God had helped him.

Sometimes we think bad thoughts instead of good ones. Bad thoughts could be: "I'm stupid." Or "It's hard to clean my room. I don't want to." Or "We always have that vegetable for dinner. Yuck!" Bad thoughts make our faces look sour. They discourage us and make us feel miserable. Excellent thoughts encourage us and make us feel better. God thinks excellent thoughts about you. Can you think of a way to remind yourself to think excellent thoughts?

Dear God, thank you for thinking excellent thoughts about me. Help me to think excellent thoughts too.

Wednesday

Read "A Gift of Sick Animals," page 484 in the *Day by Day Kid's Bible.* Or read this part of the story:

"Where are the good things my servants should say about me?" asks God. "It's you priests who treat me like nothing. . . .

"You offer me animals you don't want. You bring me the sheep that can't see. You bring me sick animals and animals that can't walk. Just try to give those animals to your rulers. Would they be happy with a gift like that?" asks God. *Malachi 1:6-8*

"**COME ON, ERICA,**" said Toni. "They're starting the game without us."

"Wait a minute," said Erica. "Mom told me to clean my room first."

"Just push the stuff under the bed," said Toni. "She'll never know the difference."

"You go on. I'll be there in a minute," said Erica as she began picking up her dirty clothes.

When people don't do their best, we might say their work is sloppy or shabby. How does it feel when you've done work that is sloppy? How does it feel when you've done work that is excellent?

Today's reading shows that the priests were not doing an excellent job. It was shabby of them to give God sheep that they wouldn't even want for themselves. Part of loving someone is doing excellent work for them. Look around. What kind of excellent work has God done for you? We love because God loved us first. We can also be excellent because God was first excellent for us.

Dear God, thank you for being excellent for me. Help me to be excellent for you.

Thursday

Read "A Good Wife," page 256 in the *Day by Day Kid's Bible.* Or read this part of the story:

> *Who can find a wife who is good?*
> *She is better than riches. . . .*
>
> *She takes care of her family. She is not lazy.*
>
> *Her children stand up and say good things about her.*
> *Her husband does too. He cheers for her.*
> *"Lots of women do good things," he says.*
> *"But you are better than all of them."*
> Proverbs 31:10, 27-29

IT SOUNDS LIKE THIS WOMAN is perfect. But we know she is not, because no one is perfect. Here's something to think about: Can you do an excellent job without doing a perfect job?

Carlton's four-year-old brother helps clean the house. He likes to spray window cleaner on the full-length mirror in the hall and wipe it with paper towels. But he can't reach all the way up. And he sometimes leaves a smudge here and there. Still, he does an excellent job for a four-year-old, and he works very hard doing it.

If a person had to be perfect to be excellent, no one would ever be excellent. Remember: being excellent means doing the best job you can. Some people feel bad when they make a mistake, because that means they did not do a perfect job. But all people make mistakes sometimes. Even parents are not perfect. But all of us can be excellent.

Dear God, help me not to worry if I'm not perfect. But help me to do the best I can.

Friday

Read "Love," page 687 in the *Day by Day Kid's Bible*. Or read this part of the story:

What if I give everything I have to poor people? What if I give up my whole life for Jesus? But I don't love people. Then it doesn't do me any good. . . .

Love always takes care of people. It always trusts. It always hopes. It always keeps going. Love never fails.
1 Corinthians 13:3, 7-8

"I LOVE CHOCOLATE CANDY." Is that the kind of love today's reading is about? No. Love for candy is only about what brings a good feeling to me, to myself. "My aunt is getting married. She fell in love with a man she met in college." Is that the kind of love today's reading is about? Part of it is. But it is easy to love someone who loves us back.

Today's reading is talking about God's kind of love. God loves all of us, whether we love him back or not. He knew that if we could love perfectly like he does, we would never do wrong. But he also knew that we could not live perfectly, because we are human—we are not God. So he sent Jesus to live a life of perfect love for us. Then Jesus took our punishment when he died on the cross. That shows just how much God loves us. Now if we receive that gift of love, we can be excellent. We can be sinless and perfect as we let Jesus' love shine through us.

Dear God, thank you for showing how much you love me by sending Jesus to make me perfect. Now help me to do my best and be excellent in all I do.

SOME THINGS YOU CAN DO THIS WEEK

* **Make a tool print.** Gather some tools from around your house (scissors, pancake turner, cheese grater, small wrench, screws, and so on). Pour a little washable paint onto some paper plates, using one paper plate for each color. Press a tool into one color of paint and then press the tool onto a piece of paper, making a print. Lay the tool on some old newspaper while you work with the other tools. One by one, print with the tools to make a design. When you are finished, wash the tools and put them back where you found them. Is there a way that you can know you've done excellent work?

* **Wash the dishes!** After dinner, wash dishes in a sink full of suds instead of putting them in a dishwasher. Pay attention to the textures you feel: smooth plates, fluffy suds, etc. Try to do an excellent job. Is there a difference between a good job, an excellent job, and a perfect job? If so, what's the difference?

* **Make a "relief."** Create a design as you glue heavy twine or string onto a piece of cardboard. Let it dry. Then lay a sheet of aluminum foil over the design and press it down over the string. Smooth it out and mold it around the design. Fold the edges of the foil around to the back of the cardboard and tape them in place. How does an artist become excellent?

* **Make a glass band.** Pour water into several glasses (or glass jars or bottles), filling each one to a different level. Then gently tap on the glasses with a plastic spoon and put them in order from the lowest sound to the highest. Try to play a simple song. You can add water or pour water out of some of the glasses in order to get the right notes. What does practice have to do with doing excellent work?

BEING THRIFTY

Keep your lives free from the love of money and
be content with what you have. Hebrews 13:5, NIV

This week you will learn

· what it means to be thrifty;
· how to fight the temptation to spend money on things you don't need;
· who was so rich he drank from gold cups and had thousands of horses;
· who prayed that God would not make him rich.

Monday

Read "Trees Will Clap," page 369 in the *Day by Day Kid's Bible*. Or read this part of the story:

Why work and pay money for things that don't do you
*   any good? . . .*

Look for God while you can find him.
*   Talk to him while he is near.*
People who do wrong should stop living that way.
*   They should turn to God.*
God will be kind and loving to them.
*   God will forgive them for free.*
Isaiah 55:2, 6-7

MIKI WAS MOVING TO A NEW HOUSE. She helped her mother clean
out the drawers in her room and put things in boxes. One of the boxes was
for things she would give away. Miki pulled a board game from the back of
the drawer. She remembered how she had begged her mother to buy it for
her. But she had played it only once. In fact, the box of things to give away
had lots of things in it that she had bought but had hardly used. Miki
decided she would try not to buy things she didn't need or wouldn't use.

Have you ever paid money for something that didn't do you any good? We can learn from mistakes like that. We can learn to be *thrifty*. That means managing our money carefully.

When you are tempted to spend money on something you don't need or won't use, you can fight temptation like Jesus did. You can say, "I will not waste my money, because God's Word says, 'Keep your lives free from the love of money and be content with what you have'" (Hebrews 13:5, NIV).

Dear God, sometimes I spend money on things I don't need. Help me to be thrifty.

Tuesday

Read "Riches," page 264 in the *Day by Day Kid's Bible*. Or read this part of the story:

> *People who love money never have enough of it. . . .*
> *You may get more things.*
> *But then more people come to you.*
>   *They want to help you use things up.*
> *So what good are things to the one who owns them?*
> *All that person can do is look at them. . . .*

Then I saw that it's good to get riches and health from God. He lets us enjoy them. . . . They're a gift from God.
Ecclesiastes 5:10-11, 18-19

THE THRONE WAS MADE of gold and ivory. All the cups were gold. There were swords and gold shields. There were 1,400 (one thousand, four hundred) chariots and 12,000 (twelve thousand) horses. There were clothes and spices and apes and baboons. And they all belonged to King Solomon. He was the richest king in the world. So he knew what he was talking about when he wrote today's reading. He was so rich that he could never use all the things he had. All he could do was look at them.

There is a danger in getting and keeping lots of money: Rich people may think they can take care of themselves, so they don't need God. But Solomon said it's God who gives us riches and lets us enjoy them. Even rich people can be thrifty. They don't have to buy things they don't need and won't use. Because the thing they need most doesn't cost any money. It's God's love.

Dear God, thank you for the money you give to me and my family. Help me to be thrifty with it.

Wednesday

Read "Rotten Riches," page 766 in the *Day by Day Kid's Bible.* Or read this part of the story:

Now you rich people, listen. . . . You'll see that your riches are rotten. Moths ate up your clothes. Your gold and silver rusted away. It all shows that you held on to your riches.

  Look! You didn't pay the people who worked for you. . . . The workers cried about it, and God heard them.

  You lived with riches all around you. You bought whatever you wanted. You made yourselves fat. *James 5:1-5*

WHY DOES GOD give people money? It's one way God takes care of people. He tells us that if we make him the most important one in our lives, he will make sure we have all we need. He knows we need money to buy food and clothes and to pay for a place to live.

Paul wrote in the Bible that God makes people rich so they can give to others. That's another way God takes care of people: through our giving. Giving is part of loving others. We love because God loved us first. So we can give our money, because God first gave it to us. When we give, we show what God is like. He enjoys giving to us, and we can enjoy giving to others.

Dear God, thank you for money that helps pay for my food and clothes and the place where I live. Help me to enjoy giving to others so they can have what they need.

Thursday

Read "Riches," page 359 in the *Day by Day Kid's Bible.* Or read this part of the story:

King Hezekiah was very rich. . . . He built places to keep his silver and gold and riches. . . .

Now the king of Babylon sent men to see Hezekiah. . . .

Hezekiah showed the men everything in his store houses. He showed them his silver and gold . . . and all his riches. . . .

Then Isaiah went to King Hezekiah. . . .

"What did they see?" asked Isaiah.

"Everything," said Hezekiah. "I showed them all my riches."

"Someday Babylon will take away all your riches," said Isaiah.
2 Kings 20:12-17; 2 Chronicles 32:27

DOMINIC GOT AN ALLOWANCE. His grandfather taught him to give some of it, save some of it, and spend some of it. Since Dominic had saved some of his money, he was able to use it to buy Christmas presents for his family. That's one way to manage money.

King Hezekiah saved a lot of his money too. But then he used it to show the men from Babylon how great he was. He wanted to impress them. That was prideful. And that was not a wise way to manage his money or his kingdom.

A man named Agur wrote something like this: "Dear God, don't let me be poor or rich. If I get rich, I might say there is no God. If I get poor, I might be tempted to steal, and that would not make you look good. So give me just as much as I need" (see Proverbs 30:8-9).

It's not bad to be rich, and it's not bad to be poor. What matters is what we do with our money—how we manage it.

Dear God, help me to be thrifty and wise with money.

Friday

Read "The Rich Man's Barns," page 544 in the *Day by Day Kid's Bible.* Or read this part of the story:

[Jesus] said to the people, "Be careful. Guard yourself against wanting more and more things. Life is not made of how many things you have." *Luke 12:15*

CLAIRE LIVED IN A POOR COUNTRY for several years because her parents were missionaries there. Then her family came back to the United States to visit. When Claire and her family started going to Sunday school, the teacher noticed something. Although Claire's family did not have much money, they all smiled a lot. Claire was the poorest one in the whole class. But she always seemed very happy.

Sometimes the more things we have, the less happy we are. We just have more things to clean and pick up. So part of being thrifty is understanding that money is not what makes us happy. Buying things might get us excited for a while, but it won't really make us happy.

We are happiest when we use our money to help and bless others, and when we thank God for every bit of what he gives us. Do we try to be thrifty because it's a rule? No. We try to be thrifty because God has shown us that's the way life works best.

Dear God, thank you for showing us how life works best. Help me to be thrifty.

SOME THINGS YOU CAN DO THIS WEEK

Collect pennies. Try to arrange your pennies by date. How old is your oldest penny? How new is your newest? Decide on some ways you will be thrifty with your money.

Make a coin rubbing. Lay several different coins out on a table and place a sheet of printer paper on top of them. If you have coins from a different country, use those too. Some of them may have different shapes. Now rub over the paper with a pencil or crayon to show the designs of the coins underneath. Remember how Agur asked God to help him not to be rich or poor, but to give him only what he needed.

Do a penny experiment. Fold a paper towel several times to make a thick padding. Place the paper towel on a plate and put a few pennies on the paper towel. Then pour vinegar onto the paper towel so that it is wet. Leave it for a day and then see what has happened. This happens because of the chemical reaction when the vinegar (acetic acid) mixes with the copper that the pennies are made of. Why might a person want more and more money?

Spin a quarter. Try to make a quarter stand on its edge by itself. Now hold the quarter on its edge with the tip of one finger while you flick it with a finger on your other hand so that it starts spinning. This will keep it on its side. See how long it can spin. Try spinning it on different kinds of surfaces. Which surface seems to work the best? Do you have a plan for managing your money? If not, think of how much you could save each week, how much you could give, and how much you could spend.

This week you will learn
· what it means to be loyal;
· what it means to betray someone;
· about two men who scared a whole army;
· about some men, each of whom had a beard on only half of his face.

Monday

Read "Fighting with a Jaw Bone," page 118 in the *Day by Day Kid's Bible.* Or read this part of the story:

The enemies got an army together. They camped around the land of Judah.

The men from Judah wondered what was happening. "Why are you coming to fight us?" they asked.

"We came to get Samson," said the enemies. . . .

So 3,000 men went from Judah to Samson's cave. "These enemies are in charge of our land," they said. . . . "We have come to take you to them." . . .

They tied Samson up with two new ropes. Then they led him away. *Judges 15:9-13*

THE 3,000 MEN WHO gave Samson to the enemy were people from Samson's own country. They were not being loyal to Samson. Being *loyal* means standing up for someone, defending and helping the person. It means not telling your friend's secrets.

We expect our friends and family to be loyal to us. When they are not, we say they have betrayed us. To *betray* or *forsake* people means to turn away from them and not support them. The 3,000 men in today's reading betrayed Samson to save themselves.

If you are ever tempted to betray a friend, you can fight temptation like Jesus did. You can say, "I will be loyal, because God's Word says, 'Do not forsake your friend'" (Proverbs 27:10, NIV).

Dear God, help me to be loyal to my friends and family.

Tuesday

Read "Jonathan Climbs up a Cliff," page 134 in the *Day by Day Kid's Bible.* Or read this part of the story:

One day Jonathan had an idea. He told it to a young man who was his helper. "Let's go where the enemy is," said Jonathan.

Jonathan didn't tell his father he was going. So no one knew Jonathan had left. . . .

"Follow me," said Jonathan to his helper. "God will help us win.". . .

Then Jonathan began to fight the enemies. His helper came right behind him. They killed about 20 men. . . .

The enemies didn't know what was going on. . . .

The Jews who were hiding heard about it. So they came out to fight. And God saved his people. *1 Samuel 14:1, 6, 13-15, 22-23*

MEL MET A NEW FRIEND named Afiba (uh–FEE–bah) at the school library. Afiba was from Africa. She could speak English, but her words sounded different. One day Mel was eating with some other friends at lunch. One friend said she thought Afiba talked funny. Another said she thought Afiba was not very smart. Afiba was sitting at a different table and couldn't hear what they said. What choices did Mel have? She could have laughed at what they said about Afiba. She could have said some bad things herself. She could have just been quiet and listened. Mel didn't do any of those things. She said, "Afiba is a good friend. I think the way she talks is beautiful. And she is very smart." Mel was loyal to her friend Afiba.

In today's reading, Jonathan's helper was loyal. Jonathan was doing something very brave but very dangerous. His helper could have said he wasn't going. Instead, he was loyal and followed Jonathan.

Part of loving is being loyal. God is loyal to us. He never leaves us. He never stops loving us, because he is loyal to us. So we can be loyal to others. When we are loyal, we show what God is like.

Dear God, thank you for being loyal to me. Help me to be loyal to my friends and family.

Wednesday

Read "A Rude King," page 165 in the *Day by Day Kid's Bible.* Or read this part of the story:

The king of Ammon died. His son became king. David thought, "I'll be kind to him. His father was always kind to me." So David sent a group of men to see the new king. They told him David was sorry that his father had died.

    But the leaders of Ammon talked to their king. . . . "Soon King David will try to take our land for himself."

    So the king took David's men. He shaved off half their beards. He cut their clothes in half across the middle. Then he sent them home. . . .

    The leaders of Ammon began to see what they had done. They had been rude to David. So their king paid for chariots to come from other lands. . . . They all got ready to fight David's army.

1 Chronicles 19:1-7

TO *BETRAY OR FORSAKE* someone means to treat the person as though he or she is not your friend. The king of Ammon betrayed David. The king was not loyal to him. That caused lots of trouble.

It's not always easy to be loyal. Thomas Edison, the man who invented the light bulb, tried lots of other ideas. Every idea that worked had to have a special paper that said Edison invented it. That way, people would know Edison did it, and he would be able get the money for it. One time a lawyer Edison trusted took some of those papers and sold them to some other men so they could say they invented one of the ideas and get the money for it. The lawyer was not loyal to Edison. Instead, he betrayed Edison for money. Still, Edison wouldn't ever say who the lawyer was, because Edison didn't want to embarrass or hurt the lawyer's family. So even though the lawyer betrayed him, Edison stayed loyal to the lawyer.

Dear God, I choose to be loyal. Thank you for showing me how.

Thursday

Read "A Chariot and Horses of Fire," page 294 in the *Day by Day Kid's Bible.* Or read this part of the story:

"You stay here," said Elijah. . . .
    "I won't leave you," said Elisha.
    So they went to Bethel together. . . .
    Elijah told Elisha, "You stay here. . . ."
    "I won't leave you," said Elisha.
    So they went to Jericho together. . . .
    Elijah told Elisha, "You stay here. . . ."
    "I won't leave you," said Elisha.
    So they walked on together. . . .

All of a sudden, horses of fire appeared. They pulled a chariot of fire. It went between Elijah and Elisha. Then a wind came, turning around and around. It took Elijah up to heaven.
2 Kings 2:2, 4, 6, 11

BEING *LOYAL* means staying with your friend or your team no matter what. Some people are loyal to a ball team. Even if the team is losing most of its games, these people still go to the games and cheer for the team.

"I won't leave you," Elisha told Elijah. And he didn't leave Elijah. That's being loyal.

Who are you loyal to? Who is loyal to you? Are we loyal because it's a rule? No. We are loyal because God has shown us that's the way life works best.

Dear God, thank you for showing us how life works best. Help me to be loyal.

Friday

Read "Thirty Silver Coins," page 607 in the *Day by Day Kid's Bible.* Or read this part of the story:

Judas was one of Jesus' 12 special friends. But Satan took control of Judas now. So Judas went to the leaders at the worship house. He told them he could show them where Jesus was. "What will you give me if I do?" he asked.

The leaders counted out 30 silver coins for Judas. Judas took the money. Then he waited and watched. He looked for a time when no crowds were around. *Matthew 26:14-16; Luke 22:3-6*

JUDAS CHOSE TO betray Jesus. What happened because of Judas's choice? Is there anyone who is always loyal to friends and family? No. All of us have times when we treat a friend or family member badly.

Even Peter betrayed Jesus. After Jesus had been taken away by the soldiers, Peter followed. But when someone said, "You were with Jesus," Peter said, "I don't know Jesus." Two more times, someone said, "You were with Jesus, weren't you?" And two more times, Peter said he never knew Jesus. After that, Peter was so sorry, he cried. (See Matthew 26:69-75.)

We sometimes make the wrong choice, like Peter did. That's why we need Jesus. He came to do for us what we cannot do for ourselves. He was always loyal to his friends. And he died to take our punishment for the times when we are not loyal. That shows just how much God loves us. Now we can feel free to try again and grow to be like Jesus.

Dear God, I'm sorry for the times when I am not loyal. Thank you for showing how much you love me by sending Jesus to forgive me. Help me to be loyal.

SOME THINGS YOU CAN DO THIS WEEK

Make a fiery design. You can do this using yellow and red tissue paper. Tear the tissue paper into pieces about three to five inches long, any shape. Pour about one-eighth cup of white glue into a bowl and add just enough water to make it like paint. Lay a piece of tissue paper onto a piece of white paper, poster board, or cardboard. Use a paintbrush to paint the glue over the tissue, completely covering the piece of tissue. Add another piece of tissue paper. It can overlap the first piece if you want. Keep adding paper and painting glue over it until you are pleased with your design. Let it dry. Remember the horses of fire and the chariot that came between Elijah and Elisha.

Make a coin bag. First you'll need to cut a circle of fabric about 10 inches across. Cut out about six small holes spaced evenly around the edge of the circle. Thread a shoestring in one hole and out the next all around the circle. Tying the ends of the shoestring together will close the top of the bag. How many coins did Judas get for betraying Jesus? Even though Judas betrayed Jesus, Jesus was still loyal. When Jesus died, he was punished for all people's sins, even those of Judas. Jesus died so everyone can be forgiven.

Play "Electricity." To do this, you will need a group of friends. Sit in a circle. Choose one person to stand in the middle of the circle and close her eyes. Everyone else holds hands. Choose a leader to start the "electric current" by squeezing the hand of the person on his right or on his left. That person squeezes the hand of the person next to him and the squeeze (the "electricity") goes from person to person around the circle. It can change direction at any time. Tell the person in the middle when she can look. She tries to see someone squeeze another person's hand. When she sees it, she points it out, and she gets to trade places with that person. Being loyal means supporting your friends. Sometimes holding hands shows that you support your friend. What else shows loyalty to a friend?

◗ **Draw "friendly feet."** On a large sheet of manila paper, trace around
your foot and a friend's foot. Across the top or bottom of the paper,
write, "I'll stand by you." What do we mean when we say we'll stand by
someone?

DILIGENCE

Lazy hands make a man poor, but diligent hands bring wealth. Proverbs 10:4, NIV

This week you will learn
· *what diligence is;*
· *how to fight the temptation to be lazy;*
· *about some animals that are diligent;*
· *about a king who made rock-throwing machines.*

Monday

Read "Working Hard or Being Lazy," page 249 in the *Day by Day Kid's Bible.* Or read this part of the story:

Think about what the ant does. Be wise.
The ant doesn't have a king to tell it what to do.
But it stores up its food in the summer. . . .

All hard work brings good things.
But if all you do is talk, you'll grow poor. . . .

I passed a lazy man's field.
Weeds were everywhere.
The stone wall was broken down.
I thought about what I saw, and I learned something.
You sleep a little. You sleep a little more.
You fold your hands to rest.
Then you grow poor.
Proverbs 6:6-8; 14:23; 24:30-34

EVERY TIME ZACHARY goes to visit his grandmother, she makes his favorite dessert: strawberry shortcake. Sometimes Zachary helps by going out to his

grandmother's garden and picking fresh strawberries. One by one, he picks them and plunks them into the bucket. It takes some time, but he is diligent, and after a while, there are plenty of berries for shortcake. The word *diligent* comes from an old word that means "to gather." When Zach gathers strawberries, he has to stay at the job until, little by little, it gets done.

If you are a diligent person, you treat your work or study as something important, doing it as soon as you can, and staying at it until it's done. A lazy person says, "I'll do it later." But if the job seems too hard, he quits.

When you are tempted to be lazy, you can fight temptation like Jesus did. You can say, "I will not be lazy, because God's Word says, 'Lazy hands make a man poor, but diligent hands bring wealth'" (Proverbs 10:4, NIV).

Dear God, sometimes I am lazy. Help me to be more diligent.

Tuesday

Read "Turning Away," page 315 in the *Day by Day Kid's Bible.* Or read this part of the story:

Joash thought he'd fix up God's worship house. He talked to the priests about it. "Gather money. . . . Use the money to fix whatever needs to be fixed. . . . Do it right away."

But the priests didn't do it right away. . . .

"Why aren't you fixing up the worship house?" asked Joash. "Stop taking money for yourselves. Give it to someone who can fix the worship house." . . .

A message went to all the people. It said to bring their tax money to God. So people from all over Judah brought money to the worship house. . . .

Then they paid workers to fix up the worship house.

The workers did good work. They worked hard.

2 Kings 12:7; 2 Chronicles 24:4-6, 9-10, 13

) ●) ●) ●) ●) ●

BARN SWALLOWS ARE BIRDS that build mud nests on barns and other tall buildings. It takes them up to two weeks to build their nests. They may fly off as many as 1,200 times to go get the mud to make their nests. They are diligent. They do their work little by little, and they stay at the job until it's done.

In today's reading, the priests were not diligent at first. They didn't act like the job was important. King Joash had to ask them a second time to fix up the worship house. Then they hired workers, and the workers were diligent.

Did you ever have to be asked more than once to do something? God is not lazy about the way he takes care of us. He never stops watching, caring, and helping. He is diligent, and he can help us be diligent too.

Dear God, thank you for being diligent in caring for me. Help me to be diligent too.

Wednesday
Read "Forts, Towers, and Rock-Throwing Machines," page 325 in the *Day by Day Kid's Bible*. Or read this part of the story:

King Uzziah built towers in Jerusalem. . . . He made them like forts. He built towers in the desert, too.

King Uzziah dug wells. He had lots of cows. People worked in his fields. He loved to grow things.

King Uzziah also made machines in the city. They were placed on the towers. They were used to shoot arrows and throw rocks when their enemies came. *2 Chronicles 26:9-10, 15*

HOW CAN YOU TELL that King Uzziah was a diligent king? You can read about all the things he planned and did.

Remember the story of Jack and the beanstalk? Jack tossed out a bean seed, went to bed, and in the morning when he woke up, there was a beanstalk, full grown.

King Uzziah made plans to build forts and wells and machines. They were not like the beanstalk. They didn't come up overnight.

We have microwave ovens that can heat food fast. We have instant soup. So we can do some things fast, fast, fast. But other jobs take time. Watch someone mowing the lawn or raking leaves. Think of how it is to clean your room. To do these jobs, a person has to be diligent, to stick with the job until it's done.

How do you feel when you know you've been diligent in doing a job? How do you feel when you know you've been lazy? Have you ever been diligent in your work, but nobody noticed, and nobody thanked you? God knows. King Solomon wrote, "All hard work brings good things" (Proverbs 14:23, DBD).

Dear God, I want to be diligent. Help me stick to doing the things that are important so that, little by little, I will get each job done.

Thursday

Read "The Wise Servant," page 544 in the *Day by Day Kid's Bible.* Or read this part of the story:

"A good servant does what his master tells him. He will be following orders when his master comes back. His master will put him in charge of everything. . . . The master may give his servant a lot," said Jesus. "Then he will want his servant to give a lot too." *Luke 12:42-44, 48*

DURING THE WINTER, eastern chipmunks hibernate in tunnels that they dig in the ground. There they store food so that when they wake about every two weeks during the cold weather, they can eat from their stored food. They have to be diligent and keep storing up their food before winter comes. So, little by little, they stay at the job of gathering nuts and seeds until the job is done.

What jobs take a while for you to do? Just as Jesus said in today's reading, people who are diligent can be trusted as good workers. People like to have diligent people working for them and with them. Diligent people get chosen to do bigger and better things.

Are we diligent because it's a rule? No. We are diligent because God has shown us that's the way life works best.

Dear God, thank you for showing us how life works best. Help me to be diligent.

Friday

Read "Lazy Busybodies," page 672 in the *Day by Day Kid's Bible.* Or read this part of the story:

Stay away from God's people who are lazy. We weren't lazy when we were with you. We paid for the food we ate. We worked hard day and night. We didn't want to be any trouble to you. . . .

We wanted to show you how to live. We told you this rule. "If a person won't work, then he shouldn't eat."

We've heard that some of you are being lazy. You're not busy.

Instead, you're busybodies. You just think about what other people should be doing. Stop this. Work for what you eat. . . .

Don't get tired of doing what's right. *2 Thessalonians 3:6-13*

HONEYBEES TRAVEL over 50,000 (fifty thousand) miles to gather the nectar that it takes to make about one medium-size jar (one pound) of honey. Yet each bee in its whole life gathers only about one teaspoon of nectar. So it takes lots of bees, diligently working together, to get the job done.

Sometimes lots of people need to work together to do a job. Jessie goes to Mexico every year with her church group. They all work together to build houses for people there who are poor. If one person got lazy and started complaining, it would discourage everyone else. That's why in today's reading, Paul said to stay away from God's people who are lazy.

Of course, sometimes we need to stop and rest. How can you tell if you are really resting and getting your energy back or if you're just being lazy?

Is anyone diligent all the time? No. All of us have times when we are lazy. That's why we need Jesus. He came to do for us what we cannot do for ourselves. He is always diligent. And he died to take our punishment for the times when we are lazy. That shows just how much God loves us. Now we can feel free to start over and try again.

Dear God, I'm sorry for the times when I am lazy. Thank you for showing how much you love me by sending Jesus to forgive me. Help me to be diligent.

SOME THINGS YOU CAN DO THIS WEEK

☀ **Play Word-It.** Write the word *diligent* across the top of a piece of paper. Try to see how many words you can make out of the letters in *diligent.*

🌙 **Make a rebus.** Write this week's Scripture verse on a piece of paper. But when you come to a word that can be drawn into a picture, draw it instead of writing it.

☀ **Go on an "Under Hunt."** With a mop or a broom, sweep under furniture that rarely gets swept under. Lift up couch cushions and chair cushions and vacuum underneath them. Did you find anything interesting under them? Why do we need to be diligent when we clean the house?

🌙 **Make a picture of a pet.** This could be of your pet or of a friend's pet. Then glue it to the inside of a box lid to make a picture frame. Decorate the inside of the lid by drawing, coloring, or painting designs around the border. Or place animal stickers around it. How can a person show diligence in taking care of a pet? Do you have a pet that is diligent in doing something?

KEEPING PROMISES

It is better to say nothing than to promise something that you don't follow through on.
Ecclesiastes 5:5, NLT

This week you will learn
· *how to fight the temptation to break a promise;*
· *who should have broken a promise;*
· *who played a trick with old bread;*
· *what promises have to do with the beginning and end of a book.*

Monday

Read "Keeping Promises," page 239 in the *Day by Day Kid's Bible.* Or read this part of the story:

> *Keep your promises.*
> > *Write them on your heart.*
> > *Then God and people will speak well of you. . . .*
> *Don't trust someone who doesn't keep his promises.*
> > *That's as bad as having a hurting tooth.*
> > *It's as bad as walking on a foot that you broke.*
> Proverbs 3:3-4; 25:19

ANOTHER WAY TO SAY "Keep your promise" is "Keep your word." Or we could say, "Be true to your word." A *promise* is saying we will or will not do something. Then the person we make the promise to can expect that we will do whatever we said. But it's not always easy to keep a promise.

Sam promised to play with his little brother, Timmy, after school. But then Sam's friend Carlos asked Sam to come to his house and play. Sam would rather play with Carlos. Sam could just tell Timmy that he has changed his mind. But how would Timmy feel? All day, Timmy has been looking forward to the time when Sam will come home from school so they can play. If Sam breaks his promise, will Timmy believe his big brother next time he makes a promise?

When you are tempted to break a promise, you can fight temptation like Jesus did. You can say, "I will keep my promise, because God's Word says, 'It is better to say nothing than to promise something that you don't follow through on'" (Ecclesiastes 5:5, NLT).

Dear God, sometimes I break my promises. Help me to do a better job of keeping them.

Tuesday

Read "John in Trouble," page 555 in the *Day by Day Kid's Bible.* Or read this part of the story:

John, who baptized people . . . had told Herod, "It's not right to marry your brother's wife." So King Herod had put John into jail. . . .

One day King Herod had a party. . . . Herodias [his wife] had a daughter who came too. She danced for the people. . . .

Herod promised to give her anything she wanted. . . .

"I want John's head on a plate! Right now!" she said.

This made Herod very upset. But he had promised. He didn't want to say no in front of everyone. *Matthew 14:3-4, 6-9*

HEROD MADE A VERY FOOLISH promise. It was a promise he didn't want to keep. In fact, it was such a bad promise that he could have told the daughter that his promise didn't include killing anyone. He could have said, "I'm sorry for making that promise and for breaking that promise. But it's better to break the promise than to kill John." But Herod did not want to admit that he had been wrong.

Sometimes we make a mistake and promise something that we later wish we had not promised. We have to decide if it would hurt someone to keep the promise or if it would hurt someone to break the promise. Most of the time, we know in our hearts what would be the right thing to do. It's important to choose the most loving thing, because God is love.

Dear God, help me to be careful about what I promise. Help me choose to show your love.

Wednesday

Read "Stale Bread and Worn-Out Shoes," page 100 in the *Day by Day Kid's Bible*. Or read this part of the story:

The people of Gibeon . . . played a trick on God's people. They put old, worn-out bags onto donkeys. . . . They carried dry, stale bread. And they went to see Joshua.

They said, "We come from a land far away. We want to make a deal with you."

God's people said, "We don't know you. Maybe you live close to us. Then God wouldn't want us to make a deal with you.". . .

Some of Joshua's men . . . saw the old bread and the worn-out bags. . . . But they didn't ask God about it.

Then Joshua and the leaders made a deal with the men. They promised not to fight them.

Three days passed. Then God's people found out that these men lived nearby. So God's people traveled to their city. But they didn't fight. They had promised not to. *Joshua 9:3-7, 14, 21*

LONG AGO, KING DAVID asked God who could come and be with him. God's answer: "Those who . . . keep their promises even when it hurts" (Psalm 15:4, NLT).

Joshua's men learned that they should ask God before making certain promises. The men from Gibeon tricked them into making a promise not to fight. Joshua's men didn't want to keep that promise, but they kept it anyway.

Tera Lynn promised to trade her monkey puppet for Daniel's king puppet. After she had promised, Tera Lynn decided she didn't really want to trade after all. But she traded, because she knew it was important to keep her promise. She decided that next time, she would try to think through her choices more carefully before she made a promise.

Do we keep promises because it's a rule? No. We keep promises because God has shown us that's the way life works best.

Dear God, thank you for showing us how life works best. Help me to keep my promises.

Thursday

Read "Money for Grain," page 493 in the *Day by Day Kid's Bible*. Or read this part of the story:

I [Nehemiah] talked to the leaders. "You're taking things from your own people!" I said. . . . This has to stop. Give their houses back. Give their fields back."

"We will," they said. . . .

I made the leaders promise to do what they said. I shook out my robe. "May God shake out people who don't keep this promise." *Nehemiah 5:7, 10-13*

PEOPLE EXPECT SOMETHING of us when we make a promise. If we break the promise, they are disappointed.

It's the same with us. We expect things of other people when they make promises to us. We are disappointed if others break a promise. We might say they "let us down." That's because when we expect something, we feel full of hope. When it doesn't happen, our feelings sag. We feel down.

Somebody once said that the biggest reason most people hold anger in their hearts is because someone broke a promise to them. But guess what? Somebody *will* break a promise to you. It might be your mother or father. It might be a teacher or a friend.

Everyone breaks a promise once in a while. Why? Because nobody is perfect but God. He is the only one who will never break a promise to you. Never, ever. So it's important to forgive people when they break their promises to us. And then we should put all our hope in God. He promises us that sooner or later, everything will be all right.

Dear God, I forgive all the people who have broken their promises to me. I will put my hope in you. Thank you for always keeping your promises.

Friday

Read "Cheer Up," page 693 in the *Day by Day Kid's Bible*. Or read this part of the story:

Two times I [Paul] made plans to visit you. I wanted to help you. Did I plan this without thinking? Do I plan like people of the world do? Do I say yes and no at the same time? God always keeps his promises. That's for sure. And we don't say yes and no at the same time. That's just as sure. *2 Corinthians 1:16-20*

FOR ANY STORYBOOK, the beginning is like a promise. In the first few pages, we read what the book is about. For example, in the story of Cinderella, we find out what her problem is: She wants to get to do the things her older stepsisters do. But they won't let her. That's like a promise that the story will take care of the problem.

If the story changed and told how Cinderella learned to bake the best pies and cakes and then opened a café, it would not keep its promise. The promise is that we will find out if Cinderella gets to do what her stepsisters get to do.

Did you know that the Bible is a story of how God loves people? The beginning is a promise. In the first few pages we learn that God made people to live with him, but there was a problem: People chose to go their own way. So we know that's what the whole Bible is about. And in the end, we find out how God took care of the problem. Now people can be with God again.

How did that happen? Jesus came to do for us what we cannot do for ourselves: to live a life of perfect love. Then he died to take our punishment for all the wrongs we do. That shows just how much God loves us.

Dear God, I'm sorry for the times when I break my promises. Thank you for keeping your promises and for showing how much you love me by sending Jesus to forgive me.

SOME THINGS YOU CAN DO THIS WEEK

Make a book bag. Fold a kitchen towel in half. The fold is the bottom of the bag. Sew the sides together. Then, using two pieces of wide ribbon, each about 10 inches long, make a handle for each side of the bag. You'll need to sew both ends of one ribbon to each side of the bag. Remember how the Bible is a book about God keeping his promises and bringing people back to himself.

Color a rainbow. Draw a rainbow on a piece of paper, and color it using colors that start with each letter in the word PROMISE. If your crayons don't have labels with names that start with all of these letters, rename some of the colors you have. For example, green can be "mint," white can be "ivory," black can be "ebony," and so on. Think about what a promise means.

Make a promise box. Cover a shoe box with Con-Tact paper and decorate it with stickers. Keep a stack of small note cards or index cards beside it. As you read your Bible, look for promises that God makes to those who love and follow him. Write each promise on a card and place it in your box. If you want to start your Bible reading at a place where there are lots of promises, try the Psalms.

Look at some storybooks. Read the first page. Can you tell what problem the rest of the book is supposed to take care of? Can you remember the end of the book? Does the book keep the promise to take care of the problem described in the first few pages? Remember how the Bible is like a promise book to us.

WANTING TO PLEASE GOD

We are not trying to please men but God. 1 Thessalonians 2:4, NIV

This week you will learn
· *how to fight the temptation to be a people pleaser;*
· *what's dangerous about being a people pleaser;*
· *how some cows and sheep pleased men, but not God;*
· *about someone who shook hands to please people.*

Monday

Read "Rules That Are in the Heart," page 704 in the *Day by Day Kid's Bible*. Or read this part of the story:

Being Jewish is great. But that's true only if you obey God's laws. . . . Let's say people obey God's laws. But they aren't Jewish. Then to God, they are his people. . . .

A real Jew has the heart of a Jew. He loves God in his heart. . . . This person wants God to cheer for him. He doesn't look for praise from people. *Romans 2:25-26, 29*

WE WERE MADE TO LIVE with friends and family all around us. So we all want people to notice us, like us, and say good things about us. That makes us feel like we are part of the group, like we are worth something.

But we were also made to live with God. So part of us wants to please God. But we don't know how to please him, because he is perfectly loving and we are not. We think God is angry with us for what we do wrong. So we give up on pleasing God, and we end up trying to please the people who will listen to us and spend time with us and make us feel like we're worth something.

But God is not angry with us. He loves us so much he gave his Son to die for us and forgive us and bring us back to him. Why would he be angry with you after showing you such love? Really, it's God who will listen to you and spend time with you and make you feel like you're worth the best love he can give: the love of his only Son, Jesus. He loves you very much. When you love him back, he is pleased.

Dear God, thank you for not being angry with me. Thank you for listening to me, spending time with me, and loving me. Help me to learn what it means to listen to you, spend time with you, and love you.

Tuesday

Read "From the Roof Tops," page 543 in the *Day by Day Kid's Bible.* Or read this part of the story:

[Jesus] said, "Watch out! What the leaders say and do isn't right." . . .

"Don't be afraid of people who can kill your body. After that, they can't do anything else," said Jesus. . . .

"Tell people you know me," said Jesus. "Then I'll tell God's angels I know you. . . . People might . . . take you to the leaders. But don't worry about what you'll say. The Holy Spirit will tell you what to say." *Luke 12:1, 4, 8, 11-12*

THE LEADERS JESUS WAS TALKING ABOUT COULD put people in jail and even kill them for following Jesus. So it makes sense that Jesus' followers were afraid of them. If Jesus' followers had been people pleasers, they might have stopped teaching about Jesus to save their lives. But they didn't.

Even today in some countries, people who tell about Jesus are in danger. If they wanted to please the leaders in those countries, they would stop talking about Jesus. But they want to please God. They know that only God knows the way life works. Only his Son, Jesus, has a love so great that it can give people peace. So Jesus' followers try to be wise and kind and loving. They are not rude. But they don't stop telling about Jesus.

Dear God, thank you that Jesus' great love can help all people have peace. Protect and help the people who tell about you in countries where they are in danger. Thank you that they are more interested in pleasing you than in pleasing people.

Wednesday

Read "Like a Mother," page 668 in the *Day by Day Kid's Bible*. Or read this part of the story:

We were brave when we told you the Good News. Many people tried to stop us. But we weren't trying to trick you. We weren't after more and more things for ourselves. It's not people that we're trying to make happy. We're trying to make God happy. He sees what's in our hearts. *1 Thessalonians 2:2, 4*

SOME PEOPLE LIKE IT so much when others praise them that they will do almost anything to please people. What's dangerous about being a people pleaser? If we are people pleasers, we might do something wrong just to please people.

Lots of people have gotten themselves into big trouble by choosing to do something wrong in order to please someone. Are there some people we should want to please? We might want to please our parents. And if they are following God's ways, they are good people to please. By pleasing them, we know we are pleasing God, too.

But when you are tempted to please people who don't love God instead of pleasing God, you can fight temptation like Jesus did. You can say, "I will please God, because God's Word says, 'We are not trying to please men but God'" (1 Thessalonians 2:4, NIV).

Dear God, I choose to please you. Thank you for showing me how.

Thursday

Read "Why Do I Hear Sheep?" page 136 in the *Day by Day Kid's Bible*. Or read this part of the story:

Samuel went to King Saul. Samuel said, "God says to fight the enemy. . . . But don't take anything that belongs to them."

So . . . they marched out to fight. . . . But Saul . . . kept the best sheep and cows. . . .

King Saul said, ". . . I did what God said."

"Then why do I hear sheep?" asked Samuel. "Why do I hear cows? . . . You have turned against God. . . ."

"I have sinned," said King Saul. "I was afraid of the people. So I let them do what they wanted." *1 Samuel 15:1-4, 9, 13-14,19, 24*

"JACK TALES" ARE STORIES that have been told for hundreds of years about a young man named Jack who does funny things or has wild adventures, like Jack and the beanstalk. One story of Jack says that his mother gave him a cow to sell at the market. On his way, Jack met a man with a donkey. The man talked him into trading the cow for the donkey. Then Jack met a man with a pig who talked him into trading his donkey for a pig. Then Jack traded the pig for a cat, and so on until Jack ended up with a stone. He let other people talk him into doing what they wanted, while all along he should have remembered that his job was to please his mother by obeying her.

King Saul let his men talk him into disobeying God. Sometimes we please people instead of God because we are afraid of what people might do or say. Do we try to please God because it's a rule? No. We try to please God because God has shown us that's the way life works best.

Dear God, thank you for showing us how life works best. Help me to please you.

Friday

Read "Absalom Takes Over," page 174 in the *Day by Day Kid's Bible.* Or read this part of the story:

Absalom [King David's son] would get up early every morning. . . . People would come into the city to see the king. . . . Absalom would meet them at the gate. He'd call to these men, "Where are you from?"

They would tell him. . . . They'd start to bow to him. But he'd shake their hand and kiss them. . . . So all the people loved Absalom. . . .

One day a man brought a message to King David. It said, "God's people are following Absalom." . . .

So King David left Jerusalem. *2 Samuel 15:1-2, 5-6, 13-14*

ABSALOM WAS NICE to the people, but not because he liked them, and not because he wanted to be kind and loving. He wanted to please the people so they would follow him instead of King David. Absalom wanted to take over his father's kingdom. If Absalom had wanted to please God, he would still have been nice to the people. But he would have done it with a kind and loving heart. And he would have helped King David.

Does anyone try to please God all the time? No. All of us have times when we try to please people instead. That's why we need Jesus. He came to do for us what we cannot do for ourselves. He always did what pleased God. And he died to take our punishment for the times when we try to please people instead of God. That shows just how much God loves us. Now we can feel free to try again and grow to be like Jesus.

Dear God, I'm sorry for the times when I try to please people instead of you. Thank you for showing how much you love me by sending Jesus to forgive me. Help me to please you.

☀ Some Things You Can Do This Week ☾

- ☀ **Please God and your parents.** Do something that you know will please your mom or dad, and you'll be pleasing God, too.

- ☾ **Play "COW."** With a basketball and a hoop, take turns shooting baskets. The first person shoots the basket any way he likes. The second person must shoot the same way. If the first person misses, he must take the first letter of the word "COW." Then the second person can shoot the ball any way she wants. If she makes the basket, the first person must copy her shot. Whenever anyone misses, he or she must take the next letter in the word. Whoever gets all the letters first begins counting his or her next misses starting with one and going up. But the other person keeps shooting until he or she has collected all the letters of the word "COW." Then you "bury the cows" and start over. Why did Saul let his people keep the cows?

- ☀ **Shake hands.** With a friend, shake hands in as many different ways as you can. Make up a handshake of your own and name it. Why did Absalom shake hands with the people?

- ☾ **Be a reporter.** Choose one of the readings for this week. Then think about how a news reporter would describe these events if they were happening in the world now. Write a headline and a newspaper article as if these things just happened.

RELYING ON GOD

We know and rely on the love God has for us. God is love.
Whoever lives in love lives in God, and God in him. 1 John 4:16, NIV

This week you will learn

· what it means to rely on someone;
· how to fight the temptation to totally rely on anything other than God;
· how God used birds to show he is reliable;
· who holds your right hand.

Monday

Read "Making a Fuss for Food," page 62 in the *Day by Day Kid's Bible*. Or read this part of the story:

God said to Moses, "Tell the people they will eat meat tonight. Tomorrow morning they'll eat bread. Then they'll know that I am the Lord."

That evening fat little birds called quail flew in. . . . The next morning . . . it looked like bits of ice covered the ground. But it wasn't ice. It was thin flakes of bread.

"What is it?" the people asked.

"It's the bread God sent you," said Moses. *Exodus 16:11-15*

IF YOU *RELY* on someone or something, you depend on that person or thing. You count on the people you rely on. You trust them to take care of things.

God's people were traveling, so they couldn't grow their own food. They were not going through cities, so they couldn't buy their own food. They had to rely on God to give them food. And God showed that he was reliable, that he could be trusted, by sending food for them.

You can rely on God too. How has he shown you and your family or friends that he is reliable?

When you are tempted to rely only on yourself or something other than God, you can fight temptation like Jesus did. You can say, "I will rely on God, because God's Word says, 'We know and rely on the love God has for us'" (1 John 4:16, NIV).

Dear God, sometimes I try to rely only on myself or something other than you. Help me to remember that you are reliable. Help me to rely on you.

Tuesday

Read "No Rain, No Food," page 280 in the *Day by Day Kid's Bible.* Or read this part of the story:

Then God told Elijah, "Go east. Hide by the brook there. Drink water from the brook. I have told the birds to bring you food."

So Elijah obeyed God. . . . Big, black birds called ravens brought food to him. They brought bread and meat every morning and every evening. Elijah drank water out of the brook. *1 Kings 17:2-6*

JEREMY'S DAD AND MOM had opened a coffee shop. But starting the shop had taken more money than they thought it would. Now their money was running out, and they didn't know how they would be able to buy food for the next week. The whole family was praying about what they should do. A few days later, a check came in the mail. It came from a business Jeremy's dad had worked for many years ago. The owners had found that they owed Jeremy's dad some money. It was enough to pay the bills for several weeks until Dad and Mom's business could start earning its own money. Jeremy's family thanked God. They had relied on him, and he had provided what they needed.

God is love. Part of loving is being reliable. No one is more reliable than God. He will never stop loving you. You can rely on him.

Dear God, thank you for being reliable. Help me to trust you and rely on your love.

Wednesday

Read "Chariots and Horses," page 215 in the *Day by Day Kid's Bible.* Or read this part of the story:

Some people trust in horses.
Some people trust in chariots.
They will fall.
But we trust in God.
We will stand strong.
Psalm 20:7-8

WHY DOES GOD want us to rely on him? When God made the first man and woman, Adam and Eve, he made them so that they would not have to worry about anything they needed. They relied on God, and he gave them all they needed. Anyone could have looked at Adam and Eve's life and said, "What a wonderful God they have. See how he loves them and takes care of them. He is great!" That would have given God glory by showing who he is.

But Adam and Eve decided they wanted the fruit they weren't supposed to eat, because then they would be wise like God. They would be able to rely on themselves and not have to trust God. After they ate the fruit, God let them find out how hard it was to rely on themselves. Still, they could grow food and make clothes. But if they said, "Look what we did," then who got the glory? Adam and Eve.

When we rely on ourselves, we often fail. If we do succeed, we often say, "Look what I did," and we take the glory for ourselves. But when we rely on God, we say, "Look what God did!" Then God gets the glory. Others see who he is and say, "Your God is wonderful. Can he be my God too?"

Dear God, I choose to rely on you. Teach me how to rely on you each day.

Thursday

Read "Don't Give Up," page 361 in the *Day by Day Kid's Bible.* Or read this part of the story:

> *"I'm the Lord. I'm your God.*
> *I hold your right hand.*
> *I tell you not to be scared, my little people.*
> *I will help you myself," says God.*
> *"I will save you. I'm your Holy One.*
> *You will have my joy.*
> *My great power will shine in you."*
> Isaiah 41:13-16

PART OF GROWING UP is realizing that no person is totally reliable. No person or thing is totally reliable except God. God will never let us down. He will never leave us.

When Jesus healed lame people, instead of lifting them up and supporting them, he told them to get up and walk. The lame people had a choice then. They could say, "You're crazy. I can't get up and walk, remember? I'm lame." Or they could rely on Jesus and trust that he really had healed them. If they relied on him, they would have to show it by obeying him. They would have to stand and walk. When they did, they found out that Jesus was reliable. He had healed them, and they really could walk!

Jesus is still reliable. We show we rely on him by obeying him. Do we rely on God because it's a rule? No. We rely on God because he has shown us that's the way life works best.

Dear God, help me to rely on you. Thank you that I can trust you to love and care for me.

Friday

Read "Do Not Trust Princes," page 218 in the *Day by Day Kid's Bible.* Or read this part of the story:

Don't trust the leaders of the land to save you.
They are only people. . . .

But good things come to people
who let God be their helper. . . .
He always keeps his promises. . . .

God is King forever.

Cheer for God!
Psalm 146:3, 5-6, 10

EVERY DAY, TAZIA RELIES on people and things. She relies on the alarm clock to wake her up. She relies on her mother to make breakfast. She relies on the bus to pick her up and take her to school. She relies on the teacher to teach her the right things and to keep order in class. She relies on her teammates when she plays ball.

We all rely on people and things all the time. That's all right as long as we realize that they are not totally reliable.

One day, the alarm didn't ring to wake Tazia up. Another time, Mom forgot to get milk at the store, so the cereal at breakfast was dry. Once the school bus broke down and her dad had to drive her to school.

The only one who is totally reliable is God. So when the people and things we rely on don't come through for us, we still have God to rely on. No matter what happens, he always loves us. And sooner or later, everything will turn out all right.

Dear God, thank you for giving me things and people to rely on. Help me not to get angry when things and people let me down. Help me to keep relying on you.

☀SOME THINGS YOU CAN DO THIS WEEK ☽

☀ **Make a bird.** First you'll need to fold a facial tissue (like Kleenex) in half. Pinch it together in the center and clip a clothespin or a paper clip across the middle. The sides now look like wings. You can tie a string to the center of the clothespin or paper clip if you want. Use this bird as a reminder of how God took care of Elijah when Elijah relied on him.

☽ **Draw a handprint.** Place your right hand on a piece of paper and trace around it. Then along the bottom of the paper write, "God holds my right hand." Let this be a reminder of the verse: "I am the Lord your God. I am holding your right hand. And I tell you, 'Don't be afraid. I will help you'" (Isaiah 41:13, ICB).

☀ **Make a calendar for next month.** Place one piece of typing paper over a calendar page. Any month, any year will do, because all you are going to do is trace the squares. When you are finished, look at a calendar that shows you the dates to place in the squares for next month. Write the dates in the squares of your calendar. Write the name of the month above it and design a border for the calendar. As you make your plans for the month, remember to let God be in charge of whatever you do. You can rely on him.

☽ **Make a montage.** Look through magazines and cut out pictures of things that people might rely on. Glue these pictures onto a poster board or piece of paper. On this montage, write, "Trust in the Lord with all your heart. Proverbs 3:5."

WHO WINS?

I have told you these things, so that in me you may have peace. In this world you will have trouble. But take heart! I have overcome the world. John 16:33, NIV

This week you will learn
· how you are like a container;
· how you are like a tree;
· what life on earth is for;
· what you don't have if you don't have Jesus.

Monday

Read "Wide, Long, High, and Deep," page 740 in the *Day by Day Kid's Bible.* Or read this part of the story:

I'm also praying that you'll know Jesus' love. I want you to know how wide his love is. I want you to know how long it is. I want you to know how high and how deep it is. God's love is greater than you can know. Still, I want you to know as much of it as you can. I want you to be filled to the top with God. *Ephesians 3:17-19*

LOOK IN THE MIRROR, and you will see an image of your body. But there's part of you that you can't see. It's not your inner stomach or your beating heart or your bones. All of your body, inside and out, is just a house where the real you lives. The part of you that is truly you and that will live forever is inside your body-house. It's your *spirit,* the center of who you are, the part of you that knows and loves. Your spirit is different from your thinking brain. It's deeper than that. It's you.

Because God is Spirit, your spirit holds the image of God in you. God is love. So you were made to be a container of God's love. If you open your spirit to him, he can fill you to the top with himself, with his love.

Dear God, help me to remember that your love is wider, longer, higher, and deeper than I will ever know. But help me understand as much of your love as I can, and fill me to the top with you.

Tuesday

Read "A Good Soldier," page 758 in the *Day by Day Kid's Bible*. Or read this part of the story:

Here's a saying you can trust.

> *If our old selves died with Jesus,*
>> *we will live with Jesus.*
> *If we keep on believing when we have hard times,*
>> *we'll rule with him. . . .*
> *If we don't keep our promises,*
>> *he will still keep his.*
>> *That's because he is who he is.*
>> *He will always be true to himself.*

2 Timothy 2:11-13

WHEN GOD PUT HIS IMAGE into people, he put a "knowing" into us. All of us know that if we are loving in all we think and say and do, we will be right and good like God. But no matter how hard we try, we can't be loving and good all the time. That's because we are not God.

Only God can be loving and good all the time. God knew this before he ever made us. And before he made us, he had a plan: He would be loving and good for us to show how much he truly loves us. That's just what God did by sending his Son, Jesus.

Jesus was loving and good all the time. And he died, taking our punishment for the times we are not loving and good. That is the gift God gave us because he loves us so much and wants us to be in his family. The Son of God came into a human family so that we could come into God's family. If we believe Jesus is God's Son and tell God we want to come into his family, he gives us his goodness and love. He helps us grow so we become more like him every day.

Dear God, thank you for sending your Son, Jesus, into a human family to be loving and good to me. Thank you for letting Jesus take the punishment for me so I can come into your family, clean from sin.

Wednesday

Read "Clay Jars Full of Riches," page 695 in the *Day by Day Kid's Bible.* Or read this part of the story:

We get pushed hard on every side. But we don't break. We wonder about things. But we don't give up. We get hurt. But God doesn't leave us. . . .

　　We know that God brought Jesus back to life. We know that he will bring us back to life too. . . .

　　Our troubles are not too bad. They only last a little while. These troubles will bring us greatness. It's a greatness that shines brighter than troubles.

　　This greatness will last forever. *2 Corinthians 4:8-9, 14, 17*

HAVE YOU EVER WATCHED a tree in a storm? A healthy tree bends in the wind, but it doesn't break. It is alive and strong, and its roots go deep. But a tree that is not healthy is stiff and weak. Or its roots don't go deep. It breaks and falls.

In a way, we are like trees. If we let God fill us with himself and his love, we don't break when stormy troubles come. If our roots go deep into God's love, we come out okay even when times are hard. In fact, hard times give us a chance to come closer to God and to enjoy seeing how God gets us out of the hard times.

Sooner or later God's love wins. And when it does, we see God's greatness, just like today's reading says. We see that God's greatness is much bigger than troubles. What's more, troubles last just for a while. God's greatness lasts forever.

Dear God, thank you that your greatness lasts forever. Take my roots deep down into your love, and fill me with yourself. Help me to grow closer to you in hard times and to know that your love always wins.

Thursday

Read "The Morning Star in Your Hearts," page 775 in the *Day by Day Kid's Bible.* Or read this part of the story:

Jesus' godly power gave us all we need to live. It gave us all we need to grow to be like God. . . .

God gave us great promises. They're very special. So you can live as a child of God. . . .

Keep doing what God wants you to do. Then you won't ever be away from God. He will give you a warm welcome into Jesus' kingdom, which lasts forever. *2 Peter 1:3-4, 10-11*

IF GOD WANTS US to live with him forever in heaven, what is life on earth for? Our life on earth is like a classroom where we learn. What does God want us to learn? For one thing, he wants us to learn that we are not God. We cannot really take care of ourselves. Only God can take care of us. For another thing, God wants us to learn that we are sinners. In other words, we can't be as good and perfect as God no matter how hard we try. So the next thing God wants us to learn is that we need his kind love to forgive us and to help us as we try to live the way life works best. Then, as we share, people see God's sharing kindness. As we help, people see God's helping kindness. As we love, people see God's loving kindness. As we tell about Jesus, people can understand just how much God loves them. Then they can accept the gift of Jesus' love for them. That's the only way they will win over death. If they accept Jesus' love, they, too, will live with God forever in heaven.

Dear God, I am not you. So I need you to take care of me. I am a sinner. I can't be as good and perfect as I know I should be. So I need your kind love to forgive me and to help me live the way you have shown me to live. Thank you for sending your Son, Jesus, so I can live with you forever. Help me to show your love to others and to tell them about Jesus so they can live with you forever too.

Friday

Read "Who Wins?" page 795 in the *Day by Day Kid's Bible.* Or read this part of the story:

Who wins over the world? It's the people who believe that Jesus is God's Son.

God gives us life forever. This life comes from his Son. If you have Jesus, you have life. If you don't have Jesus, you don't have life.

I'm writing so people who believe in Jesus will know they have life forever. *1 John 5:4-5, 11-13*

IMAGINE THAT IT IS NIGHT. One of the rooms in your house is dark, and the door to that room is closed. In all the other rooms, the lights are on. You walk to the closed door, and you open it. Does the darkness come out and make the other rooms dark? Or does the light from the other rooms go into the dark room?

Light always chases darkness away. Always. Darkness only happens if light is taken away. In the same way, life wins over death. Always. The grave of death could not win over the life of God inside Jesus. And guess what? The life of God in you will win over death. That's because sin leads to death, but God's love leads to life. And God's Son, Jesus, has paid for your sins with his love. So you are now full of Jesus' love. You are being filled more and more with his love as you follow him. And no matter what happens, God's love always wins.

Dear God, thank you for your love. Thank you that no matter what happens, your love wins. Help me to live forever in your love.

☀ SOME THINGS YOU CAN DO THIS WEEK ☽

☀ **Look in a mirror.** Get a friend or family member to help you. Ask your helper to stand beside a mirror (not in front of it), facing you. Now you stand in front of the mirror and look at yourself. Touch your right ear. Ask your helper to touch his right ear. What is different between what you see your friend doing and what you see your mirror image doing? You see your helper's right ear at the left side of your face as you look at him. In the mirror your own right ear is on the right side. That's because in a mirror, the image is reversed. Hold a page of writing up to the mirror. It's backward. Try writing this week's verse backward and holding it in front of a mirror. It will show up going the right direction, and you can read it. Remember that God made each person in his own image.

☽ **Make a vase out of play dough.** If you need to make play dough, mix one-third cup of water, one-third cup of salt, and one cup of flour. A vase is a container. What is it made to contain? How much will your vase contain? What other kinds of containers do you have around your house? Remember that you were made to contain the image of God and his love.

☀ **Make "banana candles" to eat.** Cut a banana in half and stand it on a plate. You may have to cut off the curved end too to make it flat so it will stand. Take a ring of pineapple and cut through one side of the ring so you can open it a little. Fit it around the base of the standing banana. Spoon a small bit of whipped cream onto the top end of the banana. Place a cherry on top. The banana is the candle and the cherry is the flame. Remember that light always chases away darkness, like God's love chases away sin and God's life chases away death.

☽ **Make tree bark rubbings.** Take some plain printer paper and some crayons outdoors. Holding a piece of paper up against the trunk of a tree, rub a crayon over the paper. The design of the bark will show up. Do this on several different kinds of trees to see how they are different. Remember that we are like healthy trees. Our roots grow deep down into God's love.

INDEX OF BIBLE STORIES

OLD TESTAMENT

INDEX OF WEEKLY THEME VERSES

READY TO START SOMETHING NEW?

From the Author of The Beginner's Bible

DAY BY DAY Kid's Bible

Read the Bible in 1 year, 7 minutes a day!

KARYN HENLEY

With the *Day by Day Kid's Bible*, you can read the Bible in one year! All it takes is 7 minutes a day—you've got 7 minutes, right?